Reporting for the Print Media

Reporting for the Print Media

FRED FEDLER
Florida Technological University

H:U HARCOURT BRACE JOVANOVICH, INC.

New York   Chicago   San Francisco   Atlanta

Cover photograph: David Attie

ISBN: 0-15-576615-5

Library of Congress Catalog Card Number: 73–10871

Printed in the United States of America

Contents

Reporting for the Print Media

Introduction

Reporting for the Print Media contains instructions, examples and exercises designed to help you learn how to write for the print news media. Sections 1 to 6 deal with the conventions of newswriting format and style. Sections 7 to 14 discuss the various kinds of news stories that you, as a reporter, are likely to encounter.

Most of the exercises resemble assignments given to new reporters. In some exercises, you are given a few facts and asked to write them up in acceptable newswriting style. In other exercises, the facts are more complex and require more sophisticated newswriting techniques. Still other exercises send you out of the classroom to gather information for detailed news stories.

Assume that every story in this workbook occurred on your campus or in your community unless the story specifically mentions another location. Also assume that every story you write will be published by a local newspaper.

Verify the spelling of all names that appear in the exercises by consulting the city directory at the back of the book. The city directory contains the names, addresses and occupations only of the adults who live in this fictitious community. Some names and addresses contain deliberate errors. The information in the city directory is correct.

To achieve consistent styles of capitalization, abbreviation, punctuation and spelling as you complete the exercises and assignments, follow the guidelines suggested by "The Associated Press Stylebook." The stylebook, which is used by both the Associated Press and United Press International and by most newspapers in the United States, is reprinted at the back of this workbook.

If grammar is a weak point, you should get a copy of "The Elements of Style," 2nd ed., by William Strunk Jr. and E. B. White (New York: Macmillan, 1972). The paperbound edition is available at most college bookstores for $1.25. The book is an excellent review of "the rules of usage and principles of composition most commonly violated."

Before going beyond Section 4, you should also review the libel laws in your state. Libel suits are a constant danger for journalists, and the problem of libel is dealt with throughout the workbook. Similarly, problems of good taste, ethics and responsibility are considered not in separate sections, but throughout the workbook because they continually confront journalists.

Format and Style

Type your name here
Type your course name here
Type the date the assignment is due here

Type the story slugline here — *story description*

Reporters have developed a unique format for their stories; each story you write should follow the guidelines suggested here. Begin each story one-third to one-half of the way down the first page. When you write for a newspaper, the space at the top of the page provides room for your byline, a headline and special instructions to the printers. In class, it provides room for an evaluation of your assignments. Leave a one-inch margin on each side and at the bottom of the page.

Type and double space each assignment. Do not type more than one story on each page, and type on only one side of the page. Indent each paragraph and mark it with the proper copy editing symbol: ⌐.

The slugline, typed in the upper left-hand corner of the first page, is a two- or three-word description of the story. For example, if a story describes a speech by your mayor, the slugline might say: "Mayor's Speech." The slugline is used to identify the story while it is being prepared for publication.

Do not hyphenate a word at the end of a line. If a story is continued on a second page, write and circle the word "more" at the bottom of the first page. The circle indicates that the word is not part of the story and should not be set in type. Begin the second page and all later pages about one inch from the top of the page. Type your name and the page number in the upper left-hand corner.

Double-check each fact. Your instructor may lower your grade if you misspell a person's name or make any other serious factual error. You will also be penalized for errors in diction, grammar and style. If your instructor accepts late assignments, your grades on them may also be lowered. Newspapers cannot tolerate irresponsibility. Errors may seriously injure the persons mentioned in news stories, the reporters who wrote the stories and the newspapers that published them.

(more)

Use a pencil, never a pen, to correct any errors that appear in your stories. If you use a pen and make an error, the error is difficult to correct. Also, avoid onionskin and erasable bond paper; it is difficult to edit stories typed on them.

If you indent a line, then decide that you do not want to start a new paragraph, link the lines together with a pencil, as shown here.

If you accidentally type an extra word or letter, cross out the word or or letter, then draw an arc above it to link the remaining portions of the sentence. Copy editors sometimes use another symbol to indicate that a word or letter should be deleted: ℓ

When two words or letters are inverted, use this symbol to indicate that they should be transposed. draw three lines under a letter to indicate that it should be capitalized. If a letter is capitalized but should not be, draw a slanted line Through it. If two words are accidentally run together, draw a straight line between them to indicate that a space should be added. If two letters are mistakenly separated, draw an arc above and below the space to link the letters to gether.

If you make a correction, then decide that the correction is unnecessary, write the word "stet" alongside the correction to indicate that you want to retain the original version. If you want to add a letter, word or phrase, write or type it above the line, then use a caret to indicate precisely where it fits into the sentence. Never type over a letter.

Spell out most numbers below 10 and use figures for the number 10 and most larger numbers. Consult the stylebook for more exact guidelines. If you type a numeral but want it spelled out, circle it (for example: He has 8 sisters). If you spell out a number but want to use the numeral, circle it (for example: He has thirteen sisters). Similarly, circle words that are spelled out but should be abbreviated (for example: He is from Sheboygan, Wisconsin), and words that are abbreviated but should be spelled out (for example: He is from Wis).

To add a comma, draw a comma in the proper place and put a caret over it (for example: He is tall dark and fat). If you add an apostrophe or quotation mark, place a caret under it (for example: He said, "Don't ignore these rules"). To add a period, draw either a dot or a small "x" and circle it ⊙ ⊗ A hyphen is indicated by the symbol =, and a dash by the symbol --. Beneath the last line of each news story, place either of the "end marks" shown below.

-30-

###

4

FORMAT AND STYLE: EXERCISE 1

INSTRUCTIONS: Using the proper copy editing symbols, correct the errors in the following stories.

Story 1

a judge in mobile, Ala. orderfed a young men to leavye town today.

"You sttart walking right now, Judge L. R Wilson said.

Michael A. Talley, 22, of St Louis, Mo., had been arr3sted and charged with disorderdly coduct andindecent explosure for washnig his only set of cloethes in a public laundramat. The cloethes consiste of acolored robbe, sandals and mattching Beads.

Talley said he was on his way hom from a musicfestival in Miami, Fla., when he decided to wash his cloethes.

The judge orderd the youth to pas pay a fine of $45 dollars or spend twenty-five days in Jail. He then suspendd the finE andordered him to laeve Mobil imediately.

Story 2

The citys public libray was del uGed with over due books tyesterday

it was a day of amnesty. The library board announced had that borrowers could return Overdue books yesterday without paying fines, normaly ten cents cents aday. A lirbary spo kesman said thAt at least Ten Thusand over due books pured into the main librray.

"Its amagazine. People are bringing them in shopping bags, shoe boxes, packing crates and attaché cases," said miss Mildred Troxell, director of public relations for the library. "I saw osmoe that were borrow in 1941, she added

"Not all the books Belong to the libary. "I noticed one from some library in Washington, D. c.," said Miss Troxell. That book had been overdje since 1963.

Books also were being acepted at brnanch libraries. "We may have trouble finding space for all of them before this is over," said Miss Troxell

flames extended 10 feet behind the cann as it spiralled 120 feet across the football feild.

"most people dont realize how dannggerous arosol cans are," said Capt. Carl doss training officer for the cities fire departent.

"if these products are hanlded properly, theres nothing to worry about," Dosssaid. "Improperly handled, they are killers"

"The cans don't justsit there and burst when there Heated," explained Fire Marshal Jim Carthey. "They fly like shrapnel."

Fire men have tested dozen of the cans by throwing into fires started on isolated fields.

"We started the tests for our own benefitt," said Carthey. "we wAnt to know what to expcet in case we ever encounter the cans in a burning building. But now we're also trying to warnn the public about them."

Color movies that show the cans exploding are showN during fire prevnetion progrsmas. in city schl schools

gas in the pressurized cans explands as it is heated causing the explosing.

One side blew off a spray can of cheese-spread throwed into a fire, while a rubber safety valve on the can remained in place. An exploshoh ripped a paint, cann in half, tossing both ends w 25 feet. An empty can of hairnet spray was flattened into a straight sheet tin. The bottom of a spray-on dry cleaner shot 35 feet tothe right, whil the rest of the can rocketed 75 feet in another direction.

fiRemen call the cans "unguided misiles." Doss said, it doesn't matter whether the cans are empty or full they still explode.

Doss said the worse places to leave the cans are in parked cars when the windows are rollup on, on shelves near a stove and alongisde heat registers in homes. "Theres enough heat at any of those places to cause a can to explode, and people don't expect it," dos said. "Weve also had some people seriousl hurt when theythrew the cans into trash fires."

FORMAT AND STYLE: EXERCISE 2

INSTRUCTIONS: Study the rules for capitalization, abbreviation, punctuation, numerals and spelling in "The Associated Press Stylebook," which is reprinted at the back of this workbook. Then correct the errors in the following sentences. (Not every sentence contains an error; some contain more than one.)

1. He is a government employe.

2. He collected 1435 stamps.

3. Give me some French fries.

4. The idea is anti-American.

5. The book is titled "Joy."

6. The City is in Southern California.

7. He likes the republican party.

8. He is a 6-year-old.

9. They inherited 4,200,000 dollars.

10. He lives at the Y.M.C.A.

11. It was built in the 1920s.

12. He is six feet tall and red-headed.

13. The jar contains 72¢.

14. The storm came from the west.

15. He will speak Tue. or Wed.

16. The Mayor has resigned.

17. They left at four PM Monday.

18. He lives in the U.S.

19. She hummed the song America.

20. Give me a copy of the bible.

21. The judge is a republican.

22. They work for Acme Company.

23. He ran 3/4 of a mile in 3 minutes.

24. Mr. Ralph Nader will speak.

25. The pope is catholic.

26. He is an Army sergeant.

27. It is 9 degrees above zero.

28. Tom Saule, of Boston, died.

29. "He moved to Denver", Tom said.

30. He died in Wis. on August 7.

31. He is tall, blonde, and pale.

32. It came from Tulsa Oklahoma.

33. He said, "go see a movie."

34. Andrew Kohn Junior left early.

35. He is 9 years old. His sister is 17.

36. He was transfered to Memorial hospital.

37. The debt totals $184.00.

38. He got six per cent of the votes.

39. General Douglas MacArthur is dead.

40. Chico California is a small town.

41. The city council will meet today.

42. The library is in the courthouse.

43. Ben (Deacon) Roth quit his job.

44. She has a b.a. degree.

45. He toured the capital building.

46. The address is 47 North Terry Street.

47. The dept. manager took the money.

48. Sen Proxmire (D-Wis.) has left.

49. "Can you come to the party"?

50. The highway is U.S. 141.

51. The lawmen never did arrive.

52. The thief is a white man.

53. Doctors took 5 X rays.

54. It occurred on Orange Avenue.

55. That coed is a good adviser.

56. Rev. Stuart Adler can not come.

FORMAT AND STYLE: EXERCISE 3

INSTRUCTIONS: Using the proper copy editing symbols, correct the mechanical and stylistic errors in the following sentences.

1. The president of the u.s., his wife, and 2 daughtres have anounced plans to visit the city on August 7.

2. Mary Wilson, age eight, said "the baseeball game was rather dull".

3. The General has retiRed from the army and now is President of Stazy Electronics company. The Company has an office on Central Avenue.

4. Sen. Walter Mondale, a democrat from Min nesota opposed the bill.

5. He worked for the Chicago Tribune and Life Magazine but now is writing a book titled The History of American Journalism.

6. The city hall is locafed at 2107 North Olive Road in Oshkosh, Wisconsin.

7. John Jones, Junior, of Rock Island Illionis arrived September 1 and carried about $1,400,000 in bonds for the school

8. Mr. John (Shorty) Adams, a writer from Canada, will received his Bachelor of Arts degree next Mon. and then will fly to the midwest at 7:00 P.M. in the evening.

9. The woman is studying german, History, and Physics, but says "I dont enjoy them". She says she prefers chemistry.

10. She received 14192 votes last Fall but lost the election to a the incumbent District Attorney.

11. He is seven years old, four feet tall, weighs fifty-five pounds and has saved $74.00. His sister, a beautiful blond, is 17 years old.

12. The student said, "this is certainly a difficult exercise".

13. Mr. Alton Smythe, a member of the Republican party, drove south to attend the partys presidential convention.

14. Samuel Jeffers, Junior, the Mayor of Tacoma, Washin ingtoN is expecte to arive back in the U.S. on the 14th of next month.

15. The Senattor, a Democrat from Massachusetts, sadi he visited the president att the white house at

8:00 am today and wask asked to return at 4:30 PM next Sunday for another conference.

16. His apartment is at 3114 Orchard Lane but he works at 43 River Drive.

FORMAT AND STYLE: EXERCISE 4

INSTRUCTIONS: Using the proper copy editing symbols, correct the mechanical and stylistic errors in the following stories.

Story 1

police today reco vered a stolen struck that had been abandoned ina parking ramp at third and ripley streets, but they can not understand hwo the truck got thEre

The truck was stuck. Its roof was wedged against the ramps ceiling. The truck was stolen earlier this week from Burke Dry Cleaners, Incorporated.

"We couldn't drive the dru truck straigh out", said Fred Neff, a mechafnic called by the plice. Neff explained that, "The lowest beam roof in the parking ramp was near the exist, and we would have scraped the roof and windshield off if we had triyed to drive the truck under it. But there was not enough room to turn the truck around.

"We finaly let the air out oF the rear tyres, had a couple man stand on theback bumper to weight it down, and backed the truck out." Neff said.

No one has explain how the thief awas able to drive the Truck into the ra mp while the tires were inflated.

Story 2

A new Civic Center should be constructed in the city accordiing to a report released tody by the junior chamber of comerce.

The jaycees also recommended that the City construct a "proper, convenient and thoroughly adequate youth center."

The jaycess interviewed 57 community leaders, including spokesman for governmental, educational, business, labor, and religious groups. Each of these people were asked what facilities are needed in the cijty.

The report said, "The consensus was that the most important commuinty need ifs for a civiccenter. At the present time the community has no place to hold gatherings that involve more than 5000 persons.

"Another imprtant need is a youth center for shigh school boys and girls, and for youths who hadve graduated from high school."

The Jaycees said the city also needs an incinerater at the city dump, and a meting place for Senior Citizens.

Story 3

A former Track Star at central high school did not brake any re cords but he did win a ten dollar bet when he camme out ofsretirement for an eleven minute run yestreday neen.

Don herbert, 39, the manager of a servise station at 535 Hill street told an employee that he could run toa store a Mile away and back in 15 min. The employee had just taken 55 minutes to walk the same distance.

Two friends bet Herbert $10 he could not run that fast.

Herbert acepted their bet. He ran to the stoer and backin 11 minutes but whennhe returned to the service station his friends had left, and hh was unable to collect the ten dollars.

Story 4

The crime rate in the city rose eleven percent lats yearalmost double the average increase in the Nation.

Statistics compiled by the F.B.I. revealed that 2948 serious crimss were reported in the city. during the past twelve monhts.

They include: murder, 1; mansluaghter, 2; rape, 4; robbery, 35; agravajed assault, 42; burglary and break-in, 637; larceny, 1,942; and auto theft, 306.

The total number of crimes committed in the city the previous year was 2656.

The bibbiggest increase was inn auto thefts, Which almost dudoubled from 172 the previous year.

The number of burglaries rose from 510 to 637 andtthe number of robberies increased from nine to 35.

the number of serious crimes committed here was 1,155 per 100,000 prsons, slightly below the avrage of 1,198 thruout the u.s.

The highist Rate recorded by anycity in the State were 1342 cries per 100000 people. The lowest rat was 713. The average is 1,105 in the state.

Newswriting Style

Newspapers have developed a distinctive style of writing, and every element of that style serves a specific purpose. Together, the elements enable newspapers to convey information to their readers clearly, concisely and impartially. At first the style may seem difficult and perhaps even awkward. It may also dismay some students because of its emphasis on facts; but newswriters are reporters, not creative writers.

Most daily newspapers can publish only a fraction of the information they receive each day; for example, an editor for "The New York Times" has estimated that the "Times" receives 1¼ million to 1½ million words every day but has enough space to publish only one-tenth of the material. By writing concisely, reporters try to present as much information to readers as possible. Brevity also helps readers to grasp quickly the main ideas conveyed by each story because they do not have to read any unnecessary words.

Reporters can often shorten sentences, yet retain their full meaning, by deleting unnecessary words:

A crowd of several hundred persons watched the fire.
REVISED: Several hundred persons watched the fire.

He also went on to add that the school was totally destroyed.
REVISED: He added that the school was destroyed.

He suffered the loss of his right eye.
REVISED: He lost his right eye.

Reporters can also rewrite sentences to eliminate unnecessary words and phrases:

Berkeley, Calif., is the town harboring the school.
REVISED: The school is in Berkeley, Calif.

It was not until 6 p.m. that the police were able to find the child.
REVISED: The police found the child at 6 p.m.

The average television viewer spends three hours a day at his television set.
REVISED: The average viewer watches television three hours a day.

Some sentences and paragraphs are unnecessarily repetitious, often because reporters first mention the topic, then present some specific information about it:

> Other injuries the man received include a broken arm.
> REVISED: The man also suffered a broken arm.

> Legal action has been taken by the company, which has sought an injunction to halt the strike.
> REVISED: The company has sought an injunction to halt the strike.

> This is not the first time he has been held up. He has been robbed three times in the past eight months.
> REVISED: He has been robbed three times in the past eight months.

To communicate effectively, reporters must also be precise. Every word must accurately convey the proper meaning. Imprecision creates confusion and misunderstanding:

> The blonde child and his father strolled through the park.
> REVISED: The blond child and his father strolled through the park.

> The mass media is an important source of information.
> REVISED: The mass media are an important source of information.

> The bus collided with a telephone pole.
> REVISED: The bus struck a telephone pole.

(A "blond" is a male; a "blonde" is a female. The word "media" is the plural of "medium" and thus requires a plural verb. The word "collide" means "to come together," so the pole could not have collided with the bus.)

Such considerations may seem minor, but journalists devote their lives to jobs that require a mastery of the English language, and most of them strive for perfection. Moreover, every word published by a newspaper may be read by thousands or even millions of persons. Some of these readers will detect any errors published by the newspaper, and errors inevitably damage the newspaper's (and the reporter's) credibility and reputation.

Use a forceful, direct style of writing. In general, use an active rather than a passive verb and a simple rather than a complicated sentence structure. Sentences with active verbs and simple structures tend to be more concise than passive or complicated sentences. Avoid overusing "is," "are," "was" and "were."

> A sharp criticism of the plan was voiced by the mayor.
> REVISED: The mayor sharply criticized the plan.

> Dr. Margaret Mead, an expert on marriage and families, mentioned security-loving, unadventurous people as a consequence of early marriages.
> REVISED: Dr. Margaret Mead, an expert on marriage and families, said early marriages create a security-loving and unadventurous people.

> Police officers were summoned to the scene by a neighbor.
> REVISED: A neighbor called the police.

Be specific. Avoid vague terms that convey no meaningful information. If a man is 94 years old, say so. If you simply call him "an old man," readers must guess his precise age, and few of their guesses are likely to be correct. Other examples:

He had a long history of experimentation with propulsion systems.
REVISED: He experimented with rockets for 11 years.

✓ The reporter said the hours she puts in and the pay she receives are not good.
REVISED: The reporter said she works 50 to 60 hours a week and is paid only $125.

He has gone on record as opposing the idea.
REVISED: He told reporters he will vote against higher taxes.

Use simple terms that are concise and easy to understand:

He gave assistance to the victims.
REVISED: He helped the victims.

His association with the bank began in 1968.
REVISED: The bank hired him in 1968.

Some women were engaged in conversation with their neighbors.
REVISED: Some women were talking with their neighbors.

News stories must be as impartial, as objective as possible. Journalists do express their opinions in some types of articles, particularly editorials, but not in stories that report the news. Reporters must be neutral observers, not advocates nor participants. Do not discriminate against any idea, and do not tell your readers what to think. Assume that your readers are intelligent and can make their own decisions about current issues. Your job is to gather and report the facts they need to make intelligent decisions.

Avoid adjectives and labels. They reflect your opinion. They may also be unnecessary and inaccurate, and they may unnecessarily infuriate readers who have opposite views.

When they left the roller rink, a tragic disaster occurred. A bus struck their car.
REVISED: A bus struck their car as they left the roller rink.

✓ Goligoski mentioned the interesting fact that 90 per cent of the reporters in Washington, D.C., have college degrees, compared to 80 per cent of the government employes.
REVISED: Goligoski said 90 per cent of the reporters in Washington, D.C., have college degrees, compared to 80 per cent of the government employes.

Scab workers evaded the pickets by using a back entrance at the factory.
REVISED: Some workers avoided the pickets by using a back entrance at the factory.

(A minor car accident is not a "disaster," and even if someone was killed in the accident, readers would not have to be told that the death was "tragic." Similarly, reporters should not label one statement "interesting," nor another "boring," but should simply report the statements and let readers judge for themselves. In the last example, the term "scab" is inflammatory and, depending on the circumstances, might be libelous. The word "evaded" connotes guilt and stealth; "avoided" is more objective.)

Entire sentences sometimes convey opinions rather than facts. Moreover, the opinions are often expressed as trite generalities, unsupported by facts. Such sentences must be avoided.

House trailers are not cheap. The average price is $12,000.
REVISED: The average house trailer costs $12,000.

Most of us aren't happy about going back to work on Monday. But Kris Wilcox was more than happy to return to work today. She just recovered from a heart transplant.
REVISED: Kris Wilcox returned to work today after recovering from a heart transplant.

A young hippie, typically dressed in shorts, beads and sandals, stood outside the tent.
REVISED: A youth dressed in shorts, beads and sandals stood outside the tent.

(Twelve thousand dollars is a lot of money, but people who have invested $30,000, $40,000 or more in their homes bitterly oppose the presence of mobile homes in their neighborhoods. Is it a fact or an opinion that most people hate to return to work on Monday? The sentence can be improved by simply reporting the most interesting and significant fact: that the woman returned to work after a serious operation. Reporters must avoid stereotypes and labels; a person can be described, but it should not be concluded that a particular person's style of dress is typical for any group.)

Avoid clichés, slang and profanity unless they are appropriate and essential. Trite phrases are often so vague as to be meaningless. Many of them can be replaced by facts:

A picnic ended in tragedy yesterday for two university students.
REVISED: Two university students drowned yesterday afternoon while swimming to a boat anchored 150 feet from shore.

There are hundreds of clichés and slang phrases to be avoided. Among the most common in newspaper work are the following:

a complete success	struck down by assassins
came to his rescue	gained ground
a keen mind	landed the job
decided to make tracks	leveled an attack
escaped death	made their getaway
made their home	limped into port
overwhelmed his opposition	tried their luck
quick-thinking	tipped the scales
started their mission	under their noses

Such phrases should be replaced by more original, factual wording:

He couldn't believe his eyes when he saw his score and realized that he had flunked the test.
REVISED: He was surprised when he saw his score and realized he had flunked the test.

He said the store's losses are a thing of the past.
REVISED: He said the store no longer is losing money.

He wants to hash out the details and remove the remaining stumbling blocks to graduation.
REVISED: He wants to talk to his teacher and finish the assignments so he can graduate.

Students often become self-conscious when they begin to write, and their style of writing becomes stilted. Yet students seldom have that problem when they speak to friends. After you finish writing a news story, read it aloud to yourself or to some friends. If it sounds awkward, if you would not use the same phrases and sentences in a casual conversation, you should probably rewrite the story.

NEWSWRITING STYLE: EXERCISE 2

INSTRUCTIONS: Rewrite the following sentences to eliminate any unnecessary words. When possible, use a strong verb and simple sentence structure.

1. Fire Department employes extinguished the conflagration.

2. Not until late August did she finally receive the money.

3. He is hopeful of persuading the students to vote for the incumbent president.

4. It is estimated by witnesses that the boys drowned at 4:10 p.m.

5. A pay raise increase of 8 per cent was received today by the carpenters.

6. The auto accident was due to the fact that the street was slippery.

7. It is argued by him that the United States should never have sent any troops into Vietnam.

8. The opinion of 86 per cent of the students at the school is that the price of books is outrageously high, the survey revealed.

9. They said a visit to their grandmother's was their purpose in going.

10. The booth contained a clothesline attached to which there were numerous dollar bills.

11. The council voted to wait before making its decision as to whether the city should build a new school.

12. The main reason why none of the students in the class ate three balanced meals a day was that they did not have enough time.

13. The objectives of the strikers are as follows: higher wages, a four-day work week and dental insurance.

14. First on the order of events at the meeting of the Rotary Club will be a presentation of an award to the club member with the best attendance record for the period of the past 10 years.

15. The reporter's comment on the cooperation of the police was that the police were always very polite to her, but that it was hard to obtain any information from them unless they really wanted her to have it.

16. He described the flying saucer to have been approximately 12 or 15 feet in diameter as he observed it from a distance of approximately 60 feet.

17. The student charged that he gained disfavor with his teacher because the teacher is biased against members of the male sex.

NEWSWRITING STYLE: EXERCISE 3

INSTRUCTIONS: Eliminate the unnecessary words, trite phrases and clichés in the following sentences.

1. The life of a 9-year-old boy was snuffed out early today when a school bus overturned.

2. The building burned to the ground despite the valiant efforts of firemen to save the structure.

3. The City Council last night voted to make an additional subsidy to the tune of $35,000 for the continuation of bus service within the municipality.

4. She plans to get the ball rolling to obtain a federal grant for the construction of apartments for elderly persons.

5. He has been instrumental in the attempt to formulate plans for a new swimming pool.

6. Putting it on the line, he charged that private citizens have failed to cooperate to the fullest extent with the police.

7. The department chairman made it quite clear that he fully intends to request salary increases for all the subordinates within his department.

8. Firemen sped to the scene of the fire and extinguished the blaze as an ambulance rushed the victims to a nearby hospital.

9. He went along with the idea that news about crime and violence is played up by the mass media.

10. The police officer brought out the fact that the tragic auto accident occurred on a rain-slick highway.

11. The candidate for district attorney vowed that he would leave no stone unturned and would keep his nose to the grindstone in an effort to solve the problems posed by the rising rate of crime in the city.

12. The police launched an investigation after a fusillade of shots struck an innocent bystander. However, the chief of police appeared on the scene an hour after the shooting and threw a cloak of secrecy over the entire affair.

13. The suspect took to his heels and vanished into thin air despite the cordon of heavily armed policemen.

NEWSWRITING STYLE: EXERCISE 4

INSTRUCTIONS: Make any changes necessary to improve the following sentences. Use a strong verb and a simple sentence structure. Eliminate unnecessary words, trite phrases and statements of opinion.

1. The blaze initiated at about 9:15 p.m. in the area of the school.

2. Another important concept of the author is the idea that it does not matter whether children begin to read before they are 10 years old.

3. Both women are members of the same religious denomination as their neighbor, that of Catholic.

4. A small fee of somewhere in the neighborhood of $30 a quarter will be the cost of the new student health insurance.

5. The article concluded by saying that World War II solved few basic problems in the world.

6. The crowd of protesters, which was estimated by various sources to be somewhere between the numbers of 5,000 and 10,000 strong, forced its way onto the military base and smashed hundreds of windows.

7. In the January issue of the magazine there was a guide to use in the purchase of diamonds.

8. The question that was asked every student at the school was whether he believes that newspapers report the news fairly and accurately.

9. To secure enough evidence for a conviction a police undercover agent often must buy from a drug pusher twice; otherwise not enough evidence is obtained to prove a person is actually a pusher.

10. The four were going on their way to the campus newspaper office but found themselves trapped in an elevator when it stopped between the third and the fourth floors of the building.

11. The hall in front of the courtroom slowly became filled with police officers being called in to give their testimony in the cases they were involved in.

12. One officer told of a case he had last week concerning loud mufflers. He said the judge decided to take everyone involved in the case outside to hear the car. After having the owner start the engine so everyone could hear it, and after ascertaining that the muffler was unduly loud, the judge fined the car's owner $15.

13. The maintenance man explained that it was a mechanical failure that made the elevator stop between floors of the building.

14. An amusing part of the story occurred as the man left the jail and said he really did not want to leave because the food was so much better than what his mother cooked for him at home.

15. Only one apathetic comment was made during the survey. One student said he does not care who wins the election.

16. A young driver, age 12, was involved in an accident at around 6 a.m. this morning at the north edge of town when the car he was driving went out of control and hit a tree.

17. The city sold the land for $3,000 less than the appraised value of $16,000, and one councilman complained that the property was worth much more than the price for which it was sold.

18. Another reason given by workers who are quitting their jobs at Disney World in Florida is that of being made to work for low pay at menial jobs they do not want and did not apply for.

19. No clear determination of the cause of mental retardation can be made in 75 to 85 per cent of the identified cases of retardation.

20. A spokesman for the State Highway Patrol said 24 motorists were injured last week, a drop of 54 from the 78 total the previous week.

21. The decision by the council to deny the license for the rock festival was the factor that prompted the young people to demand a hearing.

22. The group has $10,000 donated to it already by a person who wishes to remain anonymous.

23. Another important concept is the idea that every American is guaranteed by the U.S. Constitution a jury trial if he or she asks for one.

24. The suspect maintained that he had no recollection at all of the events that transpired the night the crime occurred.

25. Another complaint made by the students is the fact that tuition is too high for students who are not from the state and who must pay out-of-state tuition rates, which are three times higher than the rates paid by other students.

26. Alyce Kuchle, 97, who died yesterday, was a long-time resident of the city, having moved to this area at the age of 19.

Leads

The first paragraph in a news story is called the "lead." The lead should summarize the most interesting and important aspects of the story. The lead must arouse readers' interest and lure them into the story. Newspapers compete with other media and other activities for the attention of the public. In addition, stories within a single newspaper compete with one another for the attention of readers. If the lead bores or confuses readers, they will not finish the story.

Because the lead must summarize the entire story, it is difficult to write. The reporter must first decide what facts should be included in the lead. Traditionally, every lead was expected to answer six questions: who, how, where, why, when and what? But newspapers are abandoning that style of writing because leads that answer all six questions often become too complex. Moreover, answers to some of the questions may be unimportant. Few readers in a large city are likely to know the persons involved in most news stories, so their names need not be reported in the lead. The precise time and place that an event occurred may also be unimportant.

Leads should emphasize the answers to the most interesting and significant questions for each news story. When you write a lead, ask yourself:

1. What facts in the story are most important?
2. What facts are most likely to interest or affect my readers?
3. What is new? What are the most recent developments?
4. What facts are most unusual?

In the following examples, the first leads, although exaggerated, are the traditional kind of lead, answering all six questions. The revised leads answer only the most important and interesting questions for each story.

Andrew A. Kernan, 18, a student at Central High School and the son of Mr. and Mrs. Harry Kernan of 1432 Hillmore Lane, died at about 3:30 p.m. yesterday when his car overturned near a sharp curve on Old Highway 12.
REVISED: An 18-year-old student was killed yesterday when his car overturned while he was driving home from school.

Samuel Alston, assistant district attorney for the county, announced during a press conference at noon today in the Blackhawk Hotel that a prisoner, whom he did not identify, has confessed to the murder of a local liquor store owner seven years ago.

REVISED: A prisoner in the county jail has confessed to the murder of a local liquor store owner seven years ago.

By summarizing the story's most interesting and significant details in your lead, you can avoid a story that merely reports events in chronological order:

The weekly meeting of the City Council began at 7:30 last night in the council's chambers in City Hall.

REVISED: The City Council last night unanimously approved a proposal to begin construction on a new high school within 90 days.

The trial of Richard R. Niece for armed robbery opened in U.S. District Court yesterday morning with the testimony of his girl friend, who stated that Niece was in Chicago with her when the robbery occurred.

REVISED: Richard R. Niece abruptly stopped his trial on charges of armed robbery yesterday afternoon and admitted that he was guilty.

(Most city councils meet every week, at the same time and place. Those facts consequently are not interesting, unusual or newsworthy. The lead should report what the council said or did. Similarly, a lead should report not the way a trial started, but the outcome or the latest and most important developments.)

A lead should report the point of the story, not just its general topic:

The President discussed campus disorders last night in a speech that began at 7:30 p.m. in Northrop Auditorium.

REVISED: The President, speaking in Northrop Auditorium last night, denounced campus disorders and called them a threat to intellectual freedom.

The need for an ombudsman to represent and assist university students was the main topic considered at the Student Senate meeting last night.

REVISED: The Student Senate last night defeated a controversial plan to hire an ombudsman.

After writing dozens of stories about the same topic, some reporters tend to use the same formula for each story. As a result, all the stories begin to sound alike.

Two students reported seeing an unidentified flying object last night.

REVISED: Two students reported seeing a puzzling orange object hovering in the air above the university last night.

New safety regulations concerning automobiles were announced during a press conference in Washington, D.C., this morning.

REVISED: All cars manufactured after next Jan. 1 must be equipped with air bags that will inflate automatically whenever a car strikes another object, officials in Washington, D.C., announced today.

Specific details make leads more interesting and help reveal the uniqueness of the story:

A youth was injured in an explosion on his family's farm today.

REVISED: A high school student lost his right eye and the tip of his right thumb when a home-made rocket exploded in a shed on his family's farm today.

Students are opposed to a tuition increase for several reasons, according to a survey released today.

REVISED: Most students say they cannot afford to pay higher tuition rates and do not believe that higher rates are necessary, according to a survey released today.

Newspapers are sometimes criticized for emphasizing the unusual, but the fact remains that the unusual is more interesting than the routine and therefore attracts and holds readers' attention:

An Orlando man almost drowned yesterday while a class of lifeguards watched from a nearby dock.

A single-engine airplane overshot the grass runway at Callahan yesterday and crashed into a nearby cow pasture, injuring the two persons aboard and destroying their romance.

(The first story went on to explain that the lifeguards did not realize that the man was drowning. The second story explained that the pilot was taking his fiancee home to meet his parents. But his fiancee disliked airplanes and reluctantly agreed to fly home with him only after he assured her that the flight would be safe. She broke their engagement after the plane crash.)

Construct every lead around a strong active verb. Be careful not to overuse "is," "are," "was" and "were":

A 91-year-old woman was the victim of a purse snatching today.

OR: A 91-year-old woman was robbed of $642 while walking near her home today.

REVISED: A 12-year-old boy snatched a purse containing $642 from a 91-year-old woman today.

One person was killed and three others were injured today when their plane crashed while landing at Municipal Airport.

REVISED: A small plane lurched out of control and crashed in flames today at Municipal Airport, killing one person and injuring three others.

Paragraphs in news stories are short. Some have suggested that leads should not contain more than 30 words, but that limit is too rigid. However, as a general rule, a lead should not exceed four typed lines. Conversely, a lead may contain only a few words; there is no minimum length:

Man has reached the moon.

The last American combat troops left Vietnam at dawn today.

French scientists have discovered a cure for cancer in humans.

If your lead does exceed four typed lines, you may be trying to crowd too many facts into it. It may also be too wordy or repetitious:

No action was taken yesterday by the Seminole County Commission on the proposal by Chairman Greg Drummond that the county get completely out of the hospital business by eliminating a 200-bed disaster hospital the county has had in storage for the past 13 years.

REVISED: The Seminole County Commission yesterday failed to act on a proposal to sell a 200-bed disaster hospital.

A report released today by the U.S. Bureau of Public Roads discussed fatal accidents on interstate highways. In the report it was stated that of the approximately 2,754 fatal accidents which occurred on interstate highways last year, two-thirds involved only one vehicle and more than half of the deaths took place on Friday, Saturday and Sunday.

REVISED: Two-thirds of the fatal accidents that occurred on interstate highways last year involved only one vehicle, the U.S. Bureau of Public Roads reported today.

The bureau also reported that more than half the deaths on interstate highways occurred on Friday, Saturday and Sunday.

(In the first lead, minor details obscure the main point. The lead should stress the main point of the story, the fact that the commission failed to act on a proposal to sell its disaster hospital. The minor details can be reported in subsequent paragraphs. The second lead is too repetitious. If the lead clearly states that the U.S. Bureau of Public Roads has reported that two-thirds of the accidents on interstate highways involved only one vehicle last year, it need not be added that [1] the bureau released a report [2] that discusses fatal accidents [3] on interstate highways.)

Note that as revised, the second lead above contains two paragraphs. Some newswriters consider a lead to be a unit of thought, and that unit may include more than one paragraph. As another example, study the following lead, which was written by a reporter for United Press International:

Eugene W. Phillips stumbled and fell from his porch, punctured his back with a stick and slammed his head against the ground. It was about the nicest thing that ever happened to him.

Phillips had been blind most of the past 16 years. The accident a week ago helped him to partially regain his eyesight. (Reprinted by permission of United Press International)

Each lead should contain one or more complete sentences. The sentences must follow all the rules for proper capitalization, abbreviation, punctuation, diction and grammar. Do not use a present tense verb if an event occurred in the past, and do not delete the articles "a," "an" and "the," as did the students who wrote the following leads:

Council raises taxes, praises two.

REVISED: The City Council last night voted to raise property taxes 3.5 per cent and praised two policemen for rescuing an elderly couple from their burning home.

Offers gift to city for park.

REVISED: A retired teacher has offered the city $100,000 to buy land for a new park.

Most leads contain only one sentence. You can use two sentences in a lead, but such leads are often unnecessarily wordy:

Ralph O'Brien, police chief, commented on the danger of pistols in his speech to the Rotary Club last night. He said that family members are more likely to shoot themselves than a prowler.

REVISED: Police Chief Ralph O'Brien last night told members of the Rotary Club that citizens who buy pistols for protection are more likely to shoot themselves than a prowler.

Avoid starting a lead with a time, a location or a name, except for the rare cases when such information is what is unusual or significant about the story:

At 3:30 a.m. today, the City Council ended an 8-hour debate and approved a $47 million budget for the next fiscal year.

While flying over parts of Florida devastated by Hurricane Betsy, the President today promised to increase the federal aid being sent into the state.

Readers are most interested in stories that may affect their lives or the lives of people they know. Consequently, you should "localize" stories, mentioning details of local interest in the lead whenever possible:

> Eighty-three persons were killed today when their jet plunged into a field two miles south of the Tokyo airport.
> LOCALIZED: Eighty-three persons, including three from this area, were killed today when their jet plunged into a field two miles south of the Tokyo airport.

> The FBI reported today that the number of violent crimes in the United States rose 8.3 per cent during the last year.
> LOCALIZED: The number of violent crimes committed in the city last year rose 5.4 per cent, compared to a nationwide average increase of 8.3 per cent, the FBI reported today.

Similarly, you should emphasize the latest developments, using the words "today" or "yesterday" in leads whenever possible in order to show readers that the information is new. By stressing new developments, you can "update" an old story. Instead of reporting that a fire destroyed a store 24 hours earlier, for example, you can stress in your lead the events that have taken place since the fire, perhaps that firemen have determined the cause of the fire, identified the victims or estimated the amount of the damage:

> A three-alarm fire destroyed Higgin's Department Store on Main Street yesterday afternoon and damaged four other buildings.
> UPDATED: Firemen have discovered oily rags and an empty gas can in the basement of Higgin's Department Store, which was destroyed by fire yesterday. "It's a definite case of arson," one fireman said today.

> A 37-year-old woman gave birth to quadruplets at Memorial Hospital yesterday morning.
> UPDATED: Two quadruplets born at Memorial Hospital yesterday have died, but doctors today said the other two infants have been placed in incubators and are expected to survive.

If a story has no new developments or local angles, report it in a straightforward manner. Do not create an artificial angle:

> A high school student can smile today, since scuba divers recovered the false teeth he lost while swimming in Lake Moxie last week.
> REVISED: Scuba divers have recovered the false teeth a high school student lost while swimming in Lake Moxie.

Be as objective in your lead as you are in the body of the story. Report, do not comment, interpret or advocate:

> Late-night pedestrians, beware.
> REVISED: The police today warned that 12 pedestrians have been struck by cars during the last month, and all the accidents occurred at night.

> In a startling report issued today, 12 ministers charged that church members spend more money on beer and cigarettes than on charity.
> REVISED: Church members spend more money on beer and cigarettes than on charity, 12 ministers reported today.

Attribution is necessary whenever a lead presents an opinion or controversial statement rather than an undisputable fact. If you fail to name the source, your lead will imply that the opinion expressed is your own:

Doctors are not doing enough to curb drug abuse in the United States.
REVISED: Doctors are not doing enough to curb drug abuse in the United States,
the President today told delegates at a convention of the American Medical Association.

The wife of a serviceman will receive regular welfare payments because it is arbitrary
and inequitable to deny welfare payments to families of servicemen.
REVISED: A judge ruled today that it is arbitrary and inequitable to deny welfare
payments to the families of U.S. servicemen.

You can use direct quotes in leads. However, the quotes should (1) be brief, (2) adequately summarize the entire story and (3) be self-explanatory, as in these examples:

"Indian education is a failure and a national disgrace," a California educator declared
in a speech here today.

"All of a sudden I heard the rumble of tanks and the sound of machine-gun fire. Then
tear gas poured into the classroom."
Lorrie Kennedy, 22, reminisced about a revolution during the presidential elections in
Colombia. "I can remember every sound, every rumble, every shot," she said.

If the quote used in a lead is long, the entire lead will become too long and complex. If the quote does not adequately summarize the entire story, later segments of the story will seem disorganized and unrelated to the story's theme. If the quote is not self-explanatory, it may confuse and discourage readers and will have to be explained in a subsequent paragraph:

"It's just not worth it," advised 20-year-old Mark Thompson from his hospital bed
today. The youth was referring to his hobby of building rockets.
REVISED: A 20-year-old youth who was severely injured when a home-made rocket
exploded, today warned other youths experimenting with explosives that "It's just not
worth it."

"It was really a stupid thing to do," said Michael Schmidt, 21, a junior at the university. He was describing the actions of a scuba diver whose life he had just saved.
REVISED: A student who rescued a scuba diver from an underwater cave today said
that it had been "stupid" of the diver to enter the cave without a light and extra oxygen
tanks.

You may find it most effective to quote only a key word or phrase in a lead:

Dr. Margaret Mead, an authority on marriage and family life, today warned that student
marriages are creating "a settled, security-loving and unadventurous people."

A university student who observed an unidentified flying object last night said he was
"completely bewildered" by the experience.

A question can also make an effective lead, especially in light, humorous stories. In one case, members of a college psychology class disguised a student as an old man, placed him in a booth on campus and watched as he tried to give away dollar bills. Most passers-by refused to take money from the "old man." One re-porter, asked to write a story about the experiment, wrote the following lead:

Students in a psychology class tried to give away dollar bills yesterday, but they found
that most of their classmates were unwilling to accept them.

Another reporter began the same story with this question:

Would you accept free dollar bills from an old man?

To be effective, a question used as a lead must be specific, brief and provocative:

What do you do if you are on a ladder 20 feet above ground at 7 p.m. in an empty parking lot and a police car speeds up to you and a policeman jumps out and glares at you accusingly?
REVISED: How would you react if a policeman suspected that you were committing a burglary?

What should be done about Seminole Memorial Hospital?
REVISED: Should the county sell Seminole Memorial Hospital?

Other good question leads written by students are:

Are automobiles safe?

What is soul food?

Should colleges help coeds with the problem of birth control?

Summary leads are perhaps the easiest way to begin news stories, but as you gain experience you should experiment with other types of leads. Just make sure that every lead is clear, concise, impartial and interesting. Study the following beginning paragraphs. The first two stories appeared in the Orlando, Fla., "Sentinel Star." The third story was written by a student.

Alfred Charles Richardson, 602 Palmetto Ave., Longwood, was among 17 persons arrested Jan. 6 on burglary and grand larceny charges.
Saturday night he was released from Seminole County Jail on $8,000 bond after 37 days behind bars.
Early Sunday—as his wife vainly pleaded with him—Richardson apparently threw himself into the path of a train. The impact hurled his body 150 feet down the track, killing him. He was 23. . . .

Visibility was poor. The rain hammered on the cabin of the twin-hulled boat as it tossed about on the crests of the foaming waves.
But there was no trouble; the boat was riding the rough seas well.
Suddenly a shadow loomed out of the gray rain. It was so close there was no time to avoid the collision. The bow of the huge tanker struck the boat just forward of the cabin and sliced cleanly through both wooden hulls . . .

It begain with a raid on a watermelon patch near a small town in Minnesota.
It led to a tangle with a barbed-wire fence, a car accident and a hospital, where doctors refused to treat the two girls.
It left the girls with a few scars, several bills and two sore arms—but no watermelon.
One of the girls, in an interview today, explained that . . .

LEADS: EXERCISE 1

INSTRUCTIONS: Write *only* a lead for each of the following stories. As you write the leads, remember to:
1. Specifically summarize each story's most interesting and significant details.
2. Be concise. Most leads should not exceed four typed lines.
3. Use a complete sentence, a simple rather than a complex sentence structure and a strong verb.
4. Report when and where each story occurred. But do not begin the leads with the time and place the stories occurred unless those facts are unusually important and should be emphasized.
5. Do not comment, interpret or label.
6. Update, localize and attribute, when necessary.
7. Avoid slang, trite phrases and profanity.
8. Type and double space. Use the proper format and copy editing symbols.

1. The City Council met at 7 o'clock last night. The mayor called the meeting to order and read the minutes of the last meeting. All 12 councilmen were present. They approved the minutes of the last meeting. They discussed raising the salaries of police and firemen 7 per cent but tabled the motion until their next meeting. By a vote of 7 to 5 the council approved a controversial plan to begin a city income tax next Jan. 1. The tax will take 1 per cent of every paycheck issued within the city limits. Councilmen who favor the bill pointed out that the tax will affect persons who work in the city and use the city's facilities but do not live in the city.

2. The International Standardization Organization, which is composed of acoustics experts, today opened its annual convention. The convention is meeting in Geneva, Switzerland. Delegates from 51 countries are attending the convention, which will continue through Sunday. An annual report issued by the organization warned that noise levels in the world are rising by one decibel a year. If the increase continues, the report warned, "everyone living in cities could be stone deaf by the year 2000." The report also said that long-term exposure to a noise level of 100 decibels can cause deafness, yet a riveting gun reaches a level of 130 decibels and a jet aircraft, 150.

3. A 12-year-old boy practiced casting with his fishing rod. At 9:14 a.m. today he cast his line in his backyard. The line wound around an electric wire. The boy tried to yank the fishing line free, which pulled the wire into contact with another electric wire, causing a short circuit. Electrical service to 2,500 homes in the city was interrupted for two hours. The boy was not hurt. Police did not identify him.

4. Andrew F. Kohn, a former FBI agent, spoke to the Rotary Club at noon yesterday. Kohn said, "Serious crime in the United States is increasing 10 times faster than the population and sucks $50 million a year out of the U.S. economy because our society tolerates some kinds of crimes and criminals and refuses to deal adequately with the slums and poverty that nurture serious crime. Private citizens and government officials share the blame. They fail to act effectively against organized crime. Businessmen also feed the Mafia and other organizations by supporting their gambling activities. Some businessmen also accept mob loans and later find themselves being taken over by the criminals whose money they used."

5. A big DC10 jetliner took off from the airport at Grapevine, Tex., at 9 a.m. today. At the same time, a smaller Delta DC9 was practicing takeoffs and landings. A DC9 can carry 70 passengers, but only four persons were aboard the plane: three crewmen and an observer from the Federal Aviation Administration. The air behind the big DC10 was turbulent. As the DC9 approached the runway it became trapped in the turbulence. It tumbled out of control, slipped onto its back and crashed in flames. Everyone on the plane was killed.

6. During a press conference in his office at 8:30 a.m. today, David Kernan, president of the Security Insurance Co., which employs 630 persons, made the following statement: "We have decided to extend a new benefit to our employes and are the first company in the state to do so. We are, effective immediately,

providing our employes with legal insurance. Employes in need of legal aid may select any lawyer and this insurance plan will pay all their bills."

7. Fritz Ahl was arraigned in Municipal Court at 10:47 a.m. today. His attorney is Samuel G. Kooster. Judge Edward Failor handled the case. Ahl pleaded guilty to the charge of armed robbery at the First National Bank of about $31,000 last Sept. 3. Failor then proceeded to sentence Ahl to serve a term of 30 years in the state prison.

8. About 150 women invaded the building which houses the staff of the "Ladies Home Journal" this morning. The women brought work in the office to a standstill. A spokeswoman for the group read a statement which accused the magazine of publishing items that are "irrelevant, unstimulating and demeaning to the women of America." The magazine was also criticized for its "paternalism and sentimentality." The magazine office is in New York City.

9. Three members of a consumers' group named Concerned Americans held a press conference in Washington, D.C., today. They issued a report about the impact of tourism on cities in Florida. The report warned that tourism is causing skyrocketing prices and is endangering the state's ecological balance. The increasing population also is threatening educational, recreational and medical facilities, which are unable to keep up with increasing demands, the report said. The report added, "Millions of tourists flock to Florida every winter. As a result, the quality of life is declining. The state simply is not prepared to handle that many people. Roads are too small. There is not enough housing. The result is catastrophic. The state is experiencing a building boom, but it's haphazard. Beautiful beaches are being seized by developers. Suburbs are growing faster than cities can expand sewage facilities to them."

10. The Delta Queen is a sternwheel passenger boat. It carries passengers on the Mississippi River, from Minneapolis to New Orleans. Last year the Coast Guard condemned the boat as a fire hazard because parts of it are built of wood rather than steel. It was the last sternwheel vessel on the river, and many people argued that it should not be condemned because the Coast Guard regulations were intended primarily for ocean vessels and the Delta Queen could reach shore within minutes in an emergency. Both the U.S. House of Representatives and the U.S. Senate subsequently approved a bill to exclude the Delta Queen from the Coast Guard regulations. The President signed that bill today.

11. The U.S. Department of Commerce issued a report today. The report concerned the average family income in the United States. It compared the income of the average family in 1962 and last year. In 1962 the average family's income was $5,642. Last year it was $8,913. The average family income was highest in Alaska, where the average family had an income of $12,197 last year. The average was lowest in Mississippi and Alabama. In Mississippi the average family income was $5,884. In Alabama it was $5,952. Other states with high income averages—all over $11,000—were Wisconsin, New Jersey, Michigan, Massachusetts, California, New York and Hawaii. Generally, wages were highest in the Northeast and Midwest. They were lowest in the Southeast. The report also predicted that the average family income would rise to approximately $12,800 by 1980.

LEADS: EXERCISE 2

INSTRUCTIONS: Write *only* a lead for each of the following stories. When possible, use a full or partial quote or a question in your leads.

1. A spokesman for the Municipal Patrolmen's Association issued the following announcement last night: "We held our regular monthly meeting tonight and passed one of the most important resolutions ever to come before our group. Previous to this date, only one patrolman has been in each patrol car on our city's streets. In light of the recent attacks upon policemen in the United States, we feel this practice places the lives of patrolmen needlessly in danger. We do not want any man to work alone at night. It's too dangerous. We consequently will ask the City Council, at its meeting next week, to put a minimum of two patrolmen in each car at night—from dusk until dawn."

2. Mrs. Vera Simpson lives in the country near Enumclaw, Wash. Her children have grown up and left home. Her husband is dead. She still lives on a 160-acre wilderness ranch. The ranch has a large lake, and visitors can see the reflection of nearby mountains in the water. Living alone was too quiet for Mrs. Simpson. She loves weddings and began to invite friends to hold their weddings outdoors at the ranch, then to use a two-room guest house for their honeymoons. The idea has proved popular, and she now has about 30 weddings on the ranch every year. Couples must bring their own ministers. The audience often includes ranch animals—ducks, swans, peacocks, cattle and geese.

3. A spokesman for the U.S. Bureau of Labor Statistics held a press conference in Washington, D.C., at 10 a.m. today. He said, "The cost of living rose five-tenths of 1 per cent last month. Half the increase was caused by higher prices for clothing, automobiles, homes and food. It was the sharpest increase in the cost of living in three years. The increase pushes the Consumer Price Index up to 129.8% of its 1967 base of 100, which means it cost $12.98 last month to purchase goods that would have cost $10 in 1967."

4. The city's Human Rights Commission lost a battle last night. It wanted the City Council to ban a history book which it claims "deals erroneously and disparagingly" with American Indians. City Council members said they did not want to start banning books and refused to endorse the commission's efforts and refused to order school officials to remove the book from city schools.

5. The President recently toured Russia. Communist party chief Leonid I. Brezhnev was his host. Brezhnev is a car fancier. During his trip, the President gave Brezhnev the keys to a $9,000 Cadillac limousine. The Cadillac arrived in Moscow yesterday, and embassy officials in Moscow delivered the car to Brezhnev this morning. Brezhnev thanked the embassy officials and then drove off in the car.

6. Police received a call at 12:03 a.m. today from the manager of the Aloma Apartments, 4713 Bell Ave. The apartment manager told police someone had jumped into the apartment swimming pool and died a tragic death. Police investigating the case reported: "The pool had been closed since last Saturday night for repainting and was just being refilled with water. There were only 19 inches of water in the bottom of the pool at the time of the accident. The victim, Dr. Wesley Rue, apparently sustained a broken neck. He dove about 9 feet into the pool. The coroner pronounced him dead at the scene." Neighbors said that Dr. Rue often went swimming just before going to bed, and he apparently didn't look into the pool before diving into it last night.

7. Cab drivers in New York City have been on strike for 31 days. They are demanding higher wages. The strike involves 47,000 cab drivers who earn an average of $180 a week, with tips. They want a base salary of $250. Violence flared early today. Striking cab drivers attacked "gypsy" cabs when they tried to pick up customers in the city. Three gypsy cab drivers were hospitalized because of the injuries they sustained during the altercations. Two of their vehicles were destroyed by fire. Gypsy cabs are driven by men who are not licensed by the city and pick up passengers illegally.

8. Qantas, Australia's national airline, lost $500,000 today. A man called the airline's office in Sydney and said a bomb was on one of its planes. He promised to reveal the bomb's hiding place if the airline gave him $500,000. The airline put the money in two suitcases. The man drove up in a small yellow truck, got the money and then sped off into rush-hour traffic. He called the airline 15 minutes later, laughed and said there really was no bomb on any of its planes. No bombs were found during subsequent searches. The hoax is similar to the plot of a movie recently shown on television in Sydney. The plane was a Boeing 707 with 116 passengers. Police have not found the man nor recovered the $500,000.

9. The opposition was overwhelmed. Frederick W. Tosule got the job. The County Board of Supervisors today approved his appointment by a vote of 5 to 2. He was named the county's new welfare director. He formerly was an Army colonel. He retired from the Army two months ago. Some persons criticized his lack of experience in the field of welfare. He has no experience in the field whatsoever.

10. At 9:30 a.m. today 304 students at Central High School got a scare. Graduating seniors met in the auditorium, and each person was asked to write a statement about his or her hopes for the future. Class officers explained that they planned to read the statements at the class's 10-year reunion. But three class officers complained that the students were not taking the project seriously. With the permission of teachers, they secretly dramatized the seriousness of the world's problems. One class officer read an announcement over the public address system, warning everyone to remain seated in the auditorium because of an international crisis. Five minutes later, another announcement warned of a "red alert" because the crisis was worsening. Later, the lights in the auditorium flickered, then went out. Some students tried to leave, but discovered that the auditorium's doors were locked. Several girls began to cry. Two became hysterical. One fainted. The class officers then revealed that the affair was a hoax. School administrators, called later in the day by irate parents, promised to investigate the incident.

11. Robert J. Horten was charged with evading income taxes some time ago. The Internal Revenue Service said he has not filed a tax return since 1969 and owes $76,144 in back taxes. Horten is 37 years old. He appeared in U.S. District Court this morning and pleaded guilty to the charges against him. The judge delayed sentencing until next week. Horten has been district attorney in the city since 1968. He resigned five weeks ago.

12. The salary range for city schoolteachers is now $8,400 to $16,900. The teachers voted to accept that wage scale last night. Teachers have been teaching but have refused to participate in any extracurricular duties since their old contract expired last fall. Last night they voted to resume extracurricular duties immediately. The wage increase amounts to 7.4 per cent. New teachers will earn $8,400. To get $16,900, teachers must have a master's degree and 12 years of teaching experience.

LEADS: EXERCISE 3

INSTRUCTIONS: Write *only* a lead for each of the following stories. Use a full or partial quote in at least one lead. Use a question for at least one lead.

1. An announcement was made at a press conference in Washington, D.C., today by a spokesman for the Department of Health, Education and Welfare. The spokesman told reporters that, "The number of welfare recipients in the United States has risen to 14.4 million. The number is a record high and has increased by 1.2 million during the past year. Approximately 235,000 persons went on welfare last month, including 147,000 persons in the program of aid to families with dependent children (AFDC). The average welfare recipient is an adult who cares for two or three children. The average recipient receives $187 a month and remains on welfare for 42 months."

2. A judge today ordered the U.S. Navy to give a 10-year-old girl $57,754. She and her mother were at a resort in the Laguna Mountains to relax. Two Navy commando teams were practicing in the area. One team thought it had eluded the other and went swimming in the resort pool. The second team then stormed the resort, firing blank ammunition. A judge awarded the girl the money because her mother said she needed it "for continuing psychiatric treatment necessitated by the traumatic experience."

3. Motorists testified at last night's City Council meeting. They said they were mistreated by companies hired by the city to tow cars from no-parking zones. One man said his car was towed away while he was in it. Another said a tow-truck driver threatened him "with a tire iron." Another said he could not find his car for eight days, then "had to pay a $40 fee for storage." After a 2½-hour debate, the council unanimously adopted an ordinance regulating companies that tow cars for the city. The companies now must obtain a license from the city, report their fees to the city license inspector and paint their names and phone numbers on all their trucks. The proposal adopted by the City Council also prohibits "towing a car away if the car's driver returns to the vehicle before said vehicle is in motion behind the tow truck."

4. Three fire trucks responded to a call at 4:45 a.m. today. Mrs. Karen Bauer of 2132 S. 11th St. placed the call to the Fire Department because of a fire. In an interview later, she said, "I woke up and my throat was sore from all the smoke. I looked into the kitchen and it was just full of smoke. I got my children up and called the Fire Department while they were dressing and got out of the house. They were the first thing on my mind." Mrs. Bauer, a widow, has five children, ages 6, 11, 14, 18 and 22. Firemen said the family lives in an apartment above the Quality Drug Store, and the fire started in a neon sign outside the building, then spread to the attic. Flames were confined to the attic and a second-floor storage room. Smoke and water damage was reported throughout the building.

5. The National Fertility Study has issued its first report since its creation two years ago. It issued the report at a press conference in Washington, D.C., at 9:30 a.m. today. The report said the birthrate in the United States fell to 2.136 last year. It is the lowest rate ever recorded in the United States. A birthrate of 2.110 would mean the population would cease to increase. The National Fertility Study is financed by the federal government and conducted by researchers at Princeton University. The researchers suggested that if current trends continue, the population of the United States may begin to level off in another generation or two. A birthrate of 2.110 means the average couple of child-bearing age has 2.110 children.

6. The U.S. Department of Agriculture provides food for needy children. Because of complaints received by Congress, the department evaluated 60 school feeding programs, It reported finding "extensive waste and mismanagement." As a result, many poor children did not receive the food or received substandard food. The report compiled by the department found instances in which adult staff members ate free lunches provided for the children. In other cases, the department found instances of inadequate refrigeration. Some food was delivered 24 hours after its preparation. Some places received too many meals and other places received too few meals. The department announced the results of the study today.

7. The City Council last night settled an old argument. For the third time this year, it considered plans for an apartment complex for 840 families. Nearby homeowners continually have opposed the plans. They said the apartments will lower property values in their suburb and overcrowd roads and schools. The apartment builders last night told the City Council they would donate land for a 19-acre park between their development and the property owned by the homeowners. The suburb is located west of North Oleander Drive. After the builders promised to provide land for a park, the City Council approved the plans by a vote of 9 to 3.

8. Mrs. Marie Mitchell is a college student. She has four children, but decided to return to school, earn a degree and become a nurse. To save time, she buys groceries only twice a year. She went shopping yesterday, and her grocery list was 8 pages long. She divided the list among her husband, Fredric, and their children, and together they filled 19 shopping carts with food, and their bill totalled $481.17. All the groceries did not fit into their car, and they had to make three trips from the store to their home. The only items she buys on a weekly basis are meat, produce, bread, milk and eggs. She has fresh milk, eggs and bread delivered to her home. When they need meat, her husband buys a steer and has it butchered. They keep the food in two full-size freezers and two large refrigerators in their home. "Some people really think we're strange, but it saves gobs of time, and we save money, too," said Mrs. Mitchell.

9. The United Fund will open its annual drive in the city next Monday. The drive will end at 6 p.m. the following Saturday. Last year the United Fund set a goal of $1,240,000 but actually received only $1,213,000. The goal this year has been set at $1,320,000. The United Fund raises money for 32 charitable organizations within the city. This year's chairman is Ralph Eyles, pastor of Trinity Lutheran Church.

10. Randall Richards, 2, was playing near his home at 4:30 p.m. yesterday. Police said he apparently wandered into the street. He was struck by a truck driven by Eugene Smite, 49, of Milwaukee, Wis. Police did not file any charges against Smite. The child was taken to Memorial Hospital. A spokesman at the hospital reported this morning that the child is in critical condition. He is being treated for severe head and chest injuries. The child is the son of Mr. and Mrs. Wilfred Richards, 817 North Atlantic Ave. It is the second such tragic incident for the Richards family. Randall now is their only child. Two other children of the couple were killed in a car accident three years ago. A neighbor was taking her own daughter and the two Richards children to a movie one Saturday afternoon three years ago. Their car was struck by a bus and everyone in the car was killed.

LEADS: MISCELLANEOUS EXERCISES

1. Analyze the leads that appear on the front page of your local newspaper for three consecutive days.
   a. Count the number of words in each lead.
   b. Count the number of sentences in each lead.
   c. Analyze the sentence structure in each lead.
   d. Study the verbs, attribution and identification in each lead.

2. Find and analyze five leads that localize stories and five leads that update "old" stories.

3. Compare the leads that appear in: (1) your student newspaper, (2) a small weekly newspaper, (3) a metropolitan newspaper and (4) "Time" or "Newsweek" magazine. Analyze their similarities and differences.

4. Select 10 leads from your local newspaper which you believe are particularly good and 10 leads which you believe might be improved.
   a. Analyze the good leads and explain why they are effective.
   b. Rewrite the other leads, making any changes necessary to increase their effectiveness.

5. Select 10 stories from your local newspaper and rewrite their leads, using a full or partial quote.

6. Select 10 stories from your local newspaper and rewrite their leads, using a question.

7. Ask each student in your class to describe one interesting experience in his life.
   a. Write only the lead for a story about each student.
   b. Compare your leads with the leads written by other students.
   c. Exchange leads with other students and write critiques of one another's leads.

8. Write leads for 10 lectures given in your other courses.

The Body of a News Story

The portion of a news story that follows the lead is called the "body," regardless of its length. The body may contain one paragraph or 100 paragraphs. Each paragraph provides additional details about the main topic of the story, such as quotes, descriptions, conflicting viewpoints or explanations of various facts.

The body usually reports facts in descending order of importance, a technique that is called the "inverted pyramid" style. For example, a story about an automobile accident might contain the following sequence of paragraphs:

Lead:	Reports that a man died in an automobile accident.
Second paragraph:	Identifies the victim.
Third paragraph:	Describes the accident.
Fourth paragraph:	Names three persons injured in the same accident.
Fifth paragraph:	Describes the scene of the accident, a dangerous intersection.
Sixth paragraph:	Reports that a minor accident occurred at the same intersection a few hours later.

In the inverted pyramid style, each paragraph is typically a self-contained unit requiring no further explanation. The story ends not with a conclusion but with the least important facts; the only summary appears in the lead. The main advantage of this style is that if a reader stops reading after only one or two paragraphs, he will still have received the most important facts conveyed by the story. Moreover, the inverted pyramid style makes all the facts immediately understandable. Finally, if the story is too long for the space available, it can easily be shortened by deleting one or more paragraphs from the end.

The inverted pyramid style has several disadvantages. First, it often becomes repetitious. The lead summarizes and repeats facts discussed in greater detail later in the story. Second, a story in inverted pyramid form contains no surprises because the entire story is summarized in the lead. Third, the inverted pyramid style is complex and difficult to write well.

As an alternative, some newswriters use a summary lead, then report the remainder of the story in chronological order. Not every story can be told in chronological order, but when it is appropriate, that style provides a simple, orderly means of organizing a complex set of facts:

A 4-year-old boy was treated at Memorial Hospital yesterday after he drank a bottle of orange-colored furniture polish.

Mrs. Sandra Hansen, 494 Thorp St., told police she had gone outside at 3:30 p.m. to work in her garden. Her son, Todd, crawled outside a few minutes later.

"He was sobbing," Mrs. Hansen said. "He said his stomach hurt."

Mrs. Hansen said she found an empty bottle of furniture polish on the kitchen floor, read the label and discovered that the furniture polish was poisonous. She drove Todd to the hospital.

A spokesman at Memorial Hospital reported that Todd is in good condition and probably will be released today.

Do not overload a sentence by trying to cram too many diverse ideas into it:

A Catholic and mother of three children—two daughters ages 27 and 22 and a son age 15—and a grandmother, Mrs. Johns explained that she opposes abortion because if abortion is legalized, Americans next "might try to do away with the aged."
REVISED: Mrs. Johns, a Catholic, said she opposes abortion because if abortion is legalized, Americans next "might try to do away with the aged." Mrs. Johns has two daughters, 27 and 22, and a son, 15. She also has three grandchildren.

Thomas B. Gerald, a retired Navy chief, was on his way to the Plymouth Minute Maid plant, where he was employed as a guard, on Sunday evening when the fatal collision occurred at a railroad crossing on U.S. 141 just south of Longwood.
REVISED: Thomas B. Gerald was killed Sunday evening at a railroad crossing on U.S. 141 just south of Longwood. Gerald, a retired Navy chief, worked as a guard at the Minute Maid plant in Plymouth and was driving to work.

Similarly, each paragraph in a news story should discuss only one idea. Do not combine several diverse ideas within a single paragraph:

Living with his cousin has helped Faisal adjust to American norms. He added, "We often cook Middle Eastern dishes and invite our American friends over to our apartment."
REVISED: Faisal said living with his cousin has helped him adjust to American norms. He added, "Life is much freer here than in the Middle East. My cousin explains your ways to me and shows me what to do."

They often cook Middle Eastern dishes and invite American friends to their apartment.

Transitions are necessary whenever a news story shifts from one topic to another. A single "linkage word" may provide the necessary transition. Linkage words may refer to the time different events in the story occurred, for example "later," "earlier," "sooner." Linkage words may refer to a geographical area, for example "in other areas," "here," "there," "at the Capitol." Linkage words may also emphasize contrasts, for example "however," "conversely," "but," "nevertheless." Other common linkage words are "therefore," "also," "moreover" and "in addition."

Newswriters can also introduce new ideas by relating them to ideas already discussed. A sentence that introduces a new topic may refer to some fact mentioned earlier:

The family moved into the new house on the first of the month.
The house has five bedrooms, a fireplace and a recreation room.

Disney World is expected to attract 10 million persons to Central Florida every year.
State officials say the visitors are causing an economic boom.

(The second sentence in the first example repeats a key word, "house." The second sentence in the second example refers to a concept mentioned earlier, "the visitors.")

Transitionary sentences can also be used to link diverse ideas within a news story. Transitionary sentences should be treated as secondary leads; they should summarize the new topic, not simply name it:

> He also discussed the television coverage of the senator's funeral.
> REVISED: He said the television coverage of the senator's funeral was misleading.

> Safety experts warned of the potential danger of automobiles.
> REVISED: Safety experts said thousands of Americans are killed or injured every year because of mechanical defects in their automobiles.

(The original sentences are vague and consequently dull. They mention new topics but fail to convey any specific information about them.)

Transitions can be extremely short and, like leads, can sometimes utilize questions. Study the transitions in the following paragraphs, written by a student:

> "Sure I smoke dope," said a sophomore majoring in journalism. "There's nothing wrong with it. It isn't as harmful as alcohol."
> Has he tried LSD?
> "No, and I don't think I would," he said. "It can mess you up too much. I'll stick to pot and hash (hashish)."
> Most students said they never use any drugs.
> "I wouldn't touch that stuff," said a junior majoring in English. "It's bad for you. It's a crutch. People shouldn't need crutches. If they can't face reality without being stoned, then they aren't very good people to begin with."
> But half the students said they thought marijuana should be legalized and soon will be.
> How soon?
> "Two years," said the sophomore majoring in journalism.
> "Five years," said the junior majoring in English . . .

After completing a news story, reread it to determine whether: (1) the lead adequately summarizes the story and (2) the body adequately explains the lead. If the lead fails to summarize the story, the body will seem disorganized and unrelated to the central theme. If the body fails to explain the lead, the story will not answer all the questions that arise in readers' minds.

The more complex a story is, the more difficult it is to summarize in a single paragraph. For example, at a single meeting the student senate at your school might vote to: (1) oppose plans to raise tuition $45 a quarter, (2) discontinue subsidies for the student yearbook, (3) appoint a new vice president, (4) schedule the annual Awards Day and (5) demand more parking places for student vehicles.

Few reporters could concisely summarize all five issues in a single paragraph. As an alternative, you could summarize the most important issue in the lead, then discuss that issue in detail, introduce the second most important issue, discuss it in detail and so on through all five issues. But that kind of story would mislead too many readers. Readers interested in Awards Day or the parking problem might mistakenly assume that the entire story concerned the first topic, tuition, and stop reading before they came to the issue that interested them.

To avoid that problem, you could summarize the most important issue in the lead, then summarize the remaining issues in the second paragraph:

> The Student Senate has unanimously condemned a proposal to increase tuition $45 a quarter, beginning next fall.
> During its meeting yesterday, the senate also voted to discontinue subsidies for the student yearbook, appoint a new vice president, schedule Awards Day for May 27 and demand more parking places for student vehicles.

(Thus, readers are immediately told all five topics discussed in the story and, if they are interested in the fourth or fifth topic, will be aware that it is discussed in greater detail later in the story.)

You might prefer to summarize the main topic in the lead, then list the remaining topics in the subsequent paragraphs:

> The Student Senate has unanimously condemned a proposal to increase tuition $45 a quarter, beginning next fall.
> During its meeting yesterday, the senate also voted to:
> 1. Discontinue its annual $5,000 subsidy for the student yearbook, which consequently will cease publication after this year.
> 2. Appoint Harry Davidson, a junior, as vice president of the senate, replacing Lee Kernan, who did not return to school this fall.
> 3. Schedule the annual Awards Day for May 27.
> 4. Demand more parking places for student vehicles.

Some newspapers number each item in a list, as above; others mark each item with a dash, star, dot, check or some other typographical symbol. All the items in a list must be parallel in form: if one item is an incomplete sentence, every item must be an incomplete sentence. Lists are particularly useful when several diverse ideas must be summarized in a single story. Important ideas can be listed immediately after the lead; less important details can be summarized briefly in a list at the end of the story.

As for the end of the body of a news story, reporters seldom use a conclusion because most stories are summarized in the lead. Conclusions, therefore, are usually flat, unnecessary, subjective and sometimes confusing:

> The remainder of the meeting was concerned primarily with the gripes and comments of those present about conditions on the campus. Also discussed were some suggestions on ways those conditions could be handled.

> Is Miss Roth a good teacher? We certainly believe so.

(The first conclusion raises rather than answers questions. It fails to report precisely what conditions disturb the students and how the students hope to correct those conditions. Any topic mentioned in a news story must be fully explained. The second conclusion contains an opinion rather than a fact. Moreover, it is unnecessary. If the story has clearly described Miss Roth, her performance and her students' reactions to her, readers should be able to decide for themselves whether she is a good teacher.)

Few rules are ironclad, and reporters occasionally do try to startle readers with "suspended interest stories" that contain surprise endings. Suspended interest stories are usually brief and humorous. They do not have summary leads; instead, their leads contain interesting details that lure readers into the stories:

> Police killed an intruder after he set off a burglar alarm in a clothing store on Main Street shortly after 1 a.m. today.
> The police entered the building after customers in a nearby tavern heard the alarm and surrounded the store until police arrived.
> The police found the intruder perched on a counter and killed it with a fly swatter.
> "It was my third bat this year," declared a policeman triumphantly.

A recent story that was widely reported in the United States concerned the death of a very young suspected criminal in New York City. One version of the story, reported by United Press International, began this way:

> At the age of 9, Ricky Badden was arrested for the first time in his tough Staten Island neighborhood.
> In the next two years he was taken into custody 17 times on such charges as sexual abuse, robbery, burglary, larceny, assault and criminal mischief.
> Late Tuesday night Badden, now 11, was shot and killed by police as he fled on foot from a stolen car . . . (Reprinted by permission of United Press International)

THE BODY OF A NEWS STORY: EXERCISE 1

INSTRUCTIONS: Write complete news stories based on the information given.

1. Salley Hardee filed a suit against the city's Board of Education three months ago after the board ruled that she had to quit work because she was pregnant. Current rules state that women must leave their jobs after they reach their fifth month of pregnancy. They may return to work after a six-month leave of absence. Mrs. Hardee filed a suit against the board, demanding the right to continue teaching as long as she was physically able. Her case was scheduled for a court hearing at 9:15 a.m. today. She did not appear in court, and her case was postponed indefinitely. Her attorney explained that Mrs. Hardee had been admitted to Memorial Hospital at 11 p.m. yesterday and gave birth to a 7-pound boy at 4 a.m. today.

2. Babies sometimes are abandoned on the doorsteps of churches and homes. But the State Department of Public Welfare today issued a report that discusses another problem of abandonment that has become even more common. The report states that during the past year residents of the state have abandoned 182 adults, usually at hospitals. Most of the abandoned persons are old, poor and sick. Their ages ranged from 47 to 93. Some did not have any possessions. Others had only a grocery bag stuffed with a few meager belongings. One had a tag pinned to his shirt saying, "Do not return." Relatives often cannot take care of these people and cannot afford to place them in nursing homes. Yet the report issued by the State Department of Public Welfare said most of these persons are not sick enough to enter a hospital. Most are examined in the hospitals' emergency rooms, then transferred to a state institution.

3. Donald J. Reffstrom visited the city today. He is assistant director of the U.S. Forest Service. He spoke to the County Conservation Commission and said, "The U.S. Forest Service historically has depended upon lookout towers in our 154 national forests to detect fires. That no longer is possible. Smog has become such a problem that lookouts no longer can spot smoke. Smog has reduced visibility up to 80 per cent. Smog creates a light gray background. When a fire first starts, the smoke is almost white. It blends in with the smog and is impossible to detect. So we're already in the process of phasing out lookout towers. They're being replaced by airplanes. From a plane, you can look straight down through a much thinner layer of smog than if you were looking horizontally from a tower. We also can equip airplanes with infrared heat-sensing devices, so we can detect fires even when the smog becomes quite dense."

4. The president of the city's Board of Education thinks the time has come for the city to consider long-term teacher contracts and merit pay for superior teachers. Board President G. T. Underwood made his views known at a board meeting last night. He said salary talks last year were "lengthy and difficult." He added, "Negotiations began shortly after Jan. 1 and ran past mid-April, when such matters are commonly settled, and into late June, a time when school administrators generally concentrate on budget preparation. Budgets cannot be finalized until teacher pay is settled because salaries account for more than half of any school system's expenses. I think our board should begin to consider three- or even five-year contracts for our city's teachers. A longer contract would eliminate the need for these long negotiations every year. We also should begin to consider the issue of merit pay so we can reward our system's better teachers and give the other members of our staffs some incentive to improve their performance."

5. A boy got into a dryer in a laundromat near his home today. His name is Todd Thompson. He is 4 years old. His mother, Mrs. Alice Thompson, told police that Todd's 6-year-old sister notified her that the boy had climbed into the machine, which began to revolve when the door closed behind him. His sister's name is Mary. When Mrs. Thompson came to the rescue she could see Todd being tumbled in circles inside the machine. She estimated that he was in the machine for about five minutes. She

called the police after rescuing the boy, and a police ambulance rushed him to Memorial Hospital. He was treated for minor scratches and bruises and released from the hospital a few hours later. Doctors at the hospital said Todd temporarily lost his sense of balance, but recovered it within a few hours and did not suffer any serious injuries. The laundromat is at 406 Atherton St. The Thompsons' home is at 404 Atherton.

6. The annual art show sponsored by the city's public schools opened at 7 p.m. yesterday. For the first time, the show included art work from every grade level, from kindergarten through twelfth grade. Previously, only a few grades were selected to display their art projects. The show is being held at the Municipal Art Gallery. Stephen Souder, coordinator of art education for the city's schools, said, "We had people from all over the county attend the opening last night. There even was a crowd waiting to get in when we opened the door. I'd estimate that 500 people entered the gallery before we closed at 10 last night." The exhibits will remain on display until 5 p.m. Sunday. The gallery is open from noon until 10 p.m. Monday through Friday and from noon until 5 p.m. Saturday and Sunday. Altogether, more than 400 art projects are included in the show. Souder added, "We don't give any prizes during the show. But there is considerable merit for children just in having their paintings selected for the display. Every class in the city has art, and just a few exhibits are selected from each school. Next year we'll probably pick one or two grades and concentrate on their work. Usually we get only one room in the gallery and don't have much space. But we planned a large show this year to celebrate the 100th year that art classes have been taught in the city's schools. We've been real innovators in this area. Most schools haven't taught art for more than 20 or 30 years."

7. New York City has 1.2 million welfare recipients. About 50,000 have been classified as "employable" under new regulations. Stricter welfare laws passed by the New York State Legislature require employable welfare recipients to go to work. If they cannot find jobs with private companies, city agencies will employ them on public works projects. The welfare recipients will work as paraprofessionals in hospitals and as maintenance people in schools and parks. They will not replace regular city employes, but will be assigned to jobs that the city has not been able to afford to fill in the past. The new rules will go into effect next Monday.

8. "I just froze at the wheel," the girl said. She added, "I was just learning how to drive." She appeared in Municipal Court this morning. She was charged with making an improper left turn. Police said the car she was driving struck a light pole when she attempted to turn around in the middle of a block and her car ran up the curb. The girl, Suzanne Wilke, 16, of 4328 Melody Lane, was receiving her first driving lesson when the accident occurred. The judge did not fine her. He ordered her to attend a driver's school conducted one night a week by city policemen. She must go for three months. She must also pay for the light pole, which the judge said was worth $485.

9. The man is Harry Allenson, 83. He lives at 550 Central Ave. At about 9:30 a.m. today Allenson was walking south on a sidewalk near his home. He was struck by a car and taken to Memorial Hospital. Gerald Schwartz, 32, of 517 Garfield Ave. was driving the car. The police charged Schwartz with failure to yield the right of way when emerging from a driveway. At the hospital, Allenson is reported in satisfactory condition. He is being treated for a variety of injuries, including several broken ribs and abrasions to his left arm and hip. An ambulance rushed him to the hospital immediately after the accident.

10. Gladies Turner is a 22-year-old secretary. She lives in an apartment above a restaurant at 411 Main Street. Someone has broken into her apartment twice within the last month. When the thief broke into her apartment one month ago, he took her television set, a stereo and a half-dozen kitchen appliances. Last night Miss Turner returned home at 1 a.m. after attending a movie with some friends. When she arrived home, her apartment door was open. She called the police, and when they entered the apartment with her, they found that all the stolen items had been returned to the apartment and were piled on the floor. A note taped to the television set said, "I'm moving to another city and don't need these things any more, so you can have them back."

11. Police and firemen responded to a call at the First National Bank Building at 8:22 a.m. today. The bank is located at 482 Main Street. Kenneth Tipton, 26, of 428 N. 7th St., a window washer, began work on the 10th floor. He stepped out a window and leaned backward to wash the window's outside panes. A metal hook anchored in the window frame pulled loose. Tipton slipped from the window ledge and dangled from another hook on the other side of the window. Both hooks had been attached to a belt around his waist. People on the street below him, alerted by his screams for help, called the Fire Department. A bucket and several brushes fell to the sidewalk, but did not strike anyone. However, the bucket did smash through the back window of a parked car. In an interview after the incident Tipton said, "I was saying my prayers. I didn't know whether my belt would hold or not. I saw a lot of people below me, and I yelled for help. Then a dentist and some other men in the building came and pulled me back in the window before any of the firemen got there." Tipton is married and has a 5-year-old daughter. He said he got the window-washing job two months ago and never had any problems until today. He quit working for the rest of the day, but said he would return to work tomorrow. "I like the job," he said. "I'm outside. The pay is good, and it's interesting work."

12. City Alderman Samuel Hoffman today issued a news release. In the news release he pointed out that, while campaigning for the office he now holds, he promised voters that he would release copies of his income tax statement to the public each year. He said, "I believe this action is necessary to retain the confidence of the public and to clearly demonstrate that I am not involved in any conflicts of interest. I would also like to take this opportunity to call upon every other public official in the city to follow my example and report their income to the public." According to the income tax return, Hoffman and his wife, Ellen, earned a total of $21,232 last year. Hoffman, a fireman, earned $8,800. He received another $2,500 for serving on the City Council. His wife, a city schoolteacher, earned $9,200. Hoffman also reported that the couple received $732 in interest from bank accounts and U.S. Savings Bonds.

13. Police charged a man with disturbing the peace after an incident last night. Police filed the charge against Thomas Rielly, who is 27 years old and who resided at 1432 Center Ave. until yesterday. The following facts were revealed during testimony in court today:

Rielly appeared at the police station at 11:15 p.m. yesterday and told the sergeant on duty there that he was locked out of his apartment. When questioned further, Rielly admitted that his landlord had locked him out because he had not paid his rent for the past two months and because some neighbors complained that he made too much noise. The police sergeant said he could not help Rielly. The sergeant explained that the dispute was a civil matter, and that Rielly would have to consult a lawyer. At 11:43 p.m. Rielly called the Fire Department and reported that he was locked out of his apartment. The Fire Department sent one truck to his residence. Firemen put up a ladder and crawled through an unlocked window on the second floor, and then were able to walk downstairs and unlock the front door from the inside. The Police Department monitors all fire calls in the city and sends patrolmen to assist the Fire Department, when necessary. The police sergeant remembered Rielly and, when he determined that Rielly was the man who had talked to him earlier, ordered Rielly's arrest. Two patrolmen went to Rielly's apartment and charged him with disturbing the peace. Rielly was unable to post $25 bail and was held in jail overnight. In court this morning, he told Judge Edward Failor he did not understand the charge filed against him and did not understand why he could not call the firemen for help. "They're supposed to help people in trouble, and I was in trouble," he explained. The judge fined Rielly $20.

14. Paul Golinvaux got his wedding ring back today. Golinvaux lost the ring while swimming in Crystal Lake 16 years ago. His wife, interviewed at their home today, told the story. She said, "I couldn't believe it. The ring is just like brand new. It's in better condition than mine, and I've been wearing mine for 17 years. Paul lost his ring while we were swimming in Crystal Lake after a picnic just a few months after we got married. We didn't even look for the ring then because we thought it would be impossible to find. Then the doorbell rang this morning and some man I'd never met before asked

if my husband had lost a ring. I said, 'No.' My husband never had any ring since then, so I was sure he couldn't have lost one. Then the man showed me Paul's wedding ring, and when I saw it I recognized it. It's a plain gold band, just like mine. The man said he saw the inscription, "To Paul from Jean," and showed it to some friends. Finally someone traced it to the jewelry store where we bought it, and the store still had our name on file. So they gave him our address. I don't even know the man's name. I invited him in, and he was here for half an hour having coffee with me, but I've forgotten his name. I was just too excited to remember it. I called the jewelry store, but the people there don't know his name either."

15. Three police cars were dispatched to the First National Bank at 4:49 p.m. yesterday after a burglar alarm was set off at the bank. When the police arrived at the premises, they discovered that the bank was closed and officials at the bank did not even know that the alarm, which rings only at the police station, had been set off. The alarm does not ring in the bank itself. A subsequent investigation of the incident revealed that a janitor was sweeping the bank floor. Investigating officers concluded that his broom struck the alarm, which is on the floor beneath a cashier's desk.

16. Plans for a proposed housing project for the elderly were presented to the City Council at 9 a.m. this morning. The project involves the construction of a seven-story building with 104 apartments which would be rented to persons 55 or older. No one would be required to pay more than 25 per cent of his monthly income for rent. Rents would range from $20 to $104 a month. The project is being planned for a site at the north end of Main Street so that its occupants can easily walk to necessary facilities. Space on the first floor may be occupied by stores that could serve the building's occupants. Plans call for the floor to be occupied by a grocery store, a pharmacy and a barber shop. Plans for the project were presented to the council by the Ecumenical Housing Agency, a corporation formed by 17 churches in the city. A spokesman for the agency said that the churches feel they have an obligation to help needy persons in the city, and that the elderly have been neglected by other agencies. He added that the building is expected to cost $1.7 million, and it is hoped that it will be entirely self-supporting. However, he added that he will also ask the City Assessor's Office for a tax exemption as a nonprofit organization for the project. He explained, "We don't want to get off totally free. We fully intend to pay our fair share. We realize that we will need police and fire protection and sewage service, and we will pay for it. But taxes on a $1.7 million building normally would be $47,600 a year. We simply couldn't afford that much. However, we would be willing to give the city $6,000 a year as a contribution for its services."

17. In the past week an arsonist has caused four fires in the city. Last night a fire caused $15,000 damage at Central High School. Firemen said the blaze was confined to a basement room used by the student band. Officials at the school said that classes are meeting as usual today and that the band has been moved to the school auditorium. They added that 80 band uniforms were destroyed in the blaze. Meanwhile, the police said a 15-year-old freshman has admitted starting all four fires. The police questioned him after firemen reported that he was present in the crowd at all four fires. Fire Inspector Reynold Hunt said the youth told him he could not explain why he started the fires. Hunt said, "He says the idea to start the fires just popped into his head. He doesn't know why. I think he just threw a match into a wastebasket at the school last night. Fortunately, a janitor discovered the fire before it spread beyond that one room. This kid hasn't been in trouble before, and he comes from a real good family." Police turned the youth over to juvenile authorities. They refused to release his name because he is a minor. Hunt said the youth also admitted starting two garage fires and a fire in the sports department at Taylor's Department Store.

18. According to a police report, the Alamo Shell service station at 886 Central Ave. was robbed sometime between midnight and 6 a.m. today. The robbery was discovered when employes at the station arrived for work this morning. They noticed that a 300-pound safe was missing. Further investigation revealed that a side door had been pried open. Fred Neff, an employe at the station, said, "Someone's going to be awful mad. There wasn't anything in that safe but a bunch of comic books. We've

had so many robberies here during the past year that we never keep any money in the building at night. We always deposit it in the bank every night just after we close. My kid plays here all the time, and I usually keep a bunch of comic books around to keep him quiet while I'm working. People keep swiping the comic books. Even some of the kids that work here at night read them. So I just decided to keep them locked up when my kid's not here."

5
Improving Newswriting Style

Whenever a major news story arises, dozens and sometimes hundreds of reporters rush to the scene, gather information and then transmit that information to the public. All the newswriters report the same story, but some of their stories are more successful than others. Why?

Some reporters are particularly adept at gathering the information necessary for comprehensive news stories. They critically examine statements given to them by persons seeking publicity. They go beyond the superficial and, when necessary, ask probing questions. They also search for alternative sources of information.

Other reporters are particularly adept at writing news stories. Their stories are colorful and realistic. They arouse readers' curiosity, interest and emotions by portraying the drama inherent in some news stories. They describe vividly the people, places and events that they write about and use quotations to allow persons involved in stories to convey their ideas directly to the public.

Skilled newswriters can transform routine events into front-page stories. One reporter, bored and lazy, may write a three-paragraph story about a routine traffic accident. Because of the story's mediocrity, his editor is likely to bury the story on the bottom of page 47. Another reporter, intrigued by the same accident, may go beyond the superficial, asking more questions, looking for unusual angles and injecting some color into his story. He may write a six-page story about the same accident. Because of the story's excellence, his editor may place it on the front page.

For example: a teenager is killed when his bicycle falls directly in front of a truck. One reporter may be content to identify the victim and the truck driver and to report when, where and how the accident occurred. Another reporter may go into far more detail, not to be morbid, but to illustrate the tragic consequences of traffic accidents. He may describe the cause of the accident, the massive injuries suffered by the victim, the mob of bystanders struggling to see the corpse and the truck driver's retching anguish. He may also describe the arrival and duties of the coroner, and policemen borrowing a hose from a nearby house to wash the blood off the highway. Finally, the reporter may describe the resumption of traffic for hundreds of motorists unaware of the death and infuriated by the delay it caused. By describing the death (something newspapers almost never do), the reporter may try to show its shattering impact on a few persons—and its insignificant impact on the community, which quickly resumes its normal routine. Some persons might argue that the story is too sensational. Editors might reply that it shows life as it really is and that it might convince motorists of the need to drive more carefully.

The same principles might be applied to any type of story—a girl winning a scholarship, the construction of a new school or the election of a mayor. A good reporter will go beyond the superficial. He will describe the girl, school or mayor. He will report the story in depth and detail. He may also discuss the significance of the story and the events that led up to it.

The following guidelines are intended to help you improve your style of writing so that your news stories will be as clear, accurate and interesting as possible.

Be Specific

Avoid vague words, such as "very," "little," "much," "young" and "old." Vague words and phrases fail to communicate any meaningful information to readers. For example:

at an early age	in her later years
traveled extensively	only recently
never finished his formal education	too time-consuming
within a short time	for several years

What is "an early age"? It might be 2, 5, 10 or even 20. Similarly, a "short time" might be 5 minutes or 10 days. Someone who "never finished his formal education" might have left school after the sixth grade or after his junior year of high school. Entire sentences may also be so vague that they lack meaning:

The student said her job is unusual but fun.
REVISED: The student said she traces fraudulent telephone calls.

The response was terrific.
REVISED: More than 7,200 persons attended the rodeo, compared to 5,600 the previous year.

During a question-and-answer session after his speech he made several statements about the tax structure.
REVISED: During a question-and-answer session after his speech he said the tax structure places too heavy a burden on middle-class families.

Avoid generalities; they suggest that you failed to obtain all the specific details necessary for a good news story or failed to take the time to report those details as clearly and concisely as possible.

Identify, Define and Explain

Readers should be able to understand immediately every word, phrase and sentence in a news story. Assume that your readers have not received any previous information about your topic. Identify, define and explain difficult words and concepts. Newspapers identify individuals by reporting their age, address and occupation. College newspapers identify students by reporting their year in school, major and home town. Such identification makes stories more meaningful for readers. It also helps protect newspapers from libel suits. If a newspaper simply reports that a man named Ralph Scott has been charged with manslaughter, the newspaper has failed to identify a specific individual and consequently has libeled every man named Ralph Scott. But if the newspaper reports that Ralph Scott, 47, of 1481 Bell Ave. has been charged with manslaughter, it is identifying only one person. Other men named Ralph Scott are no longer identified and consequently cannot sue the newspaper for libel. Reporters may also have to define words:

> About half the addicts are on a methadone-maintenance program. Methadone is a synthetic narcotic used to break heroin addiction.

> Schmidt said, "I put my regulator in his mouth." A regulator is a breathing device used by scuba divers.

One student in a newswriting class wrote a seven-page story about an ombudsman but never told what an ombudsman is. As a result, other students in the class were unable to understand the story and many stopped reading after the first page.

Occasionally, reporters, particularly when they are well-informed about a topic, fail to realize the need to clearly explain every aspect of a story to readers:

> A reporter covering Indiana's senators devoted all the coverage to the senior senator because he had done a favor for the reporter concerning a drunken driving incident.
> REVISED: Goligoski said the reporter for an Indiana newspaper was charged with drunken driving and put in jail in Washington, D.C.
> The senior senator from Indiana quietly arranged for the reporter's release, and the reporter began to publish a great many favorable stories about the senator.
> "It was obvious that the reporter was paying back the favor," Goligoski said.

(Before the sentence was revised, it failed to explain the incident adequately. It mentioned a "favor" but did not specifically describe the favor. It also mentioned "a drunken driving incident" but did not provide any meaningful information about that incident.)

Use Examples

Use specific examples to clarify abstract concepts. Whenever possible, illustrate the effect a story will have on your readers. If the city council votes to raise property taxes 3.5 per cent, point out that the increase will raise the tax on the average home in your community by $37 each year. If you write a story about an individual, say a coed who became an alcoholic and flunked out of college, describe specific incidents that illustrate the problem:

> She said her grades fell from B's to D's and F's after she started drinking heavily.
> REVISED: She said school became unimportant. "I can remember staying up all night before my public health final. When I took the test I was smashed. And if that wasn't bad enough, then I ran the entire 10 blocks back to my apartment so I could drink some more. Of course, I flunked public health."

Examples are particularly important when an entire story concerns an abstract issue. If you wrote a story about the lives of young persons after they drop out of college, you would have to report the percentage of students that drop out of college every year, their reasons for dropping out and what they do afterward—join the Army, get married, get a job or enroll in another school. In addition to reporting such statistical information, a good newswriter would illustrate the story by describing the experiences of two or three students.

"The New York Times" recently began a story about the chemical contamination of fish by describing a single person.

> Sitting in his Fulton Fish Market office one morning, Abe Haymes swallowed his shot of Scotch from a small paper cup, slapped his chest and declared:
> "I've been eating fish every day of the week for the past 40 years. Do I look sick?"
> Like the rest of the city's fish dealers, Abe Haymes is angry about recent publicity concerning mercury and DDT contamination of fish . . . (Reprinted by permission of The New York Times Company)

Similarly, "Fortune" magazine (July 1971) began a story about the interstate highway system by describing the system's impact on a single truck driver:

> Five times a week Cecil Irvin swings up into the cab of his truck, carefully fits his sunglasses and leather gloves, and then starts the heavily loaded twin trailers behind him down the narrow streets of St. Louis.
>
> Six blocks later, he turns up a ramp leading to Interstate 70 and then, shifting up through 10 gears, he gradually picks up speed toward Kansas City.
>
> In Irvin's 250-mile trip westward, one sees in capsule form much of the impact, good and bad, of the $70 billion interstate highway system . . . (Reprinted by permission)

Use Quotations

Reporters obtain much of their information by listening to other persons, and they can convey a great deal of that information to readers in the form of direct, indirect or partial quotations. Direct quotations present the source's exact words and are placed in quotation marks. Direct quotes are best used to report statements that are particularly important, colorful or interesting. Indirect quotations paraphrase the source's ideas and comments and are not placed in quotation marks. Indirect quotations are used most often because they allow newswriters to report ideas most effectively. If a source fails to state his ideas clearly, the reporter can summarize the most significant facts and eliminate those that are repetitious, irrelevant, libelous or otherwise unprintable. A partial quotation is one in which only the key words or phrases in a statement are quoted directly and the remainder of that statement is summarized.

> INDIRECT QUOTE: Mrs. Ambrose said journalism students should deal with ideas, not mechanical techniques.
> PARTIAL QUOTE: Mrs. Ambrose criticized the "trade school atmosphere" in journalism schools and said students should study ideas, not mechanical techniques.
> DIRECT QUOTE: Mrs. Ambrose said, "Journalism students should be dealing with ideas of a social, economic and political nature. There's too much of a trade school atmosphere in journalism schools today. One spends too much time on minor technical and mechanical things, like learning how to write headlines."

Quotes can add depth and detail to news stories. You might make a point briefly, then use a quote to provide more detail:

> The detective said police work involves more than directing traffic and solving crimes. He said, "It's encouraging good citizenship and helping to make this a good town to live in."

> Miss Mead said there is a trend toward vocationalism on college campuses. "Many students now demand from college not a chance to think, but a chance to become qualified for some job," she explained.

> Many married students must work full-time to support their families. Miss Mead said, "This means they don't have time to think, to experiment."

Quotations also help reveal the people mentioned in news stories to be unique, interesting individuals; for example, one reporter wrote a story about a woman, the mother of five children, who returned to college. The story included this quote:

> "Very practically, I came back to college to get my degree in education because I want to be busy and couldn't quite see myself as a 50-year-old checkout girl in some super-

market. Five years of my life consisted of runny noses and coffee klatches with the neighbors. Now my kids wipe their own noses and the neighbors are still having their coffee klatches, and I'm going to be a senior next quarter."

Similarly, a story about a white woman who was dating a black man contained the following quote:

"There are some places we can't go together, but the worst part is that we can't even go to each other's homes. My dad is a giant bigot. If he ever found out about Jim, he'd kill us both.

"Jim's mom thinks all white women are rich bitches. I guess it all comes down to the fact that the sight of us together leaves a bad taste in society's mouth.

"I used to think people discriminated against me because I'm Italian Catholic. I didn't know what discrimination was."

Quotes also help emphasize dramatic moments:

Miss Nelson said she did not see the car when she stepped out onto the street. "But when I saw the headlights coming at me, I knew it was going to hit me."

Cornick shot the bear twice. "It bellowed, did a forward roll and charged toward us," Cornick said. "We ran for the car and stayed in it all night."

Some quotations require an explanation or further identification. Such information can often be inserted in parentheses:

Dr. Harold Termid, who performed the operation, said, "The technique dates back before the 20th century when it was first used by the French to study ruminants (cud-chewing animals)."

"There are a lot of things that happen that reporters never see," Smith said. "They (military officials) do a good job of covering up."

Quotations, like any other segment of a news story, should be divided into short paragraphs to increase their readability. When a quote runs to more than a half-dozen typed lines, divide it into paragraphs. Begin the quotation and every succeeding paragraph with a quotation mark. Place a closing quotation mark only at the end of the entire quotation:

Sen. Mondale added, "Perhaps the most shocking example of the insensitivity of the Bureau of Indian Affairs (educational) system is the manner in which boarding school dormitories have been administered.

"Psychiatrists familiar with the problems of Indian children have told us that a properly run dormitory system is the most crucial aspect of boarding school life, particularly in the elementary schools.

"Yet, when the 6-year-old Navajo child enters one of the boarding schools and becomes lonely or homesick, he must seek comfort from an 'instructional aide,' who has no training in child guidance and who is responsible for as many as 100 other unhappy children.

"This aide spends most of his time performing custodial chores . . . At night, the situation worsens as the ratio of dorm aides to children decreases."

The use of quotations raises an important question: if reporters quote someone, must they use that person's exact words? Some journalists believe that they can modify a quote, that they have a responsibility only to report the person's ideas fairly and accurately. But most journalists agree that a quote must consist of the person's precise words, that the only permissible modifications are the correction of grammatical errors, the deletion of profane words and the occasional deletion of unnecessary words if their deletion does not change the meaning of the sentence.

The creation of direct quotes by a reporter is likewise frowned upon as unfair to both his source and his audience. Each time a reporter places quotation marks around a statement, he is telling readers, "This is exactly what the person said." If a reporter presents his own words or his own interpretation of a source's statements as a direct quote, he is misleading readers. If he makes a mistake—however unintentionally—he may seriously injure his source's reputation and his own reputation as well.

✓ Attribute Statements

Reporters do not have to attribute statements that report undisputed facts, such as that World War II ended in 1945 or that Boston is in Massachusetts. But reporters must attribute: (1) statements about controversial issues, (2) statements of opinion and (3) all direct and indirect quotes. If you do not attribute such statements, your stories will seem to present your own opinions, not the opinions of other individuals:

> The rifle's performance is substandard, further endangering lives already threatened by military combat.
> REVISED: Sen. Hastel said the rifle's performance is substandard and is endangering the lives of soldiers.

> The workers were fooling around while they were loading the hay. Suddenly Frey's jacket sleeve became tangled in the machinery, and his hand was crushed.
> REVISED: Sheriff's deputies reported that Frey's jacket sleeve became entangled in the machinery while the workers were loading the hay, and his hand was crushed.

(Attribution is particularly important in the second example because it implies that the workers were careless. Most newspapers consequently would delete the phrase "fooling around.")

Attribution also helps readers determine the credibility of statements reported by the media. Readers may distrust statements from some sources but accept the opinions offered by other sources; for example, all the following statements report the same information, yet most American readers would find the second statement most believable:

> The U.S. government is ignoring millions of hungry and jobless citizens.

> During a Senate hearing today, Sen. Edward Kennedy testified that the U.S. government is ignoring millions of hungry and jobless citizens.

> The Soviet newspaper "Pravda" today charged that the U.S. government is ignoring millions of hungry and jobless citizens.

Each time you present another opinion, quotation or controversial statement, you must clearly attribute it. The attribution consequently may have to be repeated a dozen times in a single story:

> She said she hates college. "The teachers make us memorize. They don't teach us how to think."
> REVISED: She said she hates college. "The teachers make us memorize," she explained. "They don't teach us how to think."

> Roseau said he has attended college for three years, but never enrolled in the school, paid tuition or received a grade.

"I'm not going to get a degree, but I am getting a damned good education. I just pick the courses I really want to take and attend the classes. Most classes are so big that the teachers don't even know I'm there. I've never had any trouble."

REVISED: Roseau said he has attended college for three years, but never enrolled in the school, paid tuition or received a grade.

He added, "I'm not going to get a degree, but I am getting a damned good education. I just pick the courses I really want to take and attend the classes. Most classes are so big that the teachers don't even know I'm there. I've never had any trouble."

Avoid combining fragments of quotes with complete quoted sentences:

His mother said life is a "simple matter. I told all my children that if they really believe in God they have nothing to fear."

REVISED: His mother said life is "a simple matter." She explained, "I told all my children that if they really believe in God, they have nothing to fear."

Ross said he expects to find a job "within a few weeks. And when I do get a job, the first thing I'm going to do is buy a new car."

REVISED: Ross said he expects to find a job "within a few weeks" and, when he does, "The first thing I'm going to do is buy a new car."

The attribution can be placed at the beginning or end of a sentence. It can also be placed within a sentence, but it should not interrupt a thought:

"I sold my home," she said, "and my husband's restaurant."

REVISED: "I sold my home and my husband's restaurant," she said.

"The robber told me that he had a gun," Lien said, "and warned me to keep cool because the cops were after him."

REVISED: Lien said, "The robber told me that he had a gun and warned me to keep cool because the cops were after him."

Do not place the attribution at the end of a very long paragraph. If you do, readers will not know who is speaking until they have read the entire paragraph. Thus they will be unable to evaluate the credibility, meaning and significance of the paragraph as they read it. Place the attribution in the first sentence in a long paragraph.

The words used to attribute statements must be impartial and accurate. Newspapers often use the words "said," "commented," "stated," "replied," "declared," "added" and "explained." The word used must accurately reflect the speaker's actual behavior. Do not use the word "explained" unless the speaker actually did explain something, and do not use the word "added" unless he actually did add something to his previous comments.

The mass media can easily slant news stories by the ways in which they make attributions. For example, a study conducted by John C. Merrill ("How 'Time' Stereotyped Three U.S. Presidents," "Journalism Quarterly," Vol. 42 [Autumn, 1965], pp. 563-70) revealed that "Time" magazine disliked President Truman but favored President Eisenhower and seemed to remain undecided about President Kennedy. When "Time" attributed statements to President Truman, it reported that he "said curtly," "said coldly," "barked" and "preached." "Time" also reported that Truman spoke "with his voice heavy with sarcasm" and "flushed with anger." He grinned "slyly" and was as "cocky as ever." But when "Time" attributed statements to President Eisenhower, it reported that he "said with a happy grin," "chatted amiably," "paused to gather thought," "said warmly," "skillfully refused to commit himself" and "brushed aside misunderstanding." According to "Time," Eisenhower also was "obviously a man with a message." He made statements "serenely," "frankly," "calmly," "confidently," "sensitively" and "effectively." But President Kennedy simply "said," "announced," "concluded," "stated," "urged," "argued," "suggested," "recommended," "insisted," "contended," "maintained" or "promised."

Some editors also dislike the verbs "hopes," "feels," "believes," "wants" and "thinks." They explain that a reporter can know only what a person says, never what he hopes, feels, believes, wants or thinks. Other words are also inappropriate. People speak words; they do not grin, smile, laugh or cough them. Such words are particularly undesirable because they are easily misused:

> "We were bleeding all over the floor," she grinned.

You can use a single word, such as "said," to attribute all the statements in a news story. Using the same word a dozen times may seem awkward at first, but "said" and its synonyms are neutral and almost always appropriate. Few persons declare, announce or reveal anything. Most simply make a statement, then answer reporters' questions.

Attribution, like the remainder of news stories, must be concise. Phrases like the following are seldom necessary:

> He stated further that . . .
> In making the announcement, he said . . .
> In his present capacity as mayor, he said . . .
> He went on to say that . . .
> He also pointed out that . . .
> He let it be known that . . .
> The man made it clear that . . .
> Putting it on the line, he explained that . . .

All eight of these phrases can be replaced by "he said" or "he added." The following examples illustrate similar problems:

> He concluded by saying that, in his opinion, most teachers are underpaid.
> REVISED: He said most teachers are underpaid.
>
> "I just want to go home." These were the words of an Indiana man in U.S. District Court today.
> REVISED: "I just want to go home," said an Indiana man in U.S. District Court today.

If you quote more than one person in a single story, you must provide a clear distinction between one person's statement and another's. If you do not clearly attribute and separate each quote, readers may be unable to determine who is speaking. The problem becomes particularly acute when one quote immediately follows another:

> Vice President Spiro Agnew complained that when President Nixon finished his speech about Vietnam, "His words and policies were subjected to instant analysis and querulous criticism . . . by a small band of network commentators, the majority of whom expressed in one way or another their hostility to what he had to say."
> "The Nixon administration is trying to bring the news media under some form of covert control. This is not merely an attack on mistakes of judgment, but on the basic principle of free speech," replied Norman E. Isaacs, president of the American Society of Newspaper Editors.

These two paragraphs are confusing. Persons beginning the second paragraph might mistakenly assume, at least for a moment, that Vice President Agnew was criticizing President Nixon. To avoid confusion, the second paragraph might be revised as follows:

Norman E. Isaacs, president of the American Society of Newspaper Editors, replied, "The Nixon administration is trying to bring the news media under some form of covert control. This is not merely an attack on mistakes of judgment, but on the basic principle of free speech."

Finally, do not quote an inanimate object. You can quote a spokesman for an institution, but you cannot quote the institution itself:

In interviewing various hospitals in the area, she found that a staggering number of VD cases were treated each month.
REVISED: Spokesmen for hospitals in the area told her they treat a staggering number of VD cases each month.

Use Descriptions

Descriptions, like quotations, make a news story more interesting and help recreate the scene in the minds of readers. But reporters are reluctant to use descriptive phrases. They describe what they hear but seldom describe what they see, feel, taste or smell. One student attended a speech by the controversial Father James Groppi, and when she submitted a story about the speech, she handed her instructor a separate note that said:

The question and answer period was very brief. Father Groppi answered only three questions because he had to catch a train because the State of Wisconsin would only let him leave Wisconsin for a brief time until the legal charges filed against him are settled.

Despite the unusual circumstances surrounding Father Groppi's departure, the student failed to include this descriptive detail about his legal problems in her news story.

Descriptive phrases and sentences are most effective when they are specific. Report concrete, factual details. Avoid trite generalities. Study the following sentences, written by students asked to describe their campus:

The students seemed relaxed as they studied outside under trees on the large lawn.
The art complex appears to be a temporary structure.
Most of the buildings on campus have few windows. Those few windows are small and cleverly designed.
The library casts a knowledgeable shadow.
Here man has altered nature, but he has not destroyed it.
The campus is a lesson in harmony between man and his natural surroundings.

(All these sentences are composed of vague generalities and consequently fail to give readers a detailed picture of the campus. The first sentence, for example, presents an opinion rather than a fact. It reports that the students "seem relaxed" but it fails to report a single detail to support that conclusion. It fails to specifically describe the students' appearance, activities or positions. The sentence also refers to a "large lawn" but does not indicate how large the lawn is, where it is or what it looks like. The second sentence states that the art complex "appears to be a temporary structure," but fails to explain why the writer reached that conclusion. The third sentence reports that buildings on the campus have "few windows" and that the windows are "small and cleverly designed." If there are so few windows, the reporter might easily have counted them, estimated their dimensions and described their clever design.)

Note the specific details in the following story, which was published by the Orlando, Fla., "Sentinel Star." The story described the ordeal of one man who was struck by a bolt of lightning.

Three miles from the dock, a lightning stroke which may have been packing temperatures of up to 60,000 degrees Fahrenheit (the sun's surface is 11,000) pierced his head above and behind his right ear . . .

details

The bolt, carrying possibly 1,300 times what would be found in a normal household circuit, seared a path across his neck, down his chest, back across his waist and down his right leg, where it riddled the boat's hull with 50 to 60 small holes.

The same problems arise when reporters try to describe a person. Instead of describing factual details (height, weight, clothing, voice, mannerisms and so on), reporters sometimes mistakenly present their own overall evaluation of the person. Study the following sentences, written by students who were asked to describe one speaker:

He spoke with authority.
He gave a cool, casual speech.
He was frank about his duties.
He immediately took control of the situation.
He appeared unprepared for the occasion.
He appeared comfortable and relaxed.
His voice resonated with a maturity and sophistication rarely found in students.
He expressed some discomfort when he was called upon to speak, but he did a fine job of informing the students about his job.

(None of these sentences is an actual description. For example, the first sentence concludes that the speaker spoke "with authority," but it fails to explain why the writer reached that conclusion; the second sentence reports that he gave a "cool and casual" speech, but does not specifically describe either the speaker or his speech.)

When you describe another person, look at him carefully, then report specific facts about him. Avoid generalities, conclusions and evaluations:

POOR: He was well-dressed.
BETTER: He wore a plain blue shirt and blue-and-white striped pants.

POOR: He is a large man.
BETTER: He is 6 feet tall and weighs 210 pounds.

You can include a descriptive word or phrase almost anywhere in a news story. You can also devote an entire paragraph to a description of a person or object. Study the following descriptive phrases and sentences, all written by students:

She gazed out the window at her dead garden.

The audience applauded Galbraith, a tall, gray-haired man.

Mrs. Ambrose, a former newspaper editor, arrived breathless and five minutes late for her speech.

He leaned back in his chair, laced his fingers together across his round belly and clenched the cigar in the corner of his mouth.

She is 70 years old, but her thick brown hair is only slightly graying. As she spoke, she leaned back on a pillow and nervously smoked a cigarette. She has only a small table and a cot in her living room, and both are covered with knickknacks. She takes her guests into her bedroom to sit and talk.

Descriptions combined with quotations create even more vivid pictures for readers:

A 15-year-old girl with waist-length red hair put a Beatles' album on the stereo, then returned and asked, "Is the LSD here yet?"

A graduate student said he is "not particularly enthused" about the women's liberation movement. "I kind of enjoy the situation the way it is now," he said, smiling at his girl friend. She smiled back, raised a clenched fist and walked away.

Kent, a short, muscular man, has been selling dry ice for 10 years. Out on the dock, he cut a block of ice with a screeching band saw and explained, "These blocks are 10 inches square and weigh 60 pounds each and are 110 degrees below zero Fahrenheit. Actually, it's 109.6 below."
Despite the temperature of the blocks, sweat trickled across his forehead as he continued to cut the blocks and wrap them in insulated bags.

She smiled, got her photo album and thumbed through it. Then she said, "Fortunately for me, my mind is still here. One of the saddest things about old age is realizing that someday your mind might deteriorate before your body finally dies.
"I can still look at these pictures and remember who all the people are and exactly when and where the pictures were taken. The day I forget one is the day I'll give up."

Avoid Technical Language

Reporters often obtain their information from documents such as court records, press releases and police reports. You must critically examine such documents and present the information in terms that every reader can understand immediately. More specifically, you must eliminate technical phrases and obscure jargon:

Identification of the victims was withheld by police pending notification of their next of kin.
REVISED: Police said they will not identify the victims until their relatives are notified.

Dr. McKay added "Ethnic groups today that subsist on a vegetarian diet and practically no meat products seem to have a much lower level of serum cholesterol and a very low incidence of ischemic diseases arising from atherosclerotic disease."
REVISED: Dr. McKay added that races which eat little meat have low rates of coronary heart attacks and related illnesses.

Stress Answers

Reporters also obtain information by interviewing other persons. In your news story, you should stress a person's answer to your question, not the question itself. Do not repeat both the entire question and answer; such repetition almost always is unnecessary and dull. You can omit the question or incorporate it into the answer:

The reporter was asked whether he had any training in the laws of libel while he attended college. He replied, "I don't remember any classes like that at college."
REVISED: The reporter said he does not remember any classes in the laws of libel at his college.

OR: In response to a question, the reporter said he does not remember any classes in the laws of libel at his college.

Miss Thompsen, asked about her feelings as she received the award as the outstanding freshman at the university, said, "It's the biggest surprise of my life."
REVISED: Miss Thompsen said the award she received as the outstanding freshman at the university was "the biggest surprise of my life."

Answer Questions

News stories should answer questions, not raise them. As we have seen, you do not have to answer all six questions—who, how, where, what, why and when—in your lead, but you should answer all six questions somewhere in each news story. Moreover, you must answer all six questions about every new topic you mention in the same story. If you do not explain what you are talking about, you will only bewilder readers. For example, students have made the following statements in news stories, but failed to go on to answer the questions they raise:

He said the institution of marriage should be abolished. (Why?)
 He suggested that the civil rights movement is dead. (Why?)
He said, "Women just shouldn't be given the same opportunities as men." (Why not?)
He was reluctant to give his name because the FBI had taken his picture. (When? Where? Why?)

Other students have answered all six questions in their stories, but so obscurely that only a skilled interpreter could decipher their meaning:

John Adles said the possible deformity of the child is the only circumstance in which he felt abortions should be legal.
REVISED: John Adles said abortions should be permitted only when the child might be born deformed.

He said that before marijuana is legalized there has to be more extensive research pointing in the direction of a harmless drug.
REVISED: He said marijuana should not be legalized until research has proved that it is harmless.

Be Accurate

Newspapers are particularly careful about spelling names correctly. Spelling mistakes damage a newspaper's reputation and infuriate the persons whose names have been misspelled. Some newspapers require reporters to verify the spelling of every name they use in news stories by consulting a second source of information, usually the telephone book or city directory. The reporters then must underline the names to indicate that they have verified the spellings. Most errors occur because reporters have failed to verify spellings, to check a second source or to check for internal consistency:

Raymond Foote, editor of the newspaper, said minority groups often want publicity but do not know how to obtain it. Foot added that he tries to be fair but does not have enough space to publicize the activities of every group in the community.

Of 10 men and women interviewed, five favored the tax proposal, three opposed it and three said they had not yet reached any decision.

Sloppy proofreading also results in spelling and typographical errors, which can often be embarrassing:

Richard, Tom and two fiends reached the summit of the mountain after climbing for 17 days.

Miss Taylor's mother said, "She was lucky to get her job back. Sometimes employers are reluctant to hire hack people who have had kidney transplants."

Be Fair

Reporters have an obligation to report every significant viewpoint fully and fairly and to let readers draw their own conclusions about those viewpoints. If a group in your community names one company "The Polluter of the Year," you must contact that company and give it an opportunity to respond to the criticism. Include the reply in your story about the "award." If the reply is published later, not everyone who read the first story will see the rebuttal.

The Better Business Bureau today warned consumers about "free inspections" being offered by Doss Furnace Repair, Inc.

A spokesman for the bureau said it has received more than 200 complaints from homeowners during the past month. Some said they received bills for more than $300 after the company had offered to inspect their furnaces free.

A spokesman for the company said the customers apparently failed to read and understand its contracts.

The spokesman said customers are always told that the inspections are free, but that they will be charged for any necessary repairs or replacement parts.

If the person or institution being criticized is unavailable or refuses to speak to you, report that fact in your story to indicate that you attempted to fulfill your obligation to be fair.

Other Guidelines

1. Use contractions—"doesn't," "hasn't" and so on—only in direct quotations.

2. State where you obtained the information reported in every news story—from a press conference, speech, interview or whatever.

3. Remain impartial. You should be a neutral bystander; you should not become a participant. Except in extraordinary circumstances, you should never have to use the words "I" or "we" in a news story.

4. Fully identify persons the first or second time you mention them in news stories. Do not name a person in the first or second paragraph, continue to refer to that person throughout the story and then identify him in the final paragraph.

5. Avoid long, awkward titles, and never place two titles before a name. If you would not use a title in a casual conversation with friends, do not use it in a news story:

Junior medical technology major and Peace Corps volunteer Susan Glenn said she expects to graduate next June.

REVISED: Susan Glenn, a junior majoring in medical technology, said she expects to graduate next June. She will then enter the Peace Corps.

Seminole Education Association Salary Committee Chairman Calvin McMurray said the committee will meet Monday night.
REVISED: Calvin McMurray said the Salary Committee of the Seminole Education Association will meet Monday night. McMurray is chairman of the committee.

6. If you want to report a fact, report it clearly and emphatically. Do not slip it into a story:

The parents of 14 children, Mr. and Mrs. McCallan will celebrate their 50th wedding anniversary Sunday.
REVISED: Mr. and Mrs. McCallan, who have 14 children, will celebrate their 50th wedding anniversary Sunday.

James Bloach admitted he robbed Anders of $170 and said he tied the Vanguard drive-in theater employe's hands with a rope, but he denied that he killed the son of Central High School Principal Robert Anders.
REVISED: James Bloach admitted that he robbed Anders of $170 and said he tied Anders' hands with a rope, but he denied that he killed the youth.
Anders, the son of Central High School Principal Robert Anders, worked at the Vanguard Theater.

(The second example first mentions Anders, then refers to "the Vanguard drive-in theater employe" and to "the son of Central High School Principal Robert Anders." At best, the way these facts are presented is confusing. At worst, it is misleading, since readers might assume the story is describing three persons, not just one.)

Similarly, if you write a news story concerning Memorial Hospital, use the building's full name the first time you mention it. Later, you can refer to it as "the hospital." Do not call the building a "hospital" the first time you mention it and later refer to it as a "structure," "building," "medical facility" and "health center." Be consistent.

7. Use such words as "it," "this," "these," "those" and "that" with caution. Avoid starting a paragraph or even a sentence with one of these words unless its antecedent is obvious.

He said, "Only childless couples will be admitted, so there won't be any noise, and the trailer park won't affect schools in the area. We expect the average trailer in the park to cost $12,000, and some will cost twice that much."
Some members of the audience objected to this.
REVISED: He said, "Only childless couples will be admitted, so there won't be any noise, and the trailer park won't affect schools in the area. We expect the average trailer in the park to cost $12,000, and some will cost twice that much."
Some members of the audience disagreed and said the trailer park would still be too noisy and would lower the value of property in the area.

Commissioner Ben Benham, who represents Scott County on the Transit Authority, said the bus system no longer is losing money. He attributed this to the elimination of routes that had consistently shown losses.
REVISED: Commissioner Ben Benham, who represents Scott County on the Transit Authority, said the bus system no longer is losing money because routes that had consistently shown losses have been eliminated.

You can avoid this problem by repeating a key word or phrase or by rewriting the foggy sentence.

8. Every item in a series must be parallel in form. Place an introduction or explanation before, not after a list so that the list will be immediately meaningful.

More sheriff's deputies, the highway patrol and the FBI were sent to the bank.
REVISED: More sheriff's deputies, highway patrolmen and FBI agents were sent to the bank.

Attempting to elude a police officer, no driver's license, fleeing the scene of an accident and driving while intoxicated were the charges filed against him.
REVISED: He was charged with attempting to elude a police officer, driving without a license, fleeing the scene of an accident and driving while intoxicated.

9. Do not state the obvious. It wastes space and bores readers. For example, one student, describing the changes that had occurred during the life of a 100-year-old woman, said:

Modern superhighways, high-speed automobiles and jet planes are now common objects of the modern era.

The student might have expressed the same idea in a more interesting and relevant manner, such as:

Mrs. Hansen, who once had to spend six days on a train to visit her family in California, now flies to California in five hours every winter.

Similarly, a student writing about attempts to control the birthrate of pigeons began the story as follows:

Pigeons are common in large cities and even in small towns across the country. They are social birds and have established stable communities.
It seems acceptable that they are social and stable. However, citizens are annoyed by the messiness of pigeons and would rather not have so many around.

A more interesting lead would have been:

Some cities in the United States are experimenting with drugs to control the population of pigeons.

10. Be original. Go out and gather the information for stories yourself. Do not rewrite information that someone else has gathered and reported. By the time you rewrite the information, it is likely to be outdated. Moreover, readers may have read the original story. And you may be sued for violating a copyright law.
11. Be certain that phrases, modifiers and clauses are placed in the proper position in each sentence:

She was arrested in the restaurant by police carrying lottery tickets and almost $200 in cash.
REVISED: When police arrested her in the restaurant, she was carrying lottery tickets and almost $200 in cash.

He was found lying on the floor by a cleaning woman.
REVISED: A cleaning woman found him lying on the floor.

IMPROVING NEWSWRITING STYLE: EXERCISE 3

INSTRUCTIONS: Write complete news stories based on the following information. Unless your instructor tells you otherwise, assume that you have enough space to report every important and interesting detail in each story.

1. Shoplifting

A police sergeant today arrested a 17-year-old high school student. The police did not identify the student because he is a juvenile. But the police did describe his arrest. The student was charged with shoplifting. The sergeant was off-duty and working at the department store to supplement his income. He has arrested dozens of shoplifters at the store, but this case was particularly unusual. The sergeant stopped the student as he walked out of the store with a chain and lock valued at $1.29. The chain and lock can be used to protect a bicycle or a school locker. The youth became very upset when he was arrested and shouted that the sergeant was ruining his reputation and would ruin his future. Later, at the police station, the sergeant asked the student why he took the lock and chain. The student replied, "Because they have been stealing me blind down at school and I need it to lock my stuff up."

2. Transit System

Residents of Milwaukee, Wisconsin, will vote next Tuesday on a proposal to build a rapid transit system. The system will cost about $1 billion and include railroad and bus service for commuters. If voters approve the referendum, construction will start in about one year. The referendum includes a 1 per cent local sales tax to finance the program, and some of the money would have to be collected before work could begin on the project. The system would be operated by a county transit authority. The system, when completed in the year 1982, would include 86 miles of rapid rail transit and 142 miles of rapid busways. The plans call for reducing fares on both the bus and rail systems to a maximum of 25 cents in an effort to attract commuters to the system and to relieve congestion on freeways leading into the city. Bus fares now cost 45 cents. The transit authority also would buy 290 new air-conditioned buses to replace older equipment.

3. Telephone Deposits

The State Public Service Commission held a public hearing here yesterday. The hearing was concerned with telephones. The commission is investigating the fact that persons who want to obtain a telephone must pay a deposit before the telephone company will install a telephone in their home or place of business. The deposits range from $10 to several hundred dollars, depending on whether the customer has had a telephone before, his credit rating and his use of the telephone. If the telephone is used for business, the deposit is higher. The deposit is also higher if a person makes a great many long-distance telephone calls. The commission yesterday spent the entire afternoon listening to a lawyer for the Legal Aid Society. The lawyer said the deposits are a serious problem for the poor. He said many poor persons do not have a telephone because they cannot afford to pay the deposit. He added that a telephone is not a luxury. It is a necessity. He explained that people need telephones to call for help in the event that an emergency occurs—a crime, fire or serious illness. He said the importance of having a telephone is more critical for the poor than for the rich because, "The poor are the victims of crimes more often than the rich. Also, it is harder for poor persons to obtain and keep a job if they do not have a telephone because they are unable to call anyone, and potential or actual employers are unable to reach them."

4. Salary Proposal

Alderman Thomas Henley today announced that he will submit a proposal to raise the salaries of all 12 members of the City Council and the salary of the mayor. He will submit the proposal at the next City Council meeting, which is scheduled for 8 p.m. next Monday. The proposal would increase the salaries of the aldermen 64 per cent. The proposal would increase the salary of the mayor 130 per cent. The aldermen now are paid $14,000 a year. The proposal would raise their salaries to $23,000. The mayor now earns $15,200 a year. The proposal would raise his salary to $35,000. "It's only fair," said Henley. "This is a full-time job, and the persons who hold my job exercise as much responsibility as the key executives in any private company. The council employs more than 4,600 persons. I think we should be paid a decent salary commensurate with our responsibilities. If people in this community want a good government and a good community, they're going to have to pay for it. If they don't raise our salaries, we're going to have to continue to hold other jobs and work as aldermen part-time. That means we can't devote all our time and attention to the city's problems. You just can't administer a city and do a good job when you're only working at it 20 hours a week. I want to add that I'm not alone on this. I've discussed the matter with the other aldermen, and they're with me 1,000 per cent."

5. Swimming Death

A 6-year-old boy is dead. He died at the municipal swimming pool yesterday. But he did not drown. He apparently died after he was stung by a bee. His name was Bruce James Helget. Lifeguards saw him floundering in the pool, and they pulled him out of the water. A Medi-Alert bracelet on his wrist revealed that he was allergic to bee stings. The lifeguards found a large red welt on the back of his neck. The lifeguards proceeded to radio the information to Memorial Hospital, which dispatched a serum in an ambulance to counteract the bee sting. In the meantime, residents of the area, attracted by the excitement, rushed to the site.

The pool is located at the end of Knox Road. The pool is bounded by woods and open fields on three sides. Knox Road is the only road leading to it. The ambulance found the road blocked by traffic caused by sightseers. The ambulance driver attempted to get the serum to the pool on foot. He had to fight his way through the stalled cars and crowd. The lifeguards administered the serum to the child, but it was too late. The child died minutes later.

The swimming pool is operated by the City Parks and Recreation Commission. Lifeguards cleared the pool immediately after pulling the boy out of the water. The commission closed the pool officially a few hours later and announced that the pool will reopen later this week, after an investigation of the incident.

After the road was finally cleared, the child was rushed by the ambulance to Memorial Hospital, where a doctor, Ronald Beeker, pronounced him dead. The doctor said he understood the serum probably reached Knox Road soon enough to be of value had it reached the boy. Dr. Beeker added, "In cases like this the antidote must be administered quickly. The toxin set up by the reaction strikes within 15 minutes, and almost always fatally. I understand the ambulance arrived at 10:06 a.m. I would place the time of death at 10:15 a.m. The ambulance was stopped approximately one mile from the pool. It could have made it if the people had only moved. It's a damn shame this boy's dead. The official cause of death is heart failure, but stupidity by those sightseers is surely a contributing factor."

6. Plane Crash

Robert W. Carlson, president of Carlson Plastics Co., was killed yesterday. His sons, Robert Jr., 7, and Bradley, 12, were injured. A friend, Donald Joe Willey, 32, also was injured. All four were aboard the company's Aerostar 601 airplane. They had been vacationing in Wisconsin and were en route home when the plane crashed in a wooded area. The four had been staying at Carlson's summer home on Elkhart Lake north of Milwaukee. Eugene Rall, a farmer in the area of the crash, said he heard the airplane engines sputtering, looked up and saw the plane diving into the woods. It slammed into a hill. Authorities speculated that Carlson may have been attempting a crash landing on a nearby road. Rall said he treated the three injured persons, then drove to a nearby cottage and called the sheriff. All three of the injured persons are in good condition at Plymouth General Hospital. The two children, who were in the rear seat, escaped with cuts and bruises. Willey is being treated for a broken hip and concussion. Funeral arrangements for Carlson, who was decapitated, have not yet been scheduled. Officials at a small airport near Elkhart Lake said Carlson regularly stopped there in the company's Learjet for fuel, but yesterday was flying the firm's propeller-driven Aerostar 601. He taxied to a pump and took on 90 gallons of jet fuel, not the aviation gasoline regularly used in the Aerostar. He took off at 1 p.m. and the airplane crashed about 8 miles south of the airport.

7. Alcoholism

The Department of Health, Education and Welfare (HEW) issued a 121-page report today. Congress recently passed a law which requires the department to issue a report on alcoholism each year, and this was the first such report. The report was prepared by a committee of 11 within HEW.

The report said losses caused by alcoholism are high. It said alcohol causes 28,000 traffic deaths a year, and the deaths cost the nation a total of $15 billion. Nearly 9 million persons suffer from alcoholism or lesser drinking problems, and they constitute 10 per cent of the work force within the United States.

The report also contained some statistics about the use of alcohol. It said that in the last year, the average American drinker drank the equivalent of 44 fifths of whiskey. The report concluded that alcohol is "the major drug problem in this country." It said HEW will spend $200,000 next year to pay for advertisements to warn the public about the dangers of excessive drinking. The liquor industry has endorsed the campaign. The advertisements will be used on radio and television and in newspapers and magazines. But an official added, "We will not tell people not to drink. That is a personal decision. What we are saying is that citizens have a responsibility not to destroy themselves or society."

The 121-page report suggests that the problem of alcoholism is not adequately understood by most Americans, who seem more concerned about other drugs, such as marijuana and heroin, even though those drugs do not cause as many problems as alcohol. To prove that point the report pointed out that New York City has an estimated 600,000 alcoholics but only 125,000 heroin users. Yet the city spends 40 times more to fight narcotics addiction than it does to fight alcoholism. The report explained that most persons do not know much about alcoholism and do not consider alcohol a serious problem. People also are reluctant to admit that they have a drinking problem or are alcoholics.

Alcoholism is a particularly serious problem among certain groups. For example, the report said that on some Indian reservations alcoholism has reached epidemic proportions. On some reservations 10 per cent of the residents are alcoholics, twice the national average, and the rate of alcoholism rises to as much as 25 per cent on some reservations.

8. River Pollution

The Mississippi River has been polluted by an oil spill south of Minneapolis, Minnesota. An oil company barge collided with another barge loaded with scrap iron last Saturday. Both barges sank a few minutes after the collision. Officials of the federal Environmental Protection Agency said the barge contained about 50,000 gallons of fuel oil. The oil has been leaking out of the barge ever since it sank and covers the river for a distance of 8 miles to the south. U.S. Coast Guard officials are investigating the collision and resultant spill. But an official for the Environmental Protection Agency today issued a preliminary report concerning pollution resulting from the spill. The report said, "Every possible effort has been made to raise the barge and to plug the holes in it, but the task has proven impossible. There's absolutely nothing we can do. It will take another week to raise the barge to the surface, and we calculate that 38,000 gallons of fuel oil already have leaked from it and the remaining 12,000 gallons will enter the river water within another 48 hours. The damage to the barge is so extensive that the leak simply can't be stopped. Moreover, the amount of fuel oil leaked into the river is so massive that little can be done to save the immediate area. All the life in the river for 10 miles downriver already is dead or dying, and vegetation on shore is expected to die within a matter of weeks. We have tried to use chemicals to make the oil disperse and sink, but without success. Fortunately, a dam is located 12 miles downstrean and we consequently are concentrating our efforts there. We expect to stop all but 5 per cent of the fuel oil from proceeding any farther downstream than the dam. We also have received some information concerning the circumstances surrounding the accident and are considering a civil suit against the oil company to pay for damages. If a suit is filed, we would estimate that it would be for a sum of somewhere in the neighborhood of $100,000, and it would charge them with gross negligence."

9. Disturbing Rehearsal

Police rushed to a drugstore at 418 Dunn St. at 9:30 last night after receiving several telephone calls from persons living in the area. The callers said that they suspected a robbery was in progress and that they had heard loud shouts from inside the store. Three squad cars were dispatched to the scene. The first two officers to arrive at the store heard angry shouts and entered the store with their guns drawn. Inside, they found a crowd surrounding two young men who were yelling at each other. The officers arrested, handcuffed and searched both men, but did not find any weapons. As the other officers arrived, they ordered the crowd to leave the store. The officers at the scene then asked the young men what caused the trouble. The youths responded that there was no trouble, that they both attend a local college and were merely rehearsing their roles in a local production of Arthur Miller's play "A View from the Bridge." They showed police copies of the script. They explained that they had told several customers, who were friends of theirs, about the play and the friends urged them to run through their roles. The youths said when they began to rehearse only their friends were in the store, but the noise attracted other people, and the other customers insisted that they finish. The officers did not include the names of the youths in their report. "We've caused them enough trouble already," one officer explained. "We're sorry. It was an honest mistake."

10. World Hunger

The United Nations Food and Agriculture Organization issued a report today. Last year it set a goal of increasing world food production by 4 per cent. Today it reported that the hungry countries in the world failed to reach that goal. But other countries continued to produce a surplus of food. Overall, the report issued by the organization said food production in the world increased 3 per cent last year, but it increased only 1 to 2 per cent in underdeveloped nations. At the same time, production in the United States and Canada increased 8 per cent. The organization estimated that China did well. But production in Russia failed to increase because of bad weather. Production in Latin America actually declined about 1 per cent because of drought and other unfavorable weather conditions. The organization estimated that 300 million to 500 million persons in the world are undernourished.

11. Stewardesses

For years, airlines in the United States fired stewardesses when they became pregnant, regardless of whether or not they were married. Some of the stewardesses wanted to return to their jobs after the birth of their children, but the airlines refused to rehire them. The stewardesses belong to the Air Line Stewards and

Stewardesses Association. The union filed a lawsuit against the airlines, charging them with violating the 1965 Equal Employment Opportunity Law. The union and the airlines now have settled the case out of court. The airlines have agreed to rehire qualified stewardesses at their original seniority level. Some of the stewardesses returning to their old jobs said they were bored sitting at home and missed the excitement of their old jobs. Some said their families simply need more money. Others are divorced. Stewardesses now are paid anywhere from $800 to $1,000 a month. Moreover, they work only 72 hours a month and spend only a few nights away from home each week—often no more than two.

12. New Handcuffs

The police often use handcuffs when a suspect seems dangerous or when a suspect becomes violent. They also use handcuffs when a suspect might attempt to destroy evidence in his case. Traditionally, police have used metal handcuffs. but an officer can carry only one or two pairs. And some policemen, although they seldom admit it, have lost the keys to their own handcuffs and had to call locksmiths to free their prisoners. Prisoners also have complained that sharp edges on the metal handcuffs cut into their wrists. Now all that is changing. Local policemen are experimenting with the use of plastic handcuffs in some cases. The handcuffs are 22-inch strips of plastic and, once they're locked, cannot be reopened. Someone must cut them open when the suspect arrives at the police station. The new plastic handcuffs cost only 40 cents a pair and police say they are valuable during mass arrests—at civil disturbances, drug busts and that sort of thing. One officer can easily carry a dozen of the plastic strips in one pocket.

13. Truck Sales

Local truck dealers, who meet once a month for lunch and to discuss common problems, today revealed the following information to this newspaper. Nationwide, truck sales are expected to increase from 2.5 million this year to 3 million by 1980, primarily because more and more Americans are using trucks as recreation vehicles. In fact, many families buy trucks as second cars. So in 1962, trucks accounted for 10 per cent of the vehicle sales in the nation. Last year they accounted for 15 per cent of the sales. Many families like to buy vans or pickup trucks that can be fitted with camper units. One truck dealer, discussing his local business, said he opened for business in 1956 and sold 90 trucks that first year for a dollar volume of around $775,000. This year he expects to sell 400 trucks and to have a dollar volume of more than $7.2 million. He asked that his name not be printed so his competitors won't find out how he's doing. He added that some of his sales include big trucks priced up to $30,000 each. Overall, truck sales in the county have risen 37 per cent during the past five years, while car sales rose 28 per cent during the same period.

14. Auto Repairs

A new law went into effect at 12:01 a.m. today. The law was passed by the last session of the state legislature. It also was signed by the governor. The law is designed to help police officers find hit-and-run drivers. According to the provisions of the law, motorists who have had an accident cannot have their cars repaired until they have obtained a sticker from a law enforcement official—a highway patrolman, sheriff's deputy or city policeman. The stickers are circular and about 2 inches in diameter. They are colored orange and black. After investigating an accident, the officers are, according to the provisions of the law, to place the sticker on the windshield of each vehicle involved in the accident. If a person has a car repaired without first obtaining the sticker, he is subject to a $1,000 fine and a sentence of three months in jail. Any mechanic who repairs a car that does not have a sticker is subject to the same penalty. If a motorist damages his own car or becomes involved in an accident which causes less than $100 damage, he does not have to report the accident to the police, but he still must obtain a sticker before having his car repaired. He can obtain the sticker by driving to the nearest law enforcement agency and having an officer inspect his car. Vehicles do not need a sticker if the necessary repairs cost $25 or less. Lt. James Reedy, traffic officer for the County Sheriff's Department, said, "This law may seem like a nuisance for drivers, but it really shouldn't take more than a few minutes of their time, and it'll be a tremendous help to us. Just last year we had more than 100 hit-and-run accidents reported to us in this one county. We eventually found 17 of the drivers. If this law had been in effect, I'd estimate that we would have found three-fourths of the drivers."

15. Abortion Ruling

A 16-year-old girl whose name has been kept secret because she is a juvenile was released today from the county jail. She was placed in the jail because she refused to have an abortion. The girl appeared before County Court Judge Elmer F. Garner last Friday. The girl and her boy friend, who is also 16, had tried to obtain a marriage license but failed because neither is old enough to get married without the permission of their parents. The girl later told her parents that she was pregnant. The girl's mother then told her to get an abortion. The girl refused and ran away with her boy friend. They were apprehended by the authorities and then were taken before Judge Garner. In court Friday, the girl told Judge Garner that she "thinks an abortion is murder." She added that she loves her boy friend, wants to marry him and have the baby. Her boy friend has dropped out of high school and now earns $74 a week as a house painter. However, the judge ruled that "It is not in the interest of an unborn child to be born under these circumstances." He also ruled that both the girl and her boy friend are "children in need of supervision." He ordered the girl to obey her mother. When she still refused to submit to an abortion, he ordered that she be held in the county jail. Her attorney immediately appealed to the State Court of Appeals. In an emergency session today, the State Court of Appeals ruled that the state cannot force any person to have an abortion. The girl was released from jail at 9:45 a.m. today, minutes after Judge Garner learned of the state court's decision in the case.

16. Cargo Plane Accident

A twin-engine cargo plane took off from the airport at 9:30 a.m. today for a flight to Chicago. As the plane was gaining altitude, about 2 minutes after takeoff, the propeller from the right engine flew off. It sliced into the cockpit just behind the pilot's head, then dropped to the ground. The pilot and the copilot, the only persons aboard the airplane, were not hurt. Air traffic controllers in the airport's control tower spotted smoke caused by the mishap and immediately diverted all other airplanes approaching the airport. They also immediately stopped the takeoff of other planes and told the pilot, identified as Robert G. Sanders of Oklahoma City, Okla., to land wherever he could. Sanders, who had not yet raised the plane's landing gear, made a 180-degree turn and returned to the airport. He safely landed the plane, and both he and the copilot stepped out unhurt. The copilot was identified as John Tanner, also of Oklahoma City. As a precautionary measure, firemen blanketed the right engine with foam to prevent an outbreak of fire. The plane was towed from the runway and normal traffic resumed within 30 minutes. The propeller landed in a parking lot for airport employes. It destroyed one car and damaged 11 others.

IMPROVING NEWSWRITING STYLE: MISCELLANEOUS EXERCISES

1. Find and analyze at least 10 examples of descriptive writing in newspaper stories.

2. Analyze the use of detail and description in "Time" and "Newsweek" magazines.

3. Ask someone, perhaps one student in your class, to speak to the class for a few minutes. Write at least three descriptive paragraphs about that person. Remember to be specific and objective; do not present your own opinion or conclusions. Compare and analyze the paragraphs written by each student in your class.

4. Go out onto your campus for the first part of your class, then return to the classroom and write at least three descriptive paragraphs about the campus. Compare and analyze the paragraphs written by each student in your class.

5. Clip every story published in one edition of your student newspaper, mail the clippings to all the people mentioned in the stories and ask them to evaluate the accuracy of the stories.

6. Watch a film or a staged event, then write a news story describing it. Compare your story with the film or a record of the event.

7. Prepare a variety of statements, each attributed to a different source, then conduct a poll on campus to determine whether other students believe some of the statements more than others. You might also use different words of attribution for the same statement, such as "said," "claimed" and "alleged."

8. Invite the editor of your student newspaper to class to discuss the newspaper's problems and policies regarding the writing of news stories.

6

What Is—and Is Not—News

Reporters must learn how to recognize news, and they must also learn what their newspapers do not consider news and what should not be included in their stories.

Basically, an occurrence is considered news if it is (1) important, (2) unusual, (3) local, (4) relevant to readers' lives or (5) current.

1. Newspapers emphasize stories that are important, and they define important stories as those which involve (1) large numbers, (2) prominent individuals and institutions or (3) significant issues. A $300,000 bank robbery is more newsworthy than a $50 gas station stickup. An act of Congress is more newsworthy than a Student Senate resolution. An oil spill is more newsworthy than a building code revision.

2. The unexpected or unusual is more newsworthy than the expected. Some journalists say that news is any deviation from the normal. Thus, the fact that two persons were killed in an automobile accident is more newsworthy than the fact that 10,000 other motorists reached their destinations safely, and the fact that 30 students clashed with police is more newsworthy than the fact that 30,000 students attended classes as usual. Critics often complain that this emphasis on the unusual gives readers a distorted view of the world. Editors reply that the unusual is news and interests readers and therefore is what they must publish.

3. Local stories are more newsworthy than similar stories in distant communities. Editors assume that readers are more interested in reading stories about their own communities, since readers may be acquainted with the people, places or issues mentioned in the stories.

4. Newspapers also emphasize stories that have an immediate and direct effect on their readers' lives. Newspapers in rural areas emphasize farm news, such as current prices for crops, weather conditions and new farming techniques. College newspapers report final examination schedules and new library hours.

5. Finally, newspapers stress current information. They report what happened today or yesterday. Unless a story is unusually important, it is no longer news if the event occurred last week.

It is difficult to translate these abstract concepts into practical guidelines, but reporters can learn how their newspaper defines news by observing the work of their editors and by reading the newspaper thoroughly to determine the types of stories that are published. Each newspaper may also establish a few guidelines. For example, as a matter of policy, a newspaper in a small city may report every traffic accident, a newspaper in a larger city may report only those accidents in which at least one person is injured, and a newspaper in a major metropolitan area may report only those accidents in which at least one person is killed. Similarly, newspapers in small cities often publish all wedding announcements and obituaries, whereas newspapers in larger cities may publish only those of prominent citizens.

As to what is *not* considered news: most newspapers omit material that is (1) obscene or in poor taste or (2) libelous. Most newspapers also do not mention (3) lotteries and (4) trade names. Some newspapers also avoid (5) singling out an individual or institution for criticism, particularly when the person or persons involved live in the community, associate with the newspaper's executives or advertise in the newspaper.

1. Newspapers routinely omit obscene or scandalous details from their stories, usually on the grounds that newspapers are family publications and are read by children as well as adults. They make a distinction between news and mere gossip or sensationalism. Consequently, they ignore many cases handled by the police in their communities—a young girl's unsuccessful attempt to kill herself, family squabbles, complaints about an elderly man's foul language and so on. Newspapers also refuse to publish gruesome pictures, particularly when the pictures show the body of someone from their own community. Newspapers report accidents, but not all the bloody details. They report suicides, but seldom describe the precise methods used. Some newspapers refuse to name juvenile delinquents and victims of rape even when they have a legal right to do so. Most also refuse to report an individual's race or religion unless it is pertinent to the story. Newspapers report humorous stories, but they seldom make fun of misfortune. For example, when a fire damaged the home of a minister, a copy editor wrote this headline for the story:

**Pastor's Study
Goes to Blazes**

His editor ordered him to write a new headline.

Some newspapers publish other types of stories in an effort to help society. For example, many newspapers publish the names of every person convicted of drunken driving because they believe the adverse publicity will discourage other people from driving while drunk.

When you evaluate a potentially scandalous story, you must weigh several conflicting considerations. Ask yourself: (1) How seriously will this story injure the persons it names? (2) Will the story serve any useful purpose? (3) Does the public need and have a right to this information? (4) Does my newspaper have a right or obligation to suppress this information? (5) How will readers react to the information?

2. A libel is a written statement that damages a person's reputation. To win a libel suit, the plaintiff must prove that he has been identified and defamed and that the libel has been published. However, if a newspaper is sued for libel, it can offer three major defenses: (1) truth, (2) fair comment and criticism and (3) qualified privilege.

In most states, a newspaper will not be found guilty of libel if it can prove that the statement was true and was published for good reason. Some states require only proof of truth. The burden of that proof is on the newspaper; it must prove the substance of its story. If it reports that someone is a thief, it must prove that he is actually a thief, not just that someone else told the newspaper he was a thief.

"Fair comment" is a legal doctrine that enables newspapers to criticize public figures. If an individual deliberately seeks the public's approval, the public also has a right to criticize that individual. Thus, newspapers are free to criticize—vehemently and harshly—all public figures, including politicians, performers and authors. Newspapers can also report and comment on the activities of individuals thrust into the news involuntarily.

Newspapers have a "qualified privilege" to report official governmental proceedings. They cannot be found guilty of libel in reporting governmental proceedings if their stories are fair, accurate and complete, even though statements made during the proceedings may be false and may damage a person's reputation.

Newspapers often publish retractions, but they are only partial remedies in libel suits. The amount of money awarded the plaintiff may be reduced if the newspaper proves that it did not injure the person intentionally and that it regretted and tried to correct the error. The newspaper may also attempt to reduce the amount of damages by proving that it obtained its information from a normally reliable source.

Most newspapers are very careful to avoid making potentially libelous statements, because libel suits are expensive. Even if the newspaper wins, it must expend thousands of dollars and hours on its defense, and an unfavorable decision can cost the newspaper thousands of dollars more.

If a story you write will damage someone's reputation, ask yourself: Is the story true? Is the person a public figure? Was he involved in an official governmental proceeding, such as a trial? If you are unable to answer "Yes" to at least one of these questions, you must delete the damaging material from your story or kill the entire story. For example, you cannot report that:

> Sheriff John Tamerson today said he caught two thieves, Edward R. Shiels and Thomas J. Aldersgate, red-handed as they broke into a service station at 4702 Jefferson Ave.

This lead calls the men thieves, but the only proof of that is the sheriff's statement. The men have been convicted by the sheriff, not by a judge and jury. Moreover, the men are not public figures, and there has been no official governmental proceeding. To defend a libel suit, you would have to prove that the sheriff was correct, not just that he made the statement. Yet the sheriff might have been mistaken, or the charges against the men might be reduced or dropped, or a jury might find the men innocent.

You can avoid libel suits by reporting only that suspects have been arrested and charged with a crime:

> Sheriff John Tamerson today charged Edward R. Shiels and Thomas J. Aldersgate with burglary. Tamerson said a service station at 4702 Jefferson Ave. was broken into and that $80 was taken from a cash drawer.

This lead does not say that Shiels and Aldersgate are guilty; it says only that they have been charged with the crime—an easily proven fact.

3. The U.S. Postal Service can refuse to deliver newspapers or any other material that advertises lotteries. A lottery is any contest that involves a prize that is awarded by chance in exchange for a financial consideration, such as the price of a ticket. Because of the postal regulations, newspapers seldom report that a charitable organization will raffle off a television set or that a new car will be given to a ticket-holder at the county fair. However, newspapers can mention a lottery once it has become newsworthy, for example if a local teacher wins $50,000 in the Irish Sweepstakes or if the state government establishes a lottery to raise money for education.

4. Most newspapers in the United States refuse to mention trade names in news stories, on the grounds that mention of trade names is seldom necessary and merely provides free advertising. Thus, newspapers often replace trade names with generic terms, sometimes with unfortunate results. When an airplane crashed during a snowstorm in a mountainous area of Northern California, the family aboard the plane survived for three days by drinking melted snow and eating several boxes of Cracker Jack that one of the children had carried aboard the plane. Some newspapers, in reporting the family's ordeal and rescue, pointlessly substituted the term "candied popcorn" for "Cracker Jack."

One copy editor, disgusted because his newspaper refused to allow him to use the word "Jeep" in a story about several hundred persons who formed a caravan of Jeeps for a weekend camping trip (called a "Jeep Jamboree"), substituted the phrase, "small truck-type four-wheel-drive vehicles of various manufacture." He did not expect his newspaper to print this circumlocution, but it did. The same newspaper has substituted the term "solidified carbon dioxide" for "dry ice" and "small, beetle-shaped foreign car" for Volkswagen.

In short, common sense should dictate whether or not a trade name is used. If you believe a trade name is necessary, include it in your story.

5. Few publishers will admit that they favor any individuals or organizations. Nevertheless, most newspapers develop certain "dos" and "don'ts," which reporters call "sacred cows." Sacred cows reflect the interests of a newspaper's publisher, editor and other executives, who use their power to manipulate the news. For example, a publisher deeply involved in politics may order his staff to print only favorable information about his favorite political party and candidates. Unfortunately, it is difficult to detect a newspaper's biases until you begin to work for that newspaper. Readers can see what a newspaper did publish, but they seldom know why the newspaper published a particular story, how it slanted the facts of that story or what it did not publish. Reporters learn their newspapers' policies by talking with other members of its staff, observing and talking with their editors, noting changes made in stories they wrote and reading the newspaper to see the types of stories it emphasizes (or ignores).

WHAT IS—AND IS NOT—NEWS: DISCUSSION QUESTIONS

1. Should a reporter place quotation marks around his summary of a speaker's remarks?

2. Should a reporter eliminate speakers' grammatical errors and profane comments from news stories?

3. Should newspapers report every birth, death, marriage and divorce in their communities?

4. Should newspapers report suicides?

5. Should newspapers name juvenile delinquents?

6. Should newspapers publish trade names?

7. Should newspapers publish the names of everyone charged with drunken driving, report only the names of persons who are convicted of the charge or ignore such stories altogether?

8. How should a reporter respond if his editor instructs him to do something he considers unethical?

9. Under what circumstances should a newswriter report an individual's race or religion?

10. Reporters often describe women, particularly when they are attractive. Should they do so? Why or why not? Should they describe a female mayor as "a beautiful blonde" if they never describe men in the same manner?

11. Should a reporter show stories to the persons named in them before the stories are published?

12. How should a reporter respond when a source asks him to include or delete certain facts in a news story?

13. How should a reporter respond when someone agrees to give him information for a news story but asks him not to use his name?

14. Assume that a reporter for your newspaper interviewed a Jewish author who was visiting your community, and the story included the following quotes. Should your newspaper publish them? Why or why not?

> "Jewish women are demanding, cold, cutting and rude," the author said. "They dress for other Jewish women, not for men. There's even competition between mothers and daughters."
> Describing Jewish people on Long Island, the setting for his latest book, he said they buy obvious wealth symbols for status. "They buy big chandeliers or pianos to put in the front windows of their beautiful homes, but then have no money to pay for their furniture. And they have to have a black maid—not just a maid.
> "The kids are really spoiled," he continued. "The Jewish girls try to find the guy who can get the best prestige job and give them the biggest diamond. The third thing they consider is love.
> "All that is obvious to anyone who's ever lived on Long Island, and that's what my book is all about. I'm in town now to talk about the book."

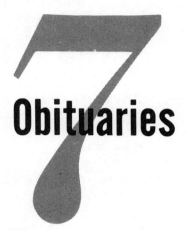

Obituaries

The obituaries published by most newspapers in the United States are poorly written and report only a few superficial facts about the lives of dead persons. The obituaries seldom convey the impression that a person with a unique personality and a unique set of experiences has just died. But newspapers cannot easily improve the quality of their obituaries. One reason is that few newspapers have enough time, space or reporters to publish adequate obituaries. Another reason is that most newspapers assign obituaries to their newest and least experienced reporters. Some newspapers even hire persons without any journalistic training to write obituaries, thus freeing experienced reporters for other assignments. Obituaries are considered an ideal assignment for new reporters because they seldom require any specialized knowledge. They are brief, simple and easy to write, and obituary writers seldom have to know anything about such fields as politics, law, urban renewal, medicine and science. Moreover, reporters can write most obituaries without leaving their desks—and the close supervision of their editors.

Funeral homes give newspapers all the information they need for most obituaries. The funeral homes, eager to have their names appear in newspapers as often as possible, obtain the information when families come in to arrange services. Some funeral homes fill out special forms provided by their local newspaper and deliver the forms to the newspaper immediately after they have been completed. Newspapers may also call every funeral home in their community at regular intervals.

When a prominent person dies, reporters review old news stories about the person in their newspaper's library. They may also call the dead person's family and business associates to obtain a photograph and more information about the person's life.

Most obituaries follow the same basic formula. The lead reports the dead person's name, age and address and the time and cause of death. Subsequent paragraphs usually list the person's accomplishments, name the surviving relatives and report the time and place of the funeral. Most obituaries also report the dead person's birthplace, education, service in the armed forces, membership in church and civic organizations, occupation and hobbies.

Newspapers in small communities try to publish an obituary for everyone who dies in their area. A single reporter may write 10 or even 20 obituaries every morning. All the obituaries usually must fit into a limited amount of space, perhaps two or three columns (about 40 to 60 inches). Because some of that space is occupied by headlines, only about 3 or 4 inches are left for each obituary. Newspapers in larger communities do not have enough space to print an obituary for everyone. Instead, they report only the deaths of the most prominent members of their community. Other deaths are reported among their classified advertisements.

Reporters could write better obituaries if they had more time and space. They might describe in detail the dead person's appearance, interests and activities, major accomplishments and goals. They could also quote the dead person or people who knew him or her.

Newspapers do publish some detailed and colorful obituaries, but primarily those of celebrities, such as politicians, entertainers and sports figures. For example, when humorist Herb Shriner died, an obituary written by the Associated Press began effectively with this quote from Shriner:

> "I'm a small town guy in a big city talking about things which folks have been thinking but just never got around to saying."

An obituary for George Syvertsen, a CBS newsman killed in Cambodia, described his last story and his quest for perfection, illustrating the latter with this anecdote:

> On one occasion I saw him argue about whether or not a story he filmed should be sent. He did not think it was good enough and his decision—so far as he was concerned—was final. He reached over a desk and opened the film can, exposing the film—argument ended.

The same obituary mentioned, as a colorful detail, Walter Cronkite's struggle to pronounce Syvertsen's name the first time he used it on the air.

Similarly, an Associated Press obituary for William Boyd described the moral philosophy of Boyd's famous character, Hopalong Cassidy:

> Hopalong pursued bad guys relentlessly, but he tried to bring them back alive. If forced into a showdown, he let the villain draw first. Smoking, drinking, swearing and romantic involvement were taboo for Hoppy.

Obituaries should not simply praise individuals, but should report their lives—both the good and the bad. Thus, Boyd's obituary also reported that, in ironic contrast with the virtuous Hoppy, Boyd had been married five times and his career had almost ended when "his name became linked with gambling and scandal" during the early 1930s. Similarly, "Newsweek" magazine's obituary for Merriman Smith, the senior wire-service correspondent at the White House, mentioned his rugged handsomeness, wit and perception and described his biggest story—the assassination of John F. Kennedy:

> Riding two cars behind President Kennedy in Dallas, Smith was one of the first to realize that JFK had been shot. He grabbed the car telephone and barked out his bulletins as the motorcade sped toward Parkland Memorial Hospital and AP correspondent Jack Bell struggled in vain to wrest the phone away. "Smith didn't apologize for keeping the phone," Bell snapped later. "Smith never apologizes." The crisp, cogent reporting of the assassination and its aftermath earned Smith his only Pulitzer Prize. (Copyright Newsweek, Inc. 1970, reprinted by permission)

But the same obituary added:

> In recent years drinking had become a recurrent problem for Smith . . . He periodically checked into hospitals for treatment, and friends concede privately that he had grown increasingly depressed over his inability to control the habit.

Thus, though obituaries are often poorly written, they do not have to be. Given enough time and space, reporters can produce well-written and interesting obituaries. As you begin to write, critically examine existing policies and work to improve the quality of every type of story you write, including obituaries.

OBITUARIES: EXERCISE 1

INSTRUCTIONS: Write obituaries based on the information given below and in the newspaper obituary forms reprinted on the following pages.

Obituary 1

Identification: Samuel Jay Kline. Born in 1897. Address: 1493 James Ave.

Circumstances of death: Death caused by pneumonia. Admitted to Memorial Hospital Friday night. Died at 12:15 a.m. today in the hospital.

Funeral Services: A memorial service will be held at Redeemer Lutheran Church at 8 p.m. tomorrow. Burial will be in Wildwood Cemetery at 10 a.m. the following day.

Survivors: Wife, Martha. Three sons, John, Lee and Bernard. Two daughters, Martha and Mildred. Eleven grandchildren. Four great-grandchildren.

Accomplishments: Born in Davenport, Iowa. Served in World War I and reached the rank of major. Moved here after the war and opened Kline's Shoe Store at 516 Main St. Store is now operated by his son, Bernard. Served as city councilman from 1943 until 1948. Ran for mayor in 1948 but was defeated by Cecil Bauer. Retired in 1962.

Obituary 2

Identification: Mrs. Lucille R. Ray. Born in 1914. Address: Jamison's Nursing Home, 1822 St. Clair Ave.

Circumstances of death: Heart attack. Had history of heart trouble and had been confined to bed for the past four years. At 7:30 a.m. today an attendant at the nursing home found her dead in bed.

Funeral Services: Not yet scheduled.

Survivors: Her husband, Fred, died six years ago. A son, Ralph, was killed in Vietnam. She had two other sons, still living, Henry of Paradise, Calif., and Louis of San Francisco, Calif.

Accomplishments: She lived here all her life, except for the time she attended college. Attended Greer Elementary School and North High School. Graduated from the University of Georgia in 1935. Returned here and taught from 1935 until her retirement four years ago because of ill health. Taught English at North High School.

Obituary 3

Identification: William David Raye. Born in 1902. Address: 112 Riverview Drive.

Circumstances of death: Suffered a heart attack at his home Sunday evening while watching television. Taken to Memorial Hospital by ambulance. Suffered a second and severe heart attack and died shortly after 10:30 a.m. today.

Funeral Services: 7 p.m. tomorrow at Hines Bros. Funeral Home. No burial, since his will specifies that his body be used for medical research or education. The family asks that, in lieu of flowers, donations be sent to the Heart Fund.

Survivors: Wife, Beth. Two daughters, Mrs. Donna Moronese of 623 N. 5th St. and Mrs. Ruth Howland, 1808 Gadsden Blvd. Five grandchildren. Two brothers, Michael and Frank, both of Miami, Fla.

Accomplishments: Born in Normandy, Tenn. Graduated from the University of Tennessee in 1925. Established the Raye Truck and Tractor Co. here immediately after graduation. Served as president of the State Trucking Association in 1930. Company went bankrupt in 1933, and he was charged with embezzlement but acquitted by a jury. Enlisted in the Army during World War II. Joined Adler's Real Estate in 1946 and rose from salesman to president. He was president of the firm, the largest in the city, at the time of his death.

Obituary 4

Identification: Leonard James Platte. Born in 1954. Son of Mr. and Mrs. Henry Platte, 1765 Edwin Blvd.

Circumstances of death: Killed in a Jeep accident. A telegram received by his parents reported that, "A Jeep he was driving went off the road and overturned about 20 miles southeast of Bonn, West Germany."

Funeral Services: Military services with an armed forces honor guard will be held at graveside in Wildwood Cemetery at 3 p.m. Friday.

Survivors: Parents, Mr. and Mrs. Henry Platte. One brother, Merle, and three sisters, Sandra, Ella Mae and Virginia, all living at home.

Accomplishments: Graduated from Colonial Elementary School and attended Central High School. Enlisted in the Army in 1971 and attained the rank of sergeant. Had been stationed in Germany for two months.

Obituary 5

Identification: Mrs. Carrie Rauscher. Born in 1889. Address: Rural Route No. 3.

Circumstances of death: Died Sunday in a hospital in Scottsdale, Ariz., where she was visiting her daughter. She had been suffering from cancer for a number of years.

Funeral services: Burial will be in Scottsdale today.

Survivors: One daughter, Mrs. Louise Pfeiffer of Scottsdale. Her husband, Marvin, died in an automobile accident 14 years ago.

Accomplishments: Born and raised here. A member of St. Paul's Methodist Church, Memorial Hospital Guild and the Rainbow Girls, Melbourne Chapter. Until her retirement at the age of 65 she had been employed by General Telephone Co. for 35 years and had been the firm's chief operator for the last 18 years.

Obituary 6

Identification: Raymond R. Shepard. Born in 1909. Address: 850 Maury Road.

Circumstances of death: Self-inflicted gunshot wound. An official report filed by Coroner Ervin Osburn said persons in an adjoining apartment heard a shot fired late last night and called the manager. He got no response when he knocked on the door of Shepard's apartment, used his own key and found Shepard's body on the bed. A gun was clutched in one of his hands.

Funeral services: Not yet scheduled.

Survivors: No known survivors. The police are trying to locate his relatives.

Accomplishments: Moved here nine months ago. Had been employed as a truck driver for Jay's Furniture but was discharged after two months and had not been employed since then.

OBITUARY BLANK

Please supply the information asked for below and send to the newspaper office as quickly as possible after the death. Relatives, friends & neighbors of the deceased will appreciate prompt reporting of this news so that they may attend funeral services or send condolences.

Full Name of Deceased___ **Howard Carl Page**

Address___ **6314 Ridge Terrace**

Age___ **74**

Date of Death___ **3:40 p.m. yesterday**

Place of Death___ **Home**

Cause of Death **Apparent heart attack**

Time and Date of Funeral___ **2 p.m. Saturday**

Place of Funeral___ **Azalea Park Methodist Church**

Place of Burial___ **Evergreen Cemetery**

Officiating Clergyman___ **The Rev. Lawrence G. Lowe Jr.**

           *   *   *

Place of Birth___ **Wichita, Kansas**

Places and Lengths of Residences___ **Moved here in 1946**

Occupation___ **Retired Army colonel**

Did Deceased Ever Hold Public Office (When and What)?___ **No**

           *   *   *

Name, Address of Surviving Husband (or Wife)___ **Wife Sally**

Maiden Name (if Married Woman)___

Form 201

Marriage, When to Whom___**Married Sally Doyle in Houston, Texas, in 1926**

                  *   *   *

Names, Addresses of Surviving Children___

   Ralph, Austin, Texas

   Samuel, Wichita, Kansas

   Howard Jr., Kansas City, Mo.

   Mary Anne, 6314 Ridge Terrace

Names, Address of Surviving Brothers and Sisters___**None**

Number of Grandchildren (Great, Great-Great, etc.)___**11**

Names, Address of Parents (if Living)___**Dead**

Additional Information___**Enlisted as private in Army in 1916. Rose to rank of captain while serving in France during WWI. Became colonel in 1942 and commanded a training camp in Texas for most of WWII. Retired in 1945 after defeat of Japan and completed 30 years of service. Numerous medals, including 3 Purple Hearts for wounds in WWI. Sold real estate here for Trust Real Estate from 1945 until 1953. Became sales manager in 1953. Retired from all business ventures 7 years ago. Commander of American Legion Post No. 4 here in 1951 and 1964. Served as State Commander in 1965. Also member of Kiwanis Club here and led drive that raised $16,000 to buy playground and picnic facilities for Riverside Park in 1961.**

OBITUARY BLANK

Please supply the information asked for below and send to the newspaper office as quickly as possible after the death. Relatives, friends & neighbors of the deceased will appreciate prompt reporting of this news so that they may attend funeral services or send condolences.

Full Name of Deceased __Frederick Daggett__

Address __777 W. Lancaster Road__

Age __64__

Date of Death __7:30 p.m. yesterday__

Place of Death __Home of daughter, Carolyn__

Cause of Death __Unknown. Autopsy scheduled for this afternoon.__

Time and Date of Funeral __4 p.m. Friday__

Place of Funeral __Church of Christ__

Place of Burial __Evergreen Cemetery__

Officiating Clergyman __Stuart Adler__

*   *   *

Place of Birth __West Berlin__

Places and Lengths of Residences __Parents moved to Milwaukee, Wis., when he was 4 years__ old. He graduated from the University of Wisconsin at Madison in 1929 and worked in Denver, Col., from 1929 to 1936. He was transferred to Boston in 1937, was drafted during WWII and moved here after the war.

Occupation

__Manager, Sears Roebuck & Co.__

Did Deceased Ever Hold Public Office (When and What)? __Member school board, 1954-1958; board__ chairman, 1958-1960. Resigned in 1960 for "personal reasons." Appointed to local draft board in 1962. Resigned in 1965 because of opposition to Vietnam War.

*   *   *

Name, Address of Surviving Husband (or Wife) __Edith__

Maiden Name (if Married Woman)

Form 201

Marriage, When to Whom___1927 in Madison to Edith Prange, then a student with

him at the University of Wisconsin_____

* * *

Names, Addresses of Surviving Children _____ _____

Frederick Jr., a lieutenant in the Air Force, stationed in Spain

John, at home_____

Debbie, at home_____

Carolyn, a teacher in the suburb of Roseville_____

_____

_____

Names, Address of Surviving Brothers and Sisters_____

_____1 brother, Ernest, in Milwaukee, Wis._____

_____

_____

_____

_____

_____

Number of Grandchildren (Great, Great-Great, etc.)__None_____

_____

Names, Address of Parents (if Living)__Gerhard and Anna Daggett, both of Milwaukee.

_____

Additional Information__Served as assistant manager of local Sears outlet from 1946

until 1962. Became manager in 1953 and held that position at the time of

his death. Refused to transfer to another city even though new job meant

promotion to larger store. Also refused job as district manager for same

reason--liked living here. Active in civic affairs. Served as President

Chamber of Commerce in 1958. Member Church of Christ. Also member of

Rotary Club. Led United Fund Drive which surpassed goal of $4.1 million

in 1964. In 1966, led $2,420,000 drive for new YMCA. Drive actually

raised $2,680,000.

OBITUARY BLANK

Please supply the information asked for below and send to the newspaper office as quickly as possible after the death. Relatives, friends & neighbors of the deceased will appreciate prompt reporting of this news so that they may attend funeral services or send messages of condolences.

Full Name of Deceased __Roger Wincek__

Address __112 Lake Ave.__

Age __26__

Date of Death __Yesterday__

Place of Death __Home__

Cause of Death __Cancer__

Time and Date of Funeral __12:30 p.m. tomorrow__

Place of Funeral __St. Mary's Catholic Church__

Place of Burial __Pleasantview Cemetery__

Officiating Clergyman __The Rev. Arthur L. Ingalls__

* * *

Place of Birth __Here__

Places and Lengths of Residences __Life-long resident of the city__

Occupation __Salesman at Belk's Sporting Goods.   Better known as long-time anti-war activist.__

Did Deceased Ever Hold Public Office (When and What)? __No__

* * *

Name, Address of Surviving Husband (or Wife) __Mary__

Maiden Name (if Married Woman) _____

Form 201

Marriage, When to Whom_____

Married the former Mary Ingram at St. Mark Lutheran Church in 1964

                                    *   *   *

Names, Addresses of Surviving Children_____

    Kathleen, 5; Lillie, 3; and Walter, 11 months, all living at home

Names, Address of Surviving Brothers and Sisters_____

    No brothers or sisters

Number of Grandchildren (Great, Great-Great, etc.) **None**

Names, Address of Parents (if Living)___**Mr. and Mrs. Gerald Wincek of 315 Parr Ave.**

Additional Information___**Graduated from Central High School. Attended college one year. Dropped out of college in 1967 to campaign for Sen. Eugene McCarthy. Co-founder of United Draft Information Center, established here in Nov., 1967, to counsel persons opposed to the draft. Classified as a conscientious objector by the draft board. Served two years as an orderly at Memorial Hospital instead of regular military service. Campaigned for Sen. McGovern in 1972 and led state organization known as "Youth For McGovern."** Inactive recently due to illness.

OBITUARY BLANK

Please supply the information asked for below and send to the newspaper office as quickly as possible after the death. Relatives, friends & neighbors of the deceased will appreciate prompt reporting of this news so that they may attend funeral services or send condolences.

Full Name of Deceased___ **Gladys Cramer**___

Address___ **1123 Hall Lane**___

Age___ **57**___

Date of Death___ **Found dead at 5 p.m. yesterday in her home**

Place of Death___ **Neighbors called police yesterday afternoon after they hadn't seen her for several days. Police found body in basement of her home.**

Cause of Death___ **Coroner investigating possibility of suicide. Body was found hanging from a clothes line. Coroner has not given official statement.**

Time and Date of Funeral___ **Not yet scheduled**

Place of Funeral___ **Redeemer Lutheran Church**

Place of Burial___ **Pleasantview Cemetery**

Officiating Clergyman___ **The Rev. Richard Knight**

*   *   *

Place of Birth___ **Here**

Places and Lengths of Residences___ **Lived here all her life in same house on Hill Lane. Her parents built the house the year before she was born.**

Occupation___ **None**

Did Deceased Ever Hold Public Office (When and What)?___

Member County Library Commission, 1952-1956 and 1958-1968

*   *   *

Name, Address of Surviving Husband (or Wife)___ **Divorced**

Maiden Name (if Married Woman)___

Form 201

Marriage, When to Whom _____

Married Bill Waundry in 1941 (His current whereabouts unknown)

                              *   *   *

Names, Addresses of Surviving Children _____

                              None

_____

_____

_____

_____

_____

Names, Address of Surviving Brothers and Sisters _____

     Richard, Miami, Fla.

     James, Des Moines, Iowa

     Margaret Williams, Des Moines, Iowa

     Dorothy Wilde, London, England

_____

_____

Number of Grandchildren (Great, Great-Great, etc.) _____

                              None

Names, Address of Parents (if Living) _____

_____

_____

Additional Information **Graduated from Central High School. Cared for her mother,**
Melba Cramer, until her death two months ago. Member St. James Church
and the League of Women Voters. Also belonged to the choir and Ladies
Guild at St. James Church.

_____

_____

_____

_____

OBITUARY BLANK

Please supply the information asked for below and send to the newspaper office as quickly as possible after the death. Relatives, friends & neighbors of the deceased will appreciate prompt reporting of this news so that they may attend funeral services or send messages of condolences.

Full Name of Deceased __Homer Turner__

Address __1410 Selma Ave.__

Age __81__

Date of Death __8 a.m. today__

Place of Death __Jamison's Nursing Home, 1822 St. Claire Ave.__

Cause of Death __Fell while shopping in Quality Appliances, 1242 Main St., 3 months ago. Lived in nursing home since release from hospital last month. Suffered a broken hip in fall. Never regained his health after the accident.__

Time and Date of Funeral __10 a.m. Saturday__

Place of Funeral __First Methodist Church. Body taken to Jordan Funeral Home.__

__Will lie in state from 7 until 10 p.m. today and from 8:30 to 9:30 a.m. Saturday.__

Place of Burial __Evergreen Cemetery__

Officiating Clergyman __Unknown__

*   *   *

Place of Birth __Detroit, Michigan__

Places and Lengths of Residences

__Moved here about 50 years ago__

Occupation

__Retired__

Did Deceased Ever Hold Public Office (When and What)?

__No__

*   *   *

Name, Address of Surviving Husband (or Wife) __Wife Patricia preceded him in death. She__

__buried in Evergreen Cemetery 20 years ago.__

Maiden Name (if Married Woman)

Form 201

Marriage, When to Whom __Married 1908 to former Patricia Tearson.   Date and__

__place of marriage unknown.__

*   *   *

Names, Addresses of Surviving Children_____

___Only known child, son, Albert, killed in Philippines during WWII___

___All funeral arrangements have been made by his attorney___

Names, Address of Surviving Brothers and Sisters___No known living relatives___

Number of Grandchildren (Great, Great-Great, etc.)___No known living relatives___

Names, Address of Parents (if Living)___Presumed dead___

Additional Information___Retired mailman.   Had same route on downtown Main St. from__

__1926 until retirement in 1951.   Served as treasurer of Mail Carriers__

__Union in 1935.   No known church affiliation.   Member of the Veterans__

__of Foreign Wars, City Sportsmans Club and Alcoholics Anonymous.   Confined__

__to bed since entered nursing home.   Filed $100,000 suit against the__

__appliance store two weeks ago.   Suit filed in court said he tripped,__

__fell over an empty cardboard box lying on floor in an aisle at store.__

__Suit charged the store with "gross negligence."__

OBITUARIES: MISCELLANEOUS EXERCISES

1. Analyze 10 obituaries published by your local newspaper.

2. Analyze 10 obituaries published by national magazines.

3. Write your own obituary.

4. Write an obituary for some person you know or another student in your class. Assume that the person died early today of a heart attack and that his death has already been reported by your local newspaper. Do not write a news story about his death, but an obituary about his life. Include the following: some interesting or unusual incidents in the person's life; a physical description of the person; at least one anecdote about the person; some of the person's favorite expressions; a quote from at least one other person who knew the dead person.

5. Write an in-depth obituary for some famous person who has not yet died. Use any appropriate sources of information. Use descriptions, anecdotes and quotes to make the obituary colorful and interesting.

8 Publicity Releases

Newspapers are besieged by individuals and organizations seeking publicity. A daily newspaper in even a medium-sized community is likely to receive 100 publicity releases in the mail every morning. Another 20 persons may call the newspaper and 10 persons may stop at the newspaper's office with requests for publicity.

Individuals and organizations prepare most publicity releases not to inform the public, but to help themselves. Business firms use publicity releases to describe their growth, name their officers and report their latest dividends. Politicians and political parties use publicity releases to win the public's support. Charities plead for money. Churches want more members. Stores want more customers. Colleges want more students. Parents want recognition for their children's achievements—and often for themselves as well.

Because publicity releases are usually self-serving, they must be examined critically before they are published. In fact, daily newspapers reject 80 to 90 per cent of the publicity releases they receive. Most publicity releases are not newsworthy because they are obvious advertisements, because they would interest only a few persons in the community, because they describe events held days earlier or because they are incomplete.

Most publicity releases that are considered newsworthy are poorly written, so they must be rewritten. The reporter must dig out and emphasize the facts that are of interest to the public, correcting any bias and discarding irrelevant details. A five-page publicity release can often be summarized in a three-paragraph news story.

Despite all this, publicity releases do constitute an important source of information for newspapers. They often provide facts that newspapers are unaware of or unable to obtain otherwise. So, when properly used, publicity releases (1) give newspapers the information necessary for legitimate news stories, (2) give individuals and organizations needed publicity and (3) give the public information about events of interest and importance.

PUBLICITY RELEASES: EXERCISE 1

INSTRUCTIONS: The following are actual, verbatim publicity releases that were mailed to newspapers. Only the names of individuals in the stories have been changed. Rewrite each of the publicity releases for publication in your local newspaper.

1. Southdale, the area's biggest and best shopping center, will host the annual City Garden Club Council Flower Show this Friday, Saturday and Sunday. The show will be in the Garden Court and on the Upper Level of beautiful Southdale. Southdale Shopping Center is located at 66th Street and France Avenue. Mrs. Vivian Dawson, vice president of the City Garden Club Council, is chairwoman of this year's flower show, which will be the biggest and best in history. Judging from 9 a.m. to 3 p.m. will be held Saturday. The show will officially open to the public for viewing from 6 until 9 p.m. Friday, and from 8 a.m. to 6 p.m. Saturday and from noon until 6 p.m. Sunday.

2. Dear Mr. Editor:

   On next Sunday the State Firemen's Association is sponsoring the 7th Annual Fire Service Day in Columbia State Historic Park. There will be a firemen's muster, muster parade and pumping contest featuring antique hand operated fire pumpers. The muster parade will consist of old and new pumpers, some of which date back to 1829. The parade will start at 12:30 p.m. at Jackson and Main Streets and proceed south on Main Street to the main parking lot.

   The pumping contest starts at 1 p.m. in the main parking lot. The contest features hundred-year-old hand-operated fire pumpers. Some of these hand pumpers can throw a stream of water two-hundred feet. This event is open to the public free of charge. It is a good time for picture taking—the old engines are colorful as are the firemen's uniforms. There is plenty of action to photograph during the pumping contest.

   As an added attraction this year, there will be a "bucket brigade" contest between teams. Anyone is welcome to form a team—youngsters or oldsters, men or women. For those who want to stay overnight, there are many good campgrounds, trailer courts and motels within four miles of Columbia.

   Columbia State Historic Park is an attraction to see also. The museum and exhibits will all be open as well as all the town businesses. You may ride a stagecoach, visit an operating gold mine and pan for gold.

   Any publicity you can give this event will be greatly appreciated. We sincerely hope that you, too, will be able to attend.

3. Dear Sirs:

   This letter is being written in behalf of the International Association of Machinests and myself, of Lodge 1209. We are submitting this letter to voice our opinion to the governor's wanting to raise tuition in the colages of this state. We feel that his beliefs and wants and his statements are uncalled for. That an increase in tution for the average student and their parents would be more of a burden and a hindrance. As things stand now most parents have a hard enough time sending their children to colage and an addition to what ever tution they do pay would cause more than one to have to drop out. This is the opinion of myself and the rest of the members of Lodge 1209, located in this community.

   We would like to see some public opinions both for and against our objections from both private citizens and other Lodges in your paper.

   Sincerely yours,
   Richard M. Reedy
   Legislative Chairman

4. Michael Morhonese, Regional Sales Manager for the State, today announced the appointment of Samuel L. Hawkins as Financial Planning Agent for American Life Insurance Agency. In this capacity, he will be responsible for the sales and service of the Company's Ordinary Life Insurance products through financial institutions in the state.

   Hawkins and his wife, Mary, reside at 504 N. Tampa Ave. They have three children, Mark, Susan and Terry.

Active in the insurance industry for over 14 years, Hawkins served the American Life Insurance Agency as an agent and staff manager. Working for that firm, he has most recently been engaged in financial security planning for banks throughout the state.

A native of the State, he attended City Business College and has completed Part I of LUTC (Life Underwriters Training Council).

American Life Insurance Agency has an office at 4231 South Main Street, with our courteous staff available to serve the public from 8 a.m. until 5 p.m. Monday through Saturday.

5. PHILADELPHIA—Physicians in the United States and Canada who have met the high standards of the American College of Physicians (ACP) have been granted Fellowship in the 56-year-old international medical specialty society. The College dedicates itself to upgrading medical care, teaching and research through stringent standards of membership and programs of continuing education.

(Ed. Note: The specialists in internal medicine or related specialties in your area are listed at the end of this release.)

Hugh R. Butt, M.D., Rochester, Minn., President of the College, said the new Fellows have earned this distinction through certification by their specialty boards, presentation of published material and evidence of scientific accomplishments and academic or hospital affiliations.

The College today is one of the leading medical societies in the provision of continuing educational opportunities for its 17,000 members. A pioneer in post-graduate courses and other means for continuing education, the ACP in 1968 started periodic self-assessment examinations by which more than 25,000 physicians have already privately judged their own degree of competence so they can direct their choice of postgraduate educational programs.

The organization, with headquarters in Philadelphia, Pa., serves the interests of doctors and their patients in many other ways. It is a founding member of the Joint Commission on Accreditation of Hospitals and provides both financial and professional support for its hospital-by-hospital surveys. Through its accreditation standards, the Joint Commission encourages hospitals to constantly improve their provision of health care.

Dr. J. E. O'Brien. Office: Professional Center, 203 Main St.
    Residence: 321 Meadowlark Drive
Dr. Phillip Tigue. Office: 843 Jamestown Drive
    Residence: 8214 Oaklando Drive

6. Dear Sirs:

Local American Legion Post #2 wishes to announce its new officers for the coming year which were elected Sunday evening as follows: Commander, Herb Grimes; 1st Vice Commander, Del McGuire; 2nd Vice Commander, Al Reeder; Finance Officer, A.L. Cannon; Chaplain, Ray Kramer; Historian, Cole Hassard; and Sgt. at Arms, Tom Henley. Grimes, a veteran of the Korean Conflict, is a biology teacher and football coach at Central High School.

7. A 2,000-pound bronze cannon salvaged from a 17th century Swedish warship is catching the eye of naval buffs and other passersby in the plaza entrance to the First National Bank, 431 Main Street. The cannon is from the Royal Warship Wasa which capsized in Stockholm harbor in 1628.

Restoration of the Wasa is the subject of an exhibit opening next Monday in the First National Bank. The exhibit is presented in association with the Royal Swedish-American Society of the county.

The Wasa, commission by King Gustav II Adolf, sank Aug. 10, 1628 while on its maiden voyage and was buried in the mud at the bottom of the harbor for 333 years. Forgotten for three centuries, the sludge-filled ship was rediscovered in 1956 and was raised from its muddy home in 18 stages over a period of two years.

Now in the process of being restored, the Wasa is a major tourist attraction in Stockholm. It is housed on the waterfront in a special aluminum-clad water bath to prevent further deterioration of the wooden vessel.

The ship was designed for a crew of 133 sailors and 300 soldiers. It was equipped with 64 cannons of varying sizes and was embellished with lavish carvings created by seven master wood carvers.

The exhibit also features artifacts from the Wasa, replicas of ornate decorations on the ship, photographs of the restoration activities, ancient maritime maps of this era and other details of life aboard a 17th Century warship. Government officials and members of the county's Swedish-American Society will be guests at a reception at First National Sunday night to mark the formal opening of the Wasa exhibit. The Wasa exhibit may be viewed Monday through Friday by the public from 8:30 a.m. to 4:30 p.m. It will remain on exhibit for a period of two weeks.

8. NEWS FROM SENATOR EDWARD J. GURNEY (R. Fla.)
   FOR IMMEDIATE RELEASE

WASHINGTON, D.C.—The Senate passed, by a unanimous consent agreement, the controversial joint resolution that would restore the name of Cape Canaveral to that area which has been designated Cape Kennedy since 1963. The resolution was introduced more than two years ago by the late Senator Spessard Holland (D. Fla.) and Senator Ed Gurney (R. Fla.), but never was reported out of committee during the 91st Congress.

Senator Lawton Chiles later joined Senator Gurney as the co-sponsor, and the resolution was re-introduced in January of this year. After the Interior Committee approved the bill, it was held up on the Senate calander. The vote was finally taken yesterday to approve the resolution. The House has not yet acted upon the resolution.

"The name Cape Canaveral is one of the earliest landmarks, appearing on maps as early as 1536," Gurney said.

"No one wants to detract in any way from the naming of the NASA installation after our late President, John F. Kennedy, but most of us believe the action to include the geographic area as Cape Kennedy was a mistake made in haste," Gurney said.

Senator Chiles said the name should be restored for the sake of history.

It is expected the House will follow the Senate in approving the resolution in the near future, and send the bill to the President for his signature.

INSTRUCTIONS: Rewrite each of the publicity releases on this and the following pages for publication in your local newspaper.

American Red Cross News Service

NATIONAL HEADQUARTERS, WASHINGTON, D.C.

Tel: Day: 857-3512
Day: 857-3627
Night: 737-8300

Mail PIB 75

RELEASE AT WILL

RED CROSS WARNS SWIMMERS ON
THE DANGERS OF HYPERVENTILATION

WASHINGTON, D. C.   --Deep breathing is fine as a part of setting-up exercises, but it's dangerous and may be fatal as a preliminary to underwater swimming, the American Red Cross warned today.

Too much deep breathing can cause "hyperventilation" and unconsciousness, Charles W. (Red) Russell, national director of Red Cross Safety Programs, said. Hyperventilation stems from an excessive rate and depth of breathing which leads to abnormal loss of carbon dioxide in the blood, he explained.

"When a swimmer hyperventilates," Mr. Russell said, "he increases his breath-holding time by blowing off carbon dioxide in his blood. When the carbon dioxide content is lowered, the stimulus for taking a breath is decreased."

When a person tries to swim under water for a long time after hyperventilating, he added, the oxygen content of the body may decline to a point where the swimmer will lose consciousness before the carbon dioxide builds up sufficiently to stimulate the breathing action. Unless someone is around to help him to the surface, the swimmer will drown.

Mr. Russell warned especially against competition by children or even adults to see how long they can stay under water.

NEWS RELEASE

THE AMERICAN LEGION
HEADQUARTERS

1608 K St., N. W.
Washington, D. C. 20006
(202) 393-4811

700 N. Pennsylvania St.
Indianapolis, Ind. 46204
(317) 635-8411

For God and Country

**NATIONAL
PUBLIC RELATIONS
DIVISION**

C. D. DeLOACH
Chairman

JAMES C. WATKINS
Director
Washington

ROD ANDERSON
Asst. Director
Indianapolis

SUBJECT SUMMARY: Viet-Time Veteran Legionnaires To Hold Special Business Session
At The American Legion's 54th Annual National Convention In Chicago

Chicago, Ill.--Vietnam-era veterans, now the second largest segment of veterans in

The American Legion, second only to World War II veterans, will meet in a special business

session Aug. 22-23 during the 54th annual Legion convention in Chicago, over the period

Aug. 18-24.

The Legion first used a special Vietnam-vet committee during its 1967 National

Convention. In that meeting and a subsequent Viet-time meeting held during a national

convention, the Legion concentrated on finding out how the Viet-time veteran sees The

American Legion, what kind of organization he wants and what programs will appeal to him.

Now that Vietnam-era veterans are emerging with increasing frequency in positions of

leadership in the Legion, this year's meeting is designed to define and clarify the role of

the Vietnam-era veteran in the Legion.

The special business session will also work to chart a course of action for The American

Legion that will be relevant to the growing number of Viet-time veterans coming into the

Legion as well as to review programs available to veterans and to plan for greater

participation from the Vietnam-era veteran group.

The first day's activities will be an all day session with several prominent speakers
scheduled to appear. They include: John H. Geiger, National Commander of The American
Legion; Donald E. Johnson, Administrator, Veterans Administration and a Past National
Commander of the Legion; William Rhatican, Staff Assistant to the President; and Robert
Hampton, Chairman, Civil Service Commission.

The second day will be an executive session limited to those Viet-time Legionnaires
authorized by each Legion Department (state) to be their official representative. They will
adopt a report which will be presented to the convention proper on Thursday morning, Aug. 24.

Both sessions will be held in Parlor C, the Conrad Hilton Hotel and will be chaired by
Mr. Frank Naylor of Kansas who was chairman of the first Viet-vet committee in 1967.

THE AMERICAN LEGION

HEADQUARTERS

1608 K St., N. W.
Washington, D. C. 20006
(202) 393-4811

700 N. Pennsylvania St.
Indianapolis, Ind. 46204
(317) 635-8411

For God and Country

**NATIONAL
PUBLIC RELATIONS
DIVISION**

C. D. DeLOACH
Chairman

JAMES C. WATKINS
Director
Washington

ROD ANDERSON
Asst. Director
Indianapolis

SUBJECT SUMMARY: American Legion's Fourth Estate Award   Goes To
                 South American Publisher, Foe Of Communism

Chicago, Ill.--The American Legion's Fourth Estate Award   for outstanding

public service in the field of communication will be presented to Paris-born Agustin

Edwards, publisher of the Santiago, Chile, newspaper El Mercurio, which fought the

Marxist coalition of Chile until Edwards, after a long struggle, left the country.

The presentation will be made by Legion National Commander John H. Geiger on the

convention platform at about 10 a.m., Aug. 24, the final day of the convention which

starts Aug. 18.

A graduate of Princeton University in 1949, Edwards had attended the law school

of the University of Chile and while a student there had worked for El Mercurio in the

morgue and on the foreign news desk. He returned to El Mercurio in 1951, by 1956

had become assistant managing editor, and in 1959 he became publisher of the El Mercurio

chain of 11 newspapers.

In addition to his work with El Mercurio, Edwards was a banker and industrialist
with board memberships, and in many instances board chairmanships, in several firms
with a combined annual business volume of about a quarter of a billion dollars. Mr.
Edwards expended much of his personal fortune in his newspapers' fight against the Marxist
government in Chile before leaving the country.

Geiger noted that it is the first time in the 15-year history of his organization's
Fourth Estate Award that the award has been given to a foreign journalist. "Our Public
Relations Commission reported that several most worthwhile entries were received from
U.S. newsmen and news organizations, but felt that Mr. Edwards' struggle on behalf of
freedom of the press and of all human freedom characterized the day-in, day-out fight
for freedom waged by the recognized news media of the United States," Geiger said.

Edwards is a long-time member of the Inter-American Press Association and was
president of that association in 1969. Presidents of the IAPA for the past decade
have been invited as distinguished guests of The American Legion to witness the
presentation to Mr. Edwards.

UNITED NATIONS ASSOCIATION of the UNITED STATES OF AMERICA

833 United Nations Plaza New York, New York 10017 OXford 7-3232 Area Code 212

For Further Information:
Jeffrey L. Hodes
(212) OX-7-3232

WASHINGTON — Warning that spreading violence and danger of major war will be the inevitable consequence of continuing neglect of issues affecting the southern half of Africa, a National Policy Panel of the United Nations Association of the U.S.A. today issued a series of recommendations to guide American business and government toward fulfilling declared policies in favor of racial equality and self-government.

In a 93-page report that is sharply critical of labor practices of most American companies in southern Africa, the Panel pointed to numerous gaps between policy and performance by both government and business. In South Africa, for example, the report pointed out that in general American firms pay less to their African employees than do South African firms.

The national interests of the United States — including defense installations in the Azores, South Africa and other areas, as well as investments, trade and strategic minerals such as chrome and gold — are analyzed by the Panel in assessing the "seeds of potentially serious conflict" in "a massive area of the world where the majority of the people are denied participation in the governments which govern them solely on the basis of the color of their skin." It pointed out that investments in all of Southern Africa, totalling about $1 billion, represent only one-third of the total U.S. investment in Africa as a whole.

The presence of 42 African states among the 131 members of the United Nations is continuously confronting the United States with difficult issues based on rising demands for racial equality and representative government, the Panel stressed. It pointed to the recent action of Congress in breaching UN sanctions against the importation of chrome from Rhodesia as one such issue, and called for Congress to repeal its action.

Headed by William Roth, San Francisco businessman and former U.S. Representative for Trade Negotiations, and William T. Coleman, Philadelphia attorney, member of President Nixon's Price Commission and Delegate to the 24th UN General Assembly, the Panel contained, in addition to business and professional leaders, the President of Princeton University, Dr. Robert F. Goheen, former State Department specialists on Africa, African scholars, a youth organization leader, and a former White House staff member.

Cyrus R. Vance, Chairman of UNA-USA Policy Studies, in presenting the report, stated that even though "the national mood is one of restricting foreign involvements ... issues of human rights, of economic opportunity, and of relations between the races, have staked out new claims to our attention and our convictions."

The Panel agreed that "solutions to the conditions which exist in southern Africa must be developed by the whites and non-whites of the area working together," and that "U.S. power and influence" are sharply limited. Nevertheless, the Panel stressed that its specific proposals could "offer aid and encouragement to internal forces for change," and help to ensure that United States policies "in no way support the oppressive policies of the white minority governments."

In relation to South Africa, the Panel urged that our government —

* Actively discourage new investments by American business.
* Discontinue guarantees and insurance to private lenders against business and political risks for U.S. exports.
* Revoke South Africa's sugar quota and reallocate it to other African nations, such as Swaziland.
* Make clear to the South African Government "that the U.S. would not go to its defense or give aid in the suppression of internal revolt related to its repressive policies."
* Assign black Americans to diplomatic and other U.S. government posts in South Africa, and insure against racial discrimination at U.S. government-sponsored functions.
* Maintain strict compliance of the arms embargo against South Africa, including a reversal of the decision to permit sales of executive-type aircraft that could be used for military reconnaissance.
* Consider "equal treatment" measures in granting visas, selective boycotts of racially-restricted sports, and selective encouragement of educational and cultural exchange.

Turning to American business in South Africa, the Panel stressed that "with notable exceptions, the nearly 300 U.S. companies operating in South Africa are not now in the forefront of the effort to improve the economic and social lot of their non-white South African workers," and suggested that the problems arise more from the parent companies in the United States than from the local representatives.

The Panel urged that American companies --

* Provide equal pay and benefits for equal work.
* Provide on-the-job and vocational training for non-whites.
* Open promotion opportunities to non-whites.
* Abolish apartheid practices in company functions.
* Withdraw from South Africa if economic feasibility requires discriminatory labor practices.
* Stop financing South African Government-sponsored commercial or military projects.

In addition, the Panel proposed the establishment within the U.S. Government of an Interdepartmental Task Force to provide continuing review of southern African issues, including priority consideration "to the monitoring of U.S. companies in their adoption of fair and non-racial labor practices and to evaluating their potential impact on non-white South African workers." The first report of the Task Force, the Panel stressed, should be issued in no less than two years time.

Ten of the report's 93 pages were taken up with individual comments, reservations or dissents on particular recommendations that were about evenly divided between those thinking the action proposed went too far and those thinking it did not go far enough.

In relation to the Portuguese territories of Angola, Mozambique and Guinea Bissau, the Panel maintained the chief thrust of U.S. policy should be to encourage Portugal to see its future in Europe rather than Africa. "Integration with Europe may, in fact, be the only way in which Portugal will be able to extricate herself from Africa," the Panel declared in urging the United States to direct loans and investment guarantees toward encouraging Portugal's economic integration with Europe. Meanwhile, the Panel recommended that until Portugal withdraws its 140,000 troops from African territory, the United States should suspend military assistance and impose an arms embargo on Portugal.

In relation to Rhodesia, the Panel not only urged that Congress repeal its action permitting the importation of chrome ore in violation of the UN sanctions voted for by the United States, but added the

United States should give strong support to the Sanctions Committee of the UN Security Council and promote exposure of violations. The present situation, the Panel said, raises "serious questions concerning the United States commitment to the United Nations."

Namibia, the former Trust Territory of Southwest Africa, the Panel pointed out, is being governed by South Africa in violation of a finding of the International Court of Justice that its presence there is illegal and in violation of resolutions adopted by large majorities in the UN General Assembly. Given the illegal status of South Africa's control of Namibia, the Panel recommended that "the Internal Revenue Service be required to disallow any deductions or credits for taxes paid by U.S. firms to the South African Government on income earned by enterprises in Namibia."

Other countires in Southern Africa also were the object of specific recommendations for business and public policy.

In relation to African nationalist movements, the Panel proposed "that the United States Government establish or maintain contact with the liberation movements and that both the U.S. Government and private organizations support the movements in the non-military aspects of their programs, including educational and medical assistance."

UNA-USA is a private, non-profit research and education organization aimed at strengthening United States participation in international organizations. Chief Justice Earl Warren (retired) is its Chairman. The National Policy Panels are set up by a Policy Studies Committee, but each Panel is free to develop its own recommendations, with UNA assuming responsibility for choosing the subject, selecting the Panel members, and publishing the Panel's report.

The Panel on Southern Africa: Proposals for Americans, carried on its research, including visits to southern Africa, over an 18-month period. The full membership of the Panel is listed below. Those names with asterisks indicate the submission of a comment, reservation or dissent.

William M. Roth, *Chairman*
San Francisco
Former U.S. Special Representative for Trade Negotiations

William T. Coleman, *Vice Chairman**
Dilworth, Paxson, Kalish, Levy and Coleman, Philadelphia
Member U.S. Delegation to the 24th UN General Assembly

Clifford L. Alexander, Jr.*
Partner
Arnold & Porter
Washington, D.C.

John R. Bunting, Jr.
President
First Pennsylvania Banking and Trust Company

Robert F. Goheen
President
Princeton University

Charles V. Hamilton †
Professor of Political Science
Columbia University

William A. Hance
Chairman
Department of Geography
Columbia University

George N. Lindsay
Partner
Debevoise, Plimpton, Lyons & Gates
Former Member, African Advisory Council,
Department of State

Ruth Schachter Morgenthau*
Professor
Brandeis University
Former Member, African Advisory Council,
Department of State

Edwin S. Munger*
Professor of Political Geography
California Institute of Technology

Waldemar A. Nielsen*
Advisor to Foundations and Corporations

Hans A. Ries*
Vice President
Continental Ore Corporation

Harvey C. Russell
Vice President
Pepsi-Cola Co.

Brad Lee Skinner*
Executive Director
Council on International Relations and UN Affairs (CIRUNA)

† Participated in the early discussions of the Panel but not in the drafting of the final report.

UNITED NATIONS ASSOCIATION of the UNITED STATES OF AMERICA

833 United Nations Plaza New York, New York 10017 OXford 7-3232 Area Code 212

For Further Information
Call: Porter McKeever
(212) OX 7-3232

For Immediate Release

The United Nations Association of the United States of America, Inc. (UNA) today announced plans to make available a four-story townhouse located at 3 Sutton Place, New York City, to the United Nations as a residence for the Secretary-General, Dr. Kurt Waldheim.

The townhouse, which was contributed to UNA by Arthur A. Houghton, Jr., President of Steuben Glass, has been appraised, by independent experts, at a fair market value in excess of One Million ($1,000,000) Dollars.

UNA President Porter McKeever said that the townhouse initially has been leased to the United Nations by UNA for one year.

"UNA appreciates very much the generosity of Mr. Houghton in contributing full owner-ship of the building to UNA," said Mr. McKeever. "Now, UNA will be in a position to initiate arrangements for the United Nations to have the property as a permanent residence for the Secretary-General. We plan to do this sometime soon. But, first, UNA's Board of Governors has to give its final approval. However, I see no reason why this cannot be done in a manner satisfactory to both origazations."

While Mr. Houghton was not able to be present when his deed was delivered to Mr. McKeever by his attorney, Mr. James J. Beha at the offices of his Counsel, Gasser and Hayes, he issued a statement indicating his pleasure that his gift to the United Nations Association should make it possible for Secretary-General Waldheim and his successors to occupy the building that had been his home for many years.

Also present at the closing were Mr. Ernest A. Gross and Mr. Robert D. Whoriskey of Curtis, Mallet-Prevost, Colt and Mosle on behalf of UNA; and on behalf of the United Nations, Mr. Robert G. Ryan, Assistant Secretary-General and Mrs. Alice E. Weil, Senior Legal Officer.

Secretary-General Waldheim presently resides at the Carlyle Hotel. His family plans to move into the townhouse sometime early this Fall. The building will be furnished by the United Nations.

The townhouse is located on the east side of Sutton Place, between East 57th Street and Sutton Square. The plot has a frontage of 40 feet and a depth of approximately 70 feet.

The rear of the townhouse looks over a community garden which faces the East River. Ownership of the garden is divided among all of the houses bordering on the garden.

The first floor of the Sutton Square townhouse has a reception hall with marble floors, a dining room with a woodburning fireplace, a fully-equipped kitchen, a pantry, and bathroom. The second floor has a drawing room across the width or the building with fireplaces at each end. It also has a ladies' sitting room and powder room, a library with antique English panelling. The beginning of an oval staircase to upper floors is also located on the second floor.

The third floor has two bedrooms in the front, each with a dressing room and bathroom. In the rear of the third floor is a sitting room with eighteenth century panelling of Scandinavian pine with bookshelves. There is also a master bedroom on the third floor adjoining an oval bathroom and dressing room. The fourth floor has two additional bedrooms, and also servants' rooms. An automatic elevator of 1800 lbs. capacity runs between the basement and the top floor. All main rooms have woodburning fireplaces.

The immediate block on which the townhouse is located, known as Suton Place Gardens, is comprised of sixteen private houses, remodeled in the early 1920's. The owners have agreed by covenants to maintain the existing compound of houses overlooking the East River in substantially the same architectural style.

The townhouse was originally built over 50 years ago for Anne Morgan, daughter of J. Pierpont Morgan. It was designed by Mott Schmidt, a noted townhouse architect. The building is brick, English Georgian in style, and has an ornamental facade both on the street and garden side. It reflects the finest design and workmanship of that period. The interiors are finished with marble floors, intricate panelling and woodwork, some of which is antique. The townhouse was improved and modernized in the 1950's by Mr. Houghton, when he acquired it.

UNA plans to contribute to the UN after its expenses are covered any funds received from the UN in connection with this property. These contributions will be to UN activities of a charitable and educational nature which UNA's Board of Governors deem to be in furtherance of UNA's goals and tax-exempt purposes. The particular activities and the exact amounts are still to be worked out by the UNA Board of Governors in consultation and agreement with the UN.

The United Nations Association in the past has contributed to various UN educational and charitable projects, which it considered to be in furtherance of its tax-exempt purposes.

The United Nations Association of the United States of America is the primary citizens organization working in support of the United States role in the United Nations. It engages in objective, non-partisan research and policy formulation, backed by nationwide education, information, and citizen-action programs aimed ar making the United Nations and other international organizations more adequate to the needs of our times. Its research and policy program involves leaders from all segments of our society whose recommendations have served to strengthen the UN and other international organizations. Its headquarters are located at 833 United Nations Plaza, New York City, on the corner of 46th Street, directly across the street from the United Nations.

UNA receives no financial support from the U.S. Government. It carries on cooperative projects with more than 140 National organizations, and conducts community activities in approximately 2,000 localities under a National UN Day Program in response to an Annual Proclamation of the President of the United States. It has approximately 70,000 individual members with directly affiliated chapters in approximately 175 communities. UNA also preforms services as requested by the U.S. Government and the UN, and publishes VISTA, an authoritative magazine reporting on international organization activities.

* * * * *

Roundup Stories

To save space, newspapers will often publish a roundup story, which summarizes several different but related events. For example, instead of publishing a separate story about each of a dozen weekend traffic deaths, most newspapers report all the deaths in a single story. Newspapers likewise may report several similar crimes or several fires in a single story.

Another type of roundup story deals with a single event but includes facts from several sources of information. Reporters may interview more than one person to (1) obtain more information, (2) verify facts they have already obtained or (3) obtain conflicting viewpoints for a balanced story. For example, if your mayor resigned unexpectedly, you might interview the mayor and ask him why he resigned, what he plans to do after leaving office, what he considers his major accomplishments and what problems will confront his successor. You might then (1) ask other city officials to comment on the mayor's performance and resignation, (2) ask the city clerk how the next mayor will be selected and (3) interview the leading contenders for the mayor's job. All this information would be included in your roundup story.

The lead of a roundup story may summarize the most important facts; or, if a story reports several different events, the lead may summarize the single most important event. After the lead, report the most important facts about the most important topic in the story. Then move on to the second, third and fourth most important topics. As you discuss each topic, report what everyone you interviewed said about it. If you report first every fact provided by one source about all the topics, then every fact provided by a second, third and fourth source, your roundup story will be disorganized and repetitious.

ROUNDUP STORIES: EXERCISE 1

INSTRUCTIONS: Write a roundup story about all three of these accidents.

Accident 1

Vehicle #1 was driven by T. J. Ortson, 51, of 810 N. 14th St. Vehicle #2 was driven by Sara Anne Talbertson, 23, of 3214 Riverview Drive. The two vehicles collided at the intersection of U.S. 141 and Carlton Avenue. The accident was reported to police at 12:35 a.m. today. The accident was investigated by Patrolmen Julius Tiller and Manuel Cortez. They reported that Ortson and his wife, Martha, suffered head and chest injuries. An ambulance rushed the couple to Memorial Hospital. A hospital spokesman later reported that both are in serious condition. Miss Talbertson was not injured, apparently, the officers said, because she was wearing a shoulder-type seat belt at the time of the accident. However, the officers charged Miss Talbertson with running a red light. Both cars were demolished. Orston was driving a 1972 Toyota valued at approximately $2,000, and Miss Talbertsen was driving a 1968 Plymouth valued at approximately $600.

Accident 2

Officers were called to the 4200 block of Wymore Road at 6:30 a.m. today to investigate a reported accident. Patrolman Cecil Roehl filed a report concerning the accident. The report said, "I arrived at the scene at 6:34 a.m. and, upon arrival, found the victim's motorcycle in the eastbound lane of traffic. The victim has been positively identified as Leon Merritt, 17, of 301 Wymore Road. Skid marks indicate that his motorcycle was traveling at excessive speeds and went out of control just past a slight dip in the road. Road signs warned of the dip. The posted speed limit is 45 miles an hour. The subject's motorcycle is estimated to have been traveling in excess of 60 miles an hour. The motorcycle went off the road and struck a fence post and then seems to have bounced back onto the road. The victim's body was thrown into a field and was lying 47 feet from the roadway. A truck driver went off the road to avoid striking the wrecked motorcycle. The driver, who was not injured, telephoned police from a nearby house. The truck had to be towed from a ditch, but no damage was apparent. The coroner pronounced Merritt dead at the scene. His motorcycle was totally destroyed."

Accident 3

The accident occurred at 8:20 a.m. today. Two vehicles were involved. A delivery van driven by Jay Gable of 1701 Woodcrest Drive and a car driven by Jean Janvier, 27, of 1338 Hope Ter. Gable was alone in his vehicle. A passenger in the Janvier vehicle has been identified as Reba Carvel. She was 23 years old. She also lived at 1338 Hope Ter. Miss Janvier and Miss Carvel taught at Colonial Elementary School, and they apparently were on their way to school when the accident occurred. Patrolman Neto, who investigated the accident, reported that: "We were unable to find any witnesses to the accident. Gable suffered a broken leg and has been taken to Memorial Hospital for treatment. He seemed in shock so I couldn't talk to him much before an ambulance took him away. Gable had stopped to pick up another man who works with him. He identified himself as Melvin McCaully, 47, of 540 Osceola Blvd. The accident occurred directly in front of his house. McCaulley said he heard Gable stop and honk. McCaully said he went to get his lunch bucket and then heard the crash. From skid marks at the scene, it appeared that Gable hadn't pulled off the road and the Janvier vehicle rammed square into the back of his van. The van was pushed off the road into a ditch, where it overturned. The car remained upright on the highway. Skid marks and the extent of the damage indicate that the car was traveling about 50 miles an hour at the time of impact. The speed limit on Osceoloa Blvd. at that point is 55 miles an hour. Both women were dead when I got to them and it took more than a half-hour for the rescue squad to pry their bodies out of the wreckage. Both bodies were badly mangled, and Miss Janvier's legs were sliced off just below the knees. Charges of manslaughter probably will be filed against Gable later today. The district attorney is looking at the evidence now."

ROUNDUP STORIES: EXERCISE 2

INSTRUCTIONS: Write a roundup story about all three of these fires.

Fire 1

Two police officers patrolling Main St. reported a fire at Frishe's Bowling Alley, 4113 Main St., at 3:32 a.m. today. They smelled smoke, got out of their squad car and traced the smoke to the bowling alley. Firemen said the fire was confined to an office, where it caused an estimated $3,700 damage. Firemen found evidence of arson and notified police that the office apparently had been set on fire after it was burglarized. Two cigarette machines, a soft-drink machine and a door leading to the office had been pried open. Police said the thieves probably set the fire to hide the robbery. The fire failed to spread beyond the office. Art Mahew, manager of the bowling alley, estimated that $20 was missing from the three machines and $50 was taken from a cash box in the office. He added, "That's all the money we keep in the building at night. Except for some change for the next day's business, we just don't keep any money in the building at night. It's too risky. This is the third robbery we've had since I started working here four years ago."

Fire 2

Firemen were called to 1314 Griese Drive at 8:23 a.m. today. They found a fire in progress on the second floor of the two-story home. The home is owned by Mr. and Mrs. Timothy Keele. Mr. and Mrs. Keel and their four children had escaped from the home before firemen arrived. Firemen extinguished the blaze within 20 minutes. The fire was confined to two upstairs bedrooms and the attic. Smoke and water damage were reported throughout the house. No one was injured. Damage was estimated at $6,000. The Keels said they do not have any fire insurance to cover the loss. Mrs. Keel also told firemen she had punished one of her children for playing with matches in an upstairs closet earlier in the morning. Firemen said the blaze started in that closet, and attributed the fire to the child playing with matches. Mrs. Keel added that she was not aware of the fire until a telephone repairman who had been working across the street noticed smoke, came over and rang her doorbell. When she answered the door, he asked her, "Do you know your house is on fire?"

Fire 3

Firemen responded to a call at the Quality Trailer Court at 10:13 a.m. today after neighbors were alerted by screams from a trailer occupied by Mrs. Susan Kopp, 71. Flames had spread throughout the trailer by the time firemen arrived at the scene. The firemen had to extinguish the blaze, then wait for the embers to cool before they were able to enter the trailer. They found Mrs. Kopp's body in her bedroom. A spokesman for the Fire Department said she had apparently been smoking in bed, then awoke when her bedding caught fire. She died of suffocation before she could get out. Neighbors who heard her screams were unable to enter the trailer because of the flames, smoke and heat. "Those mobile homes burn up in a minute," a fire marshal said later in an interview. "Four or five people die in them every year in this city alone. Most of them are just made out of cheap cardboard, wood and a lot of paint and other stuff that ignites in a matter of seconds."

ROUNDUP STORIES: EXERCISE 3

INSTRUCTIONS: Assume that a fire destroyed Central High School last night. Write a roundup story about the fire based on the following information. You may quote the sources.

Source: Patrolman Thomas Jepson

"We were patrolling the area and smelled smoke at about 9:15 but couldn't figure out where it was coming from. We got a bunch of kids in the neighborhood to help us look for the fire, but it took us 10 minutes before we pinned it down to the school. By the time we got to the school the flames were shooting out the basement windows. Some lights in the building were on, and we were afraid someone might still be inside. A lot of groups meet there at night or use the school gym. I broke in while my partner checked the outside. The smoke was so bad that I couldn't get into the basement. I checked out the other floors but didn't find anyone. I ended up on the third floor, and then I couldn't get back downstairs because the fire was coming up the stairs. I finally smashed a window and yelled for help. The first fire trucks had gotten there by then, and they put up a ladder to get me out."

Source: Janitor Ralph Cassata

"It all happened while I was home for lunch. I'm the only one working the night shift now. I usually have a partner, and we clean the building, but he quit last month, and there's still no replacement, so I gotta do everything myself. I usually take a half-hour for lunch at around 8, but I got delayed last night 'cause some Boy Scouts was playing basketball in the gym, and I had to clean up the place and lock up when they quit. So I left at just before 9. When I got back, the whole place was in flames. I always knew the place was a fire trap and so did everyone else, but no one wanted to spend the money to fix it up. Hell, the wiring was all frayed and patched. There wasn't enough storage space, so there was junk piled all over the place, even in some hallways."

Source: Fire Chief Roger Dawson

"We got the first call at 9:28, and when we got to the school there just wasn't any chance to save it. The fire had spread all through the basement and ate through the upper floors. We couldn't send any men into the building because the upper floors were collapsing. That school must have been 80 years old and was built mainly of wood. There weren't any fire walls in the place, so once the fire got a good start we couldn't keep it from spreading. We sounded a second alarm at 9:34 and a third at 9:41. That's the first three-alarm fire in the city since I became chief seven years ago. We had all but two of the fire trucks in the city there, and every off-duty fireman we could find was called in to answer other calls. Fortunately, we didn't have any other fires at the same time, or we could have been in real trouble. We do have a mutual-aid pact with the suburbs and could have called on them for help."

Source: Superintendent of Schools George Dees

"We anticipate some real difficulties because of this. We've been trying to replace the school for years, but we're just not ready yet. Somehow we'll get the students from Central back in class by Monday. We're thinking that we'll bus them to West High School and put West on a double shift. The students at West will have class from 7 in the morning to 12:30, and the Central High students will have class from 12:45 until 6:15. Each group of students will have its usual teachers. It's hardly an ideal situation, but there's nothing else we can do until we get a new building. It takes at least a year to plan and build a new high school and usually much longer. I've already checked, and the old building was insured for $1.2 million. That's all it was worth, but it'll cost at least three times that much for a new school and probably more since it'll have to be a lot larger. Central was built for 800 students, and we had 1,300 squeezed into the building this year."

ROUNDUP STORIES: EXERCISE 4

INSTRUCTIONS: Assume that a severe thunderstorm struck the city early today. Write a roundup story about the storm based on the following information. You may quote the sources.

Source: U.S. Weather Bureau Spokesman

"We recorded 3.1 inches of rain in four hours, starting at 1:22 a.m. Wind gusts reached 63 miles an hour. Those were the strongest wind gusts recorded in the city since 1952. The temperature fell 17 degrees in 15 minutes. We also received some reports of scattered hail and funnel clouds, although no touch-downs have been reported."

Source: Chief of Police Ralph O'Brien

"The department received at least a hundred calls. We've had 23 minor traffic accidents, mostly caused by slippery roads. A tree limb fell on a car at the intersection of Cedar Ave. and 35th St., killing the driver, Mrs. Kathy Murphy. Otherwise, there've been only a few minor injuries. About 60 of the calls concerned trees down and blocking roads. We referred those calls to the Department of Public Works, and it called its crews out at 3 a.m. to start cleaning up the mess. Some downtown store windows were blown out, and we've had officers stand guard until the windows could be boarded up."

Source: Fire Chief Roger Dawson

"We received 14 calls early today, all related to the storm. Electric wires were reported down in eight locations. We watched the wires until the electric company was able to shut off power to repair them. Six homes were struck by lightning. The lightning caused two small fires. It didn't hurt anyone or cause much damage. But it sure scared some people. Mostly it just caused a lot of noise."

Source: Municipal Airport Spokesman

"Three small hangars that housed private planes were flattened. Just totally destroyed. About a half-dozen small planes were blown into the woods north of the runway and 20 more were mangled on the field and in the hangars. One just danced down the runway on its nose before it finally flipped over on its back. The other planes' wings and propellers were snapped off and fuselages twisted. We'd estimate the damage here at somewhere around $150,000."

Source: Telephone Company Spokesman

"Most of our lines are underground, so the storm really didn't hurt us. We've only had two or three isolated calls, and our crews are dealing with them now."

Source: Power Company Spokesman

"Power has been off in four areas of the city. We'd estimate that a total of somewhere around 14,000 homes have been affected. But our men have been out since 2 a.m., and power was restored to 90 per cent of the homes by 9 this morning. One or two of our poles were struck by lightning, but most of the trouble was caused by trees that fell on our lines and broke them."

Source: George Dees, Superintendent of Public Schools

"The information I've received so far is still preliminary, but it seems evident that the storm really hurt us. We just finished getting the steel beams and walls up for the new Eisenhower Junior High School on Eisenhower Drive. Everything came down last night. We're going to have to start all over again. I'd estimate damage at somewhere between $300,000 and $400,000. The shell of the building had just about been finished. The walls measured 200 by 100 feet. They were concrete and brick but still didn't have much support. The wind just tore them all down. It leveled everything. The steel tubing used for scaffolds was twisted like a pretzel."

ROUNDUP STORIES: EXERCISE 5

INSTRUCTIONS: Assume that teachers at State College in your city went on strike at 12:01 a.m. today. Write a roundup story about the strike based on the following information. You may quote the sources.

Source: Joe Hawsler, President of Teamsters Local 431

"The teachers at the school went on strike at 12:01 a.m. today. As you know, we signed a contract to represent them several months ago. We've tried to negotiate a fair contract, but the school's administrators simply refused to recognize us. We're not asking for anything unreasonable. We're trying to guarantee faculty members a 40-hour week, with time-and-a-half for overtime. We're also trying to negotiate an 8 per cent raise. The administrators haven't even been willing to sit down and talk with us, so we're striking. I understand that fewer than 10 per cent of the classes at the school met this morning. Almost every single faculty member out there has joined the union, and we expect the strike to be 100 per cent effective. We don't want the strike to last long, but the administration is just going to have to bargain with us."

Source: Lee Norbratten, Chairman of the Faculty Senate

"As professionals we hate to strike, but there's no real alternative. The administration has to know that we mean business. There's no other way we can force them to recognize and bargain with our union. And we've got some pretty legitimate problems here. Right now, a Ph.D. has to go to school 20 years, including at least seven or eight years of college. After that, he's paid less than a painter or truck driver. Did you know the average faculty member here works 55½ hours a week but doesn't get an extra penny for all the overtime? We want to remedy all that."

Source: George Alson, President of the Student Senate

"I sympathize with the faculty members, but this just isn't fair to students. We're caught in the middle. Right now, some students think the whole thing is a lark, and they're enjoying the vacation. But it's serious business, and if this strike continues some students may not be able to graduate as quickly as they'd hoped."

Source: Ralph Emersen, State College Spokesman

"There has been some slight inconvenience because of the strike, but we estimate that less than a quarter of our faculty members belong to the union and more than 80 per cent of our classes met as scheduled this morning. The whole thing is being exaggerated. We expect it to end within a few days. The union is simply demanding too much. And we, the school, can't do anything more this year. There's no way we can get enough money to satisfy all the union's demands. Now next year we might raise tuition or ask the state for more money, but our budget for this year already has been settled. We expect everyone to return to their classrooms. If they don't, the school may have to impose some sort of penalties. No school can let its faculty run amok like this."

Other unions are recognizing picket lines at entrances to the college. As a result, bus and taxi service to campus has ended. No deliveries are being made. Campus stores and cafeterias report that they have only a one-day supply of food and may have to close down. The campus police reported that there has been no violence. They added that parking lots at the school this morning were about half full.

ROUNDUP STORIES: EXERCISE 6

INSTRUCTIONS: Write a roundup story based on the following information. You may quote the sources.

Background Information

"Hot lines" have been established in dozens of cities in the United States. Anyone in these cities can call a specific telephone number and report anyone he suspects is selling drugs. Most of the hot lines are operated by civic groups, particularly Chambers of Commerce. A recent survey revealed that there are five such hot lines in this state. The oldest was established four years ago and the newest was established three months ago. Altogether, they have received an estimated 6,200 telephone calls, and the calls have been credited with helping the police obtain about 40 convictions.

Source: American Civil Liberties Union Spokesman

"Hot lines that allow anonymous callers to report suspected drug sellers to police will result in investigations of innocent people who would be irreparably harmed if the information fell into the wrong hands. Use of these drug hot lines by anonymous callers is supposed to result in investigations. Such investigations will necessitate the compiling of dossiers on innocent citizens, probably based solely on mere suspicion, false information or lies. These permanent files would be available to all law enforcement agencies and possibly credit-reporting services. This opens up a whole new avenue of Big Brotherism. A guy could really get smeared with no way of fighting back because he'd never know who reported what about him or who's getting the information. If they could guarantee that the information would be kept confidential it might be okay, but we know from other experiences across the country that supposedly confidential police information has a way of turning up in credit company reports and in the hands of others who have no business having it. We believe the potential for harm presented by this gross invasion of privacy of citizens exceeds its usefulness. The ACLU urges all persons who have credible information that a crime has been committed to call the local police, identify themselves and make their report. It's the American way. But we oppose the use of this type of anonymous hot line."

Source: State Police Officers Federation Spokesman

"I'm acquainted with all five of these hot lines in the state, and I think they're doing a tremendous job. They give citizens an opportunity to aid their local police departments. It's the only way we'll ever be able to solve these drug problems. No matter how hard they try, the police can't solve the problem by themselves. All these charges about citizens being hurt are a lot of crap. No public file is ever kept on information received through the telephone calls until someone is charged in a drug case."

Source: Local Chamber of Commerce Spokesman

"We operate a hot line here. We're aware of the problems and the criticism, and we've established safeguards to make sure no one but police officers learns about any of the anonymous reports. A Police Department employe is stationed in our office and receives all of the calls. Even I don't know who's reporting what. All the information goes from here directly to the Police Department without any civilians seeing it. I also think it's important to point out that we're just extending to the general public the old police procedure of using paid informants. Police often pay street informants for information, and you can bet those informants never show up in court to testify if the police make a case on the information they provide. Yet they provide a valuable service."

ROUNDUP STORIES: EXERCISE 7

INSTRUCTIONS: During a single ceremony, the President awarded the Medal of Honor to these servicemen. Write a roundup story about all three of the following citations, which are genuine.

Citation 1

"The President of the United States of America, authorized by Act of Congress, March 3, 1863, has awarded in the name of The Congress the Medal of Honor to Platoon Sergeant Finnis D. McCleery, United States Army, for conspicuous gallantry and intrepidity in action at the risk of his life above and beyond the call of duty.

"Platoon Sergeant Finnis D. McCleery, United States Army, distinguished himself on 14 May 1968 while serving as Platoon Leader of the First Platoon of Company A, 1st Battalion, 6th United States Infantry. On that date a combined force was assigned the mission of assaulting a reinforced company of North Vietnamese Army regulars, well-entrenched on Hill 352, 17 miles west of Tam Ky, Quang Tin Province. As Sergeant McCleery led his men up the hill and across an open area to close with the enemy, his platoon and other friendly elements were pinned down by tremendously heavy fire coming from the fortified enemy positions. Realizing the severe damage that the enemy could inflict on the combined force in the event that their attack was completely halted, Sergeant McCleery rose from his sheltered position and began a one-man assault on the bunker complex. With extraordinary courage, he moved across 60 meters of open ground as bullets struck all around him and rockets and grenades literally exploded at his feet. As he came within 30 meters of the key enemy bunker, Sergeant McCleery began firing furiously from the hip and throwing hand grenades. At this point in his assault, he was painfully wounded by shrapnel, but, with complete disregard for his wound, he continued his advance on the key bunker and killed all of its occupants. Having successfully and single-handedly breached the enemy perimeter, he climbed to the top of the bunker he had just captured and, in full view of the enemy, shouted encouragement to his men to follow his assault. As the friendly forces moved forward, Sergeant McCleery began a lateral assault on the enemy bunker line. He continued to expose himself to the intense enemy fire as he moved from bunker to bunker, destroying each in turn. He was wounded a second time by shrapnel as he destroyed a bunker from which two enemy soldiers were firing rockets and hurling grenades, but Sergeant McCleery valiantly continued his attack until the friendly forces had successfully destroyed and routed the enemy from the hill. Sergeant McCleery is personally credited with eliminating several key enemy positions and inspiring the assault that resulted in gaining control of Hill 352. His extraordinary heroism at the risk of his own life, above and beyond the call of duty, was in keeping with the highest standards of the military service, and reflects great credit on him, the Americal Division and the United States Army."

Citation 2

"The President of the United States of America, authorized by Act of Congress, March 3, 1863, has awarded in the name of The Congress the Medal of Honor to Specialist Four George C. Lang, United States Army, for conspicuous gallantry and intrepidity in action at the risk of his life above and beyond the call of duty.

"Specialist Four George C. Lang, Company A, 4th Battalion, 47th Infantry, 9th Infantry Division, was serving as a squad leader on 22 February 1969 in Kien Hoa Province of the Republic of Vietnam, when his unit, on a reconnaissance-in-force mission, encountered intense fire from a well-fortified enemy bunker complex. Specialist Lang observed an emplacement from which heavy fire was coming. Unhesitatingly, he assaulted the position and destroyed it with hand grenades and rifle fire. Observing another emplacement approximately 15 meters to his front, Specialist Lang jumped across a canal, moved through heavy enemy fire to within a few feet of the position, and eliminated it, again using hand grenades and rifle fire. Nearby, he discovered a large cache of enemy ammunition. As he maneuvered his squad forward to secure the cache, they came under fire from yet a third bunker. Specialist Lang immediately reacted, assaulted this position and destroyed it with the remainder of his grenades. After returning to the area of the arms cache, his squad again came under heavy enemy rocket and automatic weapons fire from three sides and suffered six casualties. Specialist Lang was one of those seriously wounded. Although immobilized and in great pain, he continued to direct his men until his evacuation was ordered over his protests. The sustained extraordinary courage and selflessness exhibited by this soldier over an extended period of time were an inspiration to his comrades and in keeping with the highest traditions of the United States Army."

Citation 3

"The President of the United States of America, authorized by Act of Congress, March 3, 1863, has awarded in the name of The Congress the Medal of Honor to Sergeant Gordon R. Roberts, United States Army, for conspicuous gallantry and intrepidity in action at the risk of his life above and beyond the call of duty.

"Sergeant (then Specialist Four) Gordon R. Roberts distinguished himself on July 11, 1969, while serving as a rifleman in Company B, 1st Battalion, 506th Infantry, 101st Airborne Division, during combat operations in Thua Thien Province, Republic of Vietnam. Sergeant Roberts' platoon was maneuvering along a ridge to attack heavily fortified enemy bunker positions which had pinned down an adjoining friendly company. As the platoon approached the enemy positions, it was suddenly pinned down by heavy automatic weapons and grenade fire from camouflaged enemy fortifications atop the overlooking hill. Seeing his platoon immobilized and in danger of failing in its mission, Sergeant Roberts crawled rapidly toward the closest enemy bunker. With complete disregard for his own safety, he leaped to his feet and charged the bunker, firing as he ran. Despite the intense enemy fire directed at him, Sergeant Roberts continued his one-man assault on a second bunker. As he neared the second bunker, a burst of enemy fire knocked his rifle from his hands. Sergeant Roberts picked up a rifle dropped by a comrade and continued his assault, silencing the bunker. He continued his charge against a third bunker and destroyed it with well-thrown hand grenades. Although Sergeant Roberts was now cut off from his platoon, he continued his assault against a fourth enemy emplacement. He fought through a heavy hail of fire to join elements of the adjoining company which had been pinned down by the enemy fire. Although continually exposed to hostile fire, he assisted in moving wounded personnel from exposed positions on the hilltop to an evacuation area before returning to his unit. By his gallant and selfless actions, Sergeant Roberts contributed directly to saving the lives of his comrades and served as an inspiration to his fellow soldiers in the defeat of the enemy force. Sergeant Roberts' extraordinary heroism and intrepidity in action at the risk of his life were in keeping with the highest traditions of the military service and reflect great credit upon himself, his unit and the United States Army."

Speeches and Meetings

Newspapers publish at least two stories about every important speech and meeting in their communities: an "advance" story before the speech or meeting takes place and a "follow" story afterward. Advance stories are written to notify readers of an event that they may want to attend, support or oppose and to help them prepare for it. Newspapers may publish one advance story on the day an important speech or meeting is announced, a second advance story a week before the event and a third advance story on the day the event is scheduled to take place.

The advance stories for most meetings (1) name the group that is meeting, (2) report the time and place of its meeting and (3) list the major issues on its agenda. Advance stories may also (4) explain why the meeting is important and indicate whether the public (5) will be admitted, (6) will have to pay an admission charge and (7) will have an opportunity to express its opinions about the issues being discussed.

Follow stories report what was actually said or done at the speech or meeting. Follow stories for meetings are particularly difficult to write because meetings often involve a multitude of participants and issues. Twelve aldermen may attend a City Council meeting and hear a dozen witnesses, then vote on five major issues. The follow story must report the action the City Council took on all five issues, and it must do so in a limited amount of space.

The lead for an advance story should indicate why a speech or meeting is important or unusual enough to be newsworthy, usually by reporting the topics that will be considered:

> Members of the American Civil Liberties Union will meet at 8 p.m. Friday in the YWCA to discuss charges that the City Council has discriminated against a homosexual.

> The Student Senate at its meeting Thursday night is expected to vote on a proposal to support Prof. Albert Calley, whose contract for next year has not been renewed by the university.

The lead for a follow story should emphasize the latest developments. It should not simply report the topic considered at the meeting; instead, it should tell what was said or done about that topic:

> The American Civil Liberties Union last night condemned the City Council for its refusal to hire a homosexual.

> The Student Senate last night voted 14 to 3 to support Prof. Albert Calley, whose contract for next year has not been renewed by the university.

SPEECHES AND MEETINGS: EXERCISE 1

INSTRUCTIONS: Write an advance story for each of the following events.

1. Chief of Police Ralph O'Brien has scheduled a press conference. The conference will be held in his office at 8 a.m. tomorrow. O'Brien has told reporters he will make an announcement in regard to the expansion of the city's Police Department. Twenty rookies graduated from the city's new police academy and are scheduled to start work tomorrow.

2. Mayor George Markel has scheduled a press conference in his office at 8 a.m. tomorrow. The announcement about the press conference was made by his secretary, Vivian Welch. Mrs. Welch, in response to questions from reporters, said, "All I can tell you is that it's very, very important. The mayor said I'm supposed to tell all of you to be in his office by 8 tomorrow for a major announcement. He said he's got a big scoop for you. No, he didn't specifically say what he'd be talking about. All he said was that the press conference concerns 'a significant addition to the city's educational facilities.' He didn't say anything else. I know he's been working on this project for at least a year now, and it's all been kept hush-hush. He told me not to say anything else, so if you want to know any more about it, you'll have to come tomorrow."

3. The State Cattlemen's Association will hold its annual convention at the Hotel Alexander, 111 Main St. The three-day convention will open at noon tomorrow and will continue through Saturday night. A spokesman for the hotel's Convention Bureau says he expects somewhere around 900 delegates. John L. Rue, president of the State Federation of Farmers, is scheduled to speak at the convention at 8 p.m. tomorrow night. The topic of his speech is listed as: "A New Crisis in Agriculture." The speech will be given in the Rosewood Ballroom, and the Cattlemen's Association has said the public is welcome. There will be no charge if people come just to hear Rue speak, but if they want dinner, which will be served at 6:30 p.m., the charge will be $3.50.

4. The Rotary Club meets at 7 p.m. every Monday night at the YMCA. During its regular meeting next Monday, the guest speaker will be Emil Plambeck. Plambeck is superintendent of the City Park Commission. He has said he will talk about the city's park system. All members of the Rotary Club are urged to attend the meeting, which is sure to be interesting and informative. The public is also welcome.

SPEECHES AND MEETINGS: EXERCISE 2

INSTRUCTIONS: Write a follow story based on the following announcement made by Chief of Police Ralph O'Brien at a press conference in his office at 8 a.m. today.

Source: Chief of Police Ralph O'Brien

"I would like to announce that 20 rookie officers have just finished our new three-month training program and began working regular 8-hour shifts at 7 a.m. this morning. Since I became chief 12 years ago, this unquestionably is the finest group of men to join the force. They're smarter, more mature and better trained. It is the first group to complete the three-month training program which we established just last year. Seven of the rookies are college graduates, and most of the others have had some college courses. We fully intend to encourage every one of these men to get a college degree. A federal grant that we've already received lets us pay their college tuition. We're also able to pay college graduates $100 a month more than our other officers.

"These new men are dedicated professionals. They're interested in helping society every bit as much as teachers, social workers and even doctors, and I'm confident that they can help society through good police work. Police work isn't just directing traffic and solving crimes. That's only a part of it. It's encouraging good citizenship and helping make this community a good place to live.

"I would like to make two other points. First, these men can't do their job alone. Every resident of this community has a responsibility to help them, both by conscientiously obeying the laws and by helping our department apprehend those persons who violate the laws. And second, even with the addition of these men, our department is still understaffed. We still don't have nearly as many men as we need, and I expect to ask the City Council to authorize the addition of another 20 men in about a year. If the further addition is approved we should reach our goal of having 1.5 officers for every 1,000 persons in the city. We now have roughly 1.3."

Background Information

Rookie policemen are paid $720 a month if they do not have a college degree, $770 a month if they have completed two years of college and $820 a month if they have a college degree. Rookies must serve a one-year probationary period before becoming regular patrolmen, at which time their base pay rises to $780 a month.

The city's Police Department now has 119 men, plus 11 civilian employes. The Federal Bureau of Investigation recommends 2.0 police personnel, including civilian workers, per 1,000 population, but requirements vary with the size of each town and its rate of crime. The 15 largest cities in the state have an average of 1.4 police personnel per 1,000 people, according to statistics compiled by the State Crime Commission. The commission also reports that the number ranges from a high of 1.87 to a low of 1.05 in other cities.

About 350 men applied for the 20 positions on the police force. Civil Service spokesmen said the number is unusually large and probably is explained by the high rate of unemployment in the area and by the fact that many college graduates have not been able to obtain jobs in their chosen fields.

SPEECHES AND MEETINGS: EXERCISE 3

INSTRUCTIONS: Write a follow story based on the following announcement made by Mayor George Markle at a press conference in his office at 8 a.m. today.

"I've got an announcement of major significance. I've been working on this proposal for several months and today am pleased to announce that the proposal tentatively has been approved by the City Council, the County Board of Supervisors and area educators. For some time I've been disturbed because the educational facilities in the area are not balanced. We've got an excellent elementary and high school system and a good college. But one gap remains. We don't have anything for the hundreds of students who want some training after high school but who don't want to go to college. By that I mean vocational training for some type of trade.

"There seems to be a real demand for vocational training. We've got a lot of unemployed in this area, but at the same time there're literally thousands of jobs that aren't filled, and employers say it's because they can't find anyone trained in the proper skills. We consequently are planning a vocational technical center that will be built in the downtown area. As we visualize it, the center will offer vocational training in a variety of fields. Most of the courses will last one or two years, at the very most. The basic fields of study will include such things as auto mechanics, printing, electronics, welding, salesmanship, bookkeeping, office management, nursing, cooking and secretarial work. If there's a demand for other courses, we'll add them as we go along.

"In addition to that, the school will serve as an adult education center with a wide variety of night courses. We'll offer any courses that the people of this city want to take, provided we can find qualified instructors. As a start, we expect to offer courses in art; homemaking; different kinds of hobbies, like knitting and bridge; and the traditional academic fields of history, languages and the like.

"We want to put the center downtown so it will be accessible to the largest possible number of students. We hope to rent some space in an existing building so we can open the school next fall. Then, as soon as we can, we hope to erect a new building. We expect that building will cost somewhere in the neighborhood of $3.6 million. State and federal grants should pay two-thirds of the cost, and the remainder will be jointly financed by the city and county. We anticipate that the center eventually will serve somewhere around 1,000 full-time students during the day, plus 2,000 to 3,000 students enrolled part-time at night. We anticipate only a small fee, somewhere around $50 a semester, for the full-time students. These people, after they're trained, should be stable, responsible citizens, and we expect that the taxes they'll pay to the city after they graduate and become employed will more than repay the additional cost of their training.

"We've kept this idea quiet until now because we wanted to see if we could get some cooperation between the city and county, and we were afraid that a lot of premature publicity might have caused some confusion. But now I'm happy to announce that formal proposals will be submitted to both the City Council and the County Board of Supervisors at their next regular meetings, and both bodies already have indicated, informally, that they are favorably disposed toward the passage of those proposals."

SPEECHES AND MEETINGS: EXERCISE 4

INSTRUCTIONS: Write a follow story based on the following speech given by John L. Rue, president of the State Federation of Farmers, before the 720 persons attending the annual convention of the Cattlemen's Association at the Hotel Alexander.

"I want to speak tonight about a new problem, a problem that seriously threatens our way of life. That problem is Emotional Environmentalists.

"Emotional Environmentalists are one of the greatest threats to agriculture today. They are the real obstacle to the job of feeding 220 million people in the United States and substantial numbers abroad. Critics forget that American farmers are so productive that, even though the number of farmers in these United States has been declining for years, they create a surplus that our government is able to ship to less fortunate people in other nations.

"These Emotional Environmentalists are a disaster lobby. They are leading an environmental binge. A few years ago these same people were concerned about hunger and malnutrition. Just before that everyone seemed to be an expert on how to accomplish racial integration.

"Some of these people advocate organic farming. They insist that food should be produced, packed and marketed without the use of pesticides and fertilizers, other than those derived from animal waste and compost, or fungicides to prevent decay on its trip from farm to table. But these people don't know what they're talking about. They just don't know anything about agriculture. Not one that I've ever talked to was raised on a farm. They just don't understand their demands are impossible. If we followed their suggestions, the quality and variety of food in this country would decline by half in a matter of months.

"America can go back to organic farming, as these critics demand. It can be done. But we could not raise enough food to feed every American. We first would have to decide which 50 million Americans should starve to death—literally die for lack of food—not just malnutrition, but no food at all to eat. Without chemicals our production rates would fall back to the level they were 100 years ago—less than a third of today's standards. And then half the crop we did produce would rot by the time we transported it to consumers.

"These critics want a nice sirloin steak for dinner, but they want it without cattle feedlots. These Emotional Environmentalists forget that nature is harsh, with extremes of flood, drought, storms, cold and heat. When nature shows some extremes the Emotional Environmentalists tend to blame not nature, but the people who are trying to temper the extremes—in many cases farmers.

"The big job for American agriculture is to make sure we don't overreact, to make sure we don't go do some silly asinine things because of the attacks on farming. America and the rest of the world are going to continue to feed more and more people from less farmland. And we are going to do it with the same things the Emotional Environmentalists are trying to destroy, because agricultural science has not succeeded in developing alternative methods for producing and distributing the massive food supplies needed that meet the quality standards consumers demand."

SPEECHES AND MEETINGS: EXERCISE 5

INSTRUCTIONS: Write a follow story based on the following speech given by Emil Plambeck, superintendent of the City Park Commission, at the regular meeting of the Rotary Club at the YMCA at 7 p.m. yesterday.

"I'm pleased to be here this evening and intend to discuss a topic of concern to all of us—the city's park system. You gentlemen, as businessmen, know the value of an attractive community. It promotes growth and helps attract both new residents and new industry. An attractive community with a good park system also improves the quality of life for those of us already living here.

"Members of this community long have boasted of one of the finest park systems in the United States. But now, because of financial problems, we are beginning to fall behind. We simply are not getting enough money to expand our park system to meet the needs of a growing community or even enough money to maintain our old system properly. As a result, the parks are becoming overcrowded and all the people utilizing them every weekend are endangering the vegetation and wildlife we've worked so hard to preserve.

"We used to feel that we were among the top-ranking communities in the United States, but now there definitely are several other cities that have gone ahead of us, even within this very state. We still look pretty good on paper, but some of the statistics are misleading. Neighborhood parks in the new suburbs are lagging badly behind our needs. We do have several excellent parks, with a lot of acreage, but they're concentrated in the older sections of the city.

"City planners recommend that we provide one acre of playground for each 100 persons living in the city. We now have 1.3 acres—30 per cent more than the minimum requirement. But that lead is slipping. Just five years ago we had 1.45 acres per 100 residents. And you have to keep in mind the fact that 1 acre for every 100 persons is a minimum—not the ideal. An ideal ratio would be 1.5 acres for every 100 persons, and we're falling farther and farther away from that goal.

"We need some laws to force developers to provide property in new subdivisions for schools and playgrounds. My office is working on a new code to help the city obtain land for parks in each new suburb constructed around the city. I haven't revealed that fact before, but we expect to submit the proposal to the City Council within a few days. If the council accepts it, the developers will be required to set aside 3.5 per cent of their land for miniparks. That way we'll be able to have wooded areas in every neighborhood, maybe with baseball diamonds or a few tennis courts.

"The city hasn't been totally inactive in this area since I took office five years ago. We have acquired three parks. One of them—near Ridgeview School—has two ball fields and a large picnic area. The other new areas include Petersen Park, on West Dover Court and Hillandale Road, and Riverview Park. In the case of the Ridgeview and Petersen Parks, the land was purchased by the park board with funds provided by the City Council. The city inherited the land for Riverview Park. Altogether, the city now has 27 parks and playgrounds, which include 1,168 acres valued at more than $10 million. But I'd like to see the city develop at least a half-dozen more parks, all in the newer subdivisions."

SPEECHES AND MEETINGS: EXERCISE 6

INSTRUCTIONS: Write an advance story about each of the following meetings.

1. American Legion Post 257 will meet in its Post Clubrooms at 8 p.m. next Tuesday, with Commander Albert Knudsen presiding. The post's Finance, Welfare, House and Activities committees are expected to give their reports. The House Committee will reveal plans for a new building. The Activities Committee will report on the Legion's annual circus, which raises money to pay medical bills for needy children in the city. The circus has been scheduled for next June 15-17 at the county fairground. Knudson said, "We want to remind members that this is a very important meeting, and it's essential that everyone attends." Refreshments will be served and the recreation rooms opened after the meeting adjourns.

2. The City Council will meet in its chambers in the city hall at 7 p.m. today for its regular weekly meeting. Mayor George Markle will preside. Three issues are listed on the council's agenda. They involve reports by the (1) Streets, (2) Tax and (3) Police and Fire committees. The Streets Committee has been working on a plan to alleviate the parking problem in the downtown business district and is expected to give its report tonight. But the Streets Committee, which is composed of five members of the City Council, has not yet revealed anything about the content of its report. The Tax Committee, according to the agenda, will review various proposals for increasing tax revenue for the city next year. It has been studying the problem for five months. Earlier, members of the Tax Committee warned that the city would go $2.3 million into debt next year unless it finds some way to get more money. Some of the money is needed to grant raises to city employes. A proposal to raise the salaries of police and firemen will be presented by the Police and Fire Committee.

3. Wilson Shorey, chairman of the County Zoning Commission, provided the following information. "A special public hearing of the commission has been scheduled for 7:30 p.m. tomorrow in Room 34 at the county courthouse to consider a proposed trailer park. The Hawkeye Investment Corp. of Atlanta, Ga., has announced plans to develop a park for 180 mobile homes on land three miles north of the city along Highway 141 and has asked the commission to rezone the land to permit the development of the trailer park. The commission will make its decision after hearing comments from persons interested in the proposal. Representatives from the Hawkeye Investment Corp. will be on hand to describe their proposal in detail and to answer questions about the proposal. Note that the commission, in the past, normally has conducted its hearings during the day. Many persons have expressed interest in the proposal to come before the commission tomorrow night and, as a result, I decided to schedule this hearing at night so more persons would be free to attend the hearing. Many times in the past people have complained they work during the day and cannot attend hearings unless they are willing to lose a day's wages, which they can ill afford to do."

SPEECHES AND MEETINGS: EXERCISE 7

INSTRUCTIONS: Write a follow story based on the following information. Assume that the newspaper was unable to send a reporter to the American Legion's meeting, which was held last night, but that the paper received a copy of these minutes, taken by Harry Felton, post secretary.

The monthly meeting of American Legion Post 257 was held last evening in the Post Clubrooms. The meeting was called to order by Commander Albert Knudson at 8:06 p.m. with 87 members in attendance. After the Advance of the Colors and the recitation of the Pledge of Allegience, Chaplain Louis Small gave an opening prayer.

The Finance Committee reported a balance of $42,754 in funds after payment of all outstanding bills, noting that the balance represents an increase of $4,821 during the last year, primarily because of fund raising events for our new building.

The Welfare Committee reported that two members undergoing treatment at Memorial Hospitel were sent baskets of fruit, and that nice letters of thanks have been recieved from them.

The House Committee revealed plans to build a new building in the 600 block of Main Street next to the Plaza Motel. The committees plans estimate the cost of the new structure at $740,000. The building would contain two meeting rooms, plus a bar, bingo parlor, small gym, recreation room and cafeteria, or small resturant. The committee discussed the possibility of including a rifle range, swiming pool and bowling alley but reported that it rejected them because they were to expensive. The building will have a basement and two stories. It will be constructed primarly of brick and concrete.

Members of the House Commitee said money could be raised by selling our old building, which they estimated is worth about $45,000. They also said we could raise money by letting other civic and fraternal groups rent the new building when the Legion is not using it. The House Committee also noted that we should mount a membership drive and try to get more men who have served in Vietnam, since there are hundreds of veterans in the city, but not many have been signed up yet. The committee members promised to send copys of the proposal to each Legion member. The proposal will be discussed again at the next meeting. No action was taken on it last night, but most members seemed to favor the idea.

The Activitys Committee said the anual circus sponsored to raise money to pay medical bills for needy children will be held June 15-17 at the County Fair Ground. Members said they are planing for the best circus ever this year, with new exhibits, carnival rides and refreshment stands. In some years, the circus has raised more than $30,000 in profits. But it lost $732 last year, and the committee members warned that unless the circus was improved and showed a profit this year it might have to be discontinued. Committe members said they thought bad weather hurt the circus last year. They also noted that a lot of people saw circuses on television and might be reluctant to pay any money to see one in the city.

No further business appearing, the meeting was adjourned at 10:43 p.m., and the bar was reopened.

SPEECHES AND MEETINGS: EXERCISE 8

INSTRUCTIONS: Write a follow story based on the following information.

The weekly meeting of the City Council opened at 7:34 p.m. yesterday in the city hall with all councilmen in attendance and with Mayor George Markel presiding. The mayor opened the meeting with a brief prayer. Minutes from the last meeting were read and approved.

Under old business, Alderman Ron Cairns of the Second Ward raised the zoning problems of the Old Town area. He said construction had begun on a drive-in restaurant on 4th Street, and that five smaller businesses had been torn down to make room for it. Cairns said, "We have to do something, and we have to do it fast. The businessmen in this area worked for years to develop a distinctive style for their neighborhood. Their buildings have been restored. They offer a lot of unique merchandise. The area has become a real tourist attraction. Now other businesses are trying to move in, and they're destroying the flavor of the area. They're tearing down everything old and colorful and putting up a neon jungle. We waited too long on this and couldn't stop the restaurant. We need a comprehensive plan to develop a pedestrian-orientated atmosphere in the area. We need some tough zoning laws to force new businesses to conform to the area's style of architecture and to prohibit the use of any more neon light." City Council members voted 11-1 to refer the issue to the Zoning Committee and instructed the committee to come up with some recommendations.

The Streets Committee presented a plan to restrict downtown parking and to speed traffic through the downtown area. Its preliminary report was approved by a vote of 10 to 2. But it is only a preliminary proposal and details and final plans still must be worked out. They will be subject to the approval of the mayor and City Council. The Streets Committee suggested raising parking meter fees from 10 cents to 25 cents an hour. It also proposed banning all parking on Main St. And it would ban parking on the right-hand side of all one-way streets. Aldermen Greenstein and Hulich opposed the plan. They said the meter rates were too high and would hurt small businessmen.

The Police and Fire Committee presented a plan to give police and firemen an 8 per cent raise. Starting salaries would rise to $734 a month. Police and firemen had asked for 12 per cent, but the 8 per cent figure was agreed upon after lengthy negotiations. They got a 10 per cent raise last year. The proposal, unanimously approved by the City Council, also will add 34 men to the Police Department, raising its size to 820 men.

The Tax Committee, which reported last, recommended that the city levy a 1 per cent income tax on all those who work in the city, regardless of where they live. The committee members said the tax would raise $12 million a year, would be easy to collect and would tax people who use city facilities but do not pay property taxes to the city. The committee added that the revenue from the income tax could be used, in part, for property tax relief. Copies of the proposal were given to all the aldermen. They then voted to delay action until they have had more time to study the proposal—perhaps next week. However, Alderman Cairns, chairman of the Tax Committee, noted that, unlike other types of taxes, this one would place the heaviest burden on the rich, not the poor. He added, "Any new tax is unpopular, but this is the best possible tax for the people who actually live in the city. Sure, they're going to have to pay it, too. But we estimate that the average worker would pay only about $72 a year. More than half the $12 million will come from people who don't live in the city but have been burdening its facilities for years."

SPEECHES AND MEETINGS: EXERCISE 9

INSTRUCTIONS: Write a follow story based on the following information.

Background Information

The County Zoning Commission conducted a special public hearing last night to consider plans to develop a 35-acre trailer park three miles north of the city. The hearing began at 7:30 p.m. and was held in the county courthouse. All five members of the commission were present. They scheduled the hearing in the evening rather than the afternoon, they said, so that persons interested in the topic would have an opportunity to attend the hearing and express their views. About 120 persons attended the hearing and janitors had to bring in extra chairs so everyone could be seated. Some members of the audience submitted a petition signed by 310 persons opposed to the plans. The commissioners began the meeting by asking representatives of the Hawkeye Development Corp., which developed the plans, to explain its position.

Harvey Rabb, Vice President of the Hawkeye Development Corp.

"We want to develop a park for 180 mobile homes. The park won't hurt anyone. In fact, it should upgrade the neighborhood. Only childless couples will be admitted, so there won't be any noise, and the park won't affect schools in the area. We expect the average mobile home in the park to cost $12,000, and some will cost twice that much. They're not cheap, and they look good. When you mention trailer parks, some people still think of a bunch of trailers clumped together on a bare piece of ground. Our park won't be anything like that. We've already hired a professional landscape artist and fully intend to preserve the area. As you know, it's wooded, and we don't expect to have to cut more than a half-dozen trees. No one wants to bulldoze the area. The trees add shade and privacy and beauty for our tenants. That's worth money to us. We're also planning a swimming pool and community center. And we'll have a redwood fence or some type of shrubbery around the entire park for added privacy. Some people are worried about the sewage problem, but we'll have a three-acre lagoon."

Roy Andersen, County Health Inspector

"The lagoon is the big question here for many people. But they don't know what they're talking about when they criticize the plans. Lagoons are an ideal solution to the sewage problem for small towns that can't afford a sewage disposal plant, and they're quite appropriate here. They're regulated by the State Department of Health and seldom create any odor or any other problems. A three-acre lagoon is capable of handling the sewage from 300 persons. There would be no problem about meeting the necessary specifications at the trailer court."

Paul LeMayy, Attorney for the Petitioners Opposed to the Plans

"People living in this area have spent $15,000 to $50,000 for their homes. Now you're being asked to change the character of the neighborhood. That isn't fair. These people's investments should be protected. The present development pattern of single-family homes should be maintained. I don't care what these people say. Trailer homes lower property values, and experience elsewhere clearly has shown that they lead to higher taxes and crowded roads and schools. Yet their owners don't pay any property taxes. None at all. You have a responsibility to protect the people of this county and to respect their wishes. I ask you to reject these plans."

Commission Chairman Wilson Shorey

"It's 12:15 and I think we can adjourn. We'll make a decision later this week and give it to the County Board of Supervisors at their next meeting. I think I personally should add, though, that people who own trailers spend a lot of money for them, have good educations and high salaries. They shouldn't have to live in the least desirable places. We have a responsibility to them too."

SPEECHES AND MEETINGS: EXERCISE 10

INSTRUCTIONS: Assume that the local school board conducted a public hearing last night at North High School to consider its proposed budget for the next school year. The budget totals $42.3 million, an increase of $4.1 million from the previous year. Write a follow story based on the following statements.

George Dees, Superintendent of Schools

"I realize that the increase is large, but we need 80 per cent of the $4.1 million to hire 23 teachers for a new elementary school and to raise the salaries of our other teachers. We've made every possible cut. Every last penny of our budget is necessary to ensure a quality education for our children. If we cut the budget, we'll hurt them."

George Knight, President of the Taxpayers' Party

"Why don't we cut the size of the administrative staff in half? That budget wouldn't be half so big if we cut down on all the big-shots in your department. I understand we've got 824 teachers and 214 administrators, and a lot of those administrators are making more than $20,000 a year. I say fire half the administrators and hire more teachers. We need more people in classrooms, not behind desks in their plush offices."

Alan Costello, 112 E. Elmwood Ave.

"I wouldn't mind paying all that money if we got something for it. Your teachers can't even maintain discipline in their classrooms. Each of my kids is worse than the last one. They just want to go out and do as they damn please. I want to know why teachers aren't showing them how to be good Americans and making them respect their parents."

Diana Powers, 4132 Oakland Ave.

"I disagree with those last comments. Sure, teachers have to maintain discipline in their classrooms. But you can't expect teachers to do it alone. The job of the schools is not discipline. That's the job of parents. Parents have to help."

John Halvens, President of Concerned Parents for Hale School

"No one's brought up the real reason for all this money. We never had these problems before busing. Now this year you're going to start busing students between Hale and Bonnebrook schools. If the federal government wants us to integrate those schools, let them pay for it. I don't want to. If we had any guts, we'd fight it."

Ernest Green, 807 Broadway

"Before you let any children into schools, I think someone should go through all the libraries and really examine the books you've got there. My son brought books home last year by Eldridge Cleaver, Richard Wright, Gordon Parks, Claude Brown and other writers like that. I don't want my children exposed to that kind of garbage."

Linda Fort, 2713 Stacy Drive

"Why do we need so many teachers? When I was in school I just had one teacher, and that was it. Anyone who needs outside help to teach 5-year-olds shouldn't be a teacher. Now you've got a special person for music and another for guidance and another for physical education and another for art. If you hired one decent teacher, she could take care of all that by herself."

SPEECHES AND MEETINGS: EXERCISE 11

INSTRUCTIONS: Write a follow story about the following speech, which was given at Southern Illinois University by John Seigenthaler, editor of the Nashville "Tennessean." Assume that Seigenthaler appeared before the Press Club in your community last night. (Portions of the speech have been deleted.)

There is a crisis confronting the editors of the nation's newspapers; an intimately personal crisis. The problem is a crisis of credibility; a crisis of self-credibility. The press of this country has always been under attack. But always in the past there has been something close to unanimity among those within the management of the press—even those who disagreed among themselves on public issues—that their rights were inviolate and unassailable under the First Amendment of the Constitution. Free press issues were clearly drawn and clearly understood.

No more. Within the last few weeks a news executive told me at a press meeting in Florida: "I'm afraid if we don't crack down on some of these despoilers of a free press (he was talking about the impact of the underground press) we are all going to be in trouble."

A few months ago I was in Washington for the annual meeting of the American Society of Newspaper Editors. During a panel discussion it was suggested that there be a straw poll—an unofficial show of hands—to indicate how those editors present felt about the role of "The New York Times" in the Pentagon Papers affair. The room was full. The vote was taken. "The Times" won an informal vote of confidence—barely. I was distressed. Men who had lived and prospered under a free press, who are charged by the First Amendment to serve as an adversary to and watchdog on government, raised their hands against a newspaper that exercised its freedom and was already under the protection of a United States Supreme Court ruling when we met.

If there are that many news management people opposed to the actions of "The Times," the Washington "Post" and others in the Pentagon Papers case, with a supportive Supreme Court finding, how many more are there who stand against the full protection of the First Amendment in the many controversial press questions facing us? How many are willing to say they support Earl Caldwell of "The New York Times" in his challenge of the government's right to demand his presence, by subpoena before a federal grand jury, together with his notes and tape recorded interviews with members of the Black Panthers in San Francisco?

And how many of us are willing to take a stand against the increasing practice by police to assume the guise of newsmen for the purpose of spying on radical groups?

There are those who are utilizing the First Amendment who need its protection and the support of those of us who have lived by it and benefited from it. But too many of us are reluctant to give that support. We are reluctant to give it to the underground press. We are reluctant to give it to the student press. We are reluctant to give that support to the television news media, whose subservience to federal regulatory power can become absolute—because it includes the power to license or not to license. We are reluctant, even, to give it to many within our own industry, those within the print media.

The First Amendment was written so that we might contest authority; so that we might exercise authority on our own and of our own. We never envisioned a press establishment we did not control. Now there is one upon us, and it includes diverse, disagreeable and even disrespectful elements. Because we know not how to protect ourselves from them and are loath to join with them in work we should be about, we are confronted by this crisis of credibility.

SPEECHES AND MEETINGS: EXERCISE 12

INSTRUCTIONS: Write a follow story about the following speech on crime and drug abuse, which was given by President Richard Nixon during his 1972 campaign for reelection and which was broadcast live on radio from Camp David, Md.

Good Afternoon.

Four years ago, at the close of a turbulent decade which had seen our Nation engulfed by a rising tide of disorder and permissiveness, I campaigned for President with a pledge to restore respect for law, order and justice in America. I am pleased to be able to report to you today that we have made significant progress in that effort.

. . .

. . . We have fought the frightening trend of crime and anarchy to a standstill. The campuses which erupted in riots so often in the late '60s have become serious centers of learning once again. The cities which we saw in flames summer after summer a few years ago are now pursuing constructive change.

The FBI crime index showed an increase of only 1 percent during the first half of this year. That is the closest we have come to registering an actual decrease since these quarterly statistics began 12 years ago. And in 72 of our largest cities, we have already begun to see a decrease in crime this year as compared to last.

We have moved off the defensive and onto the offensive in our all-out battle against the criminal forces in America. We are going to stay on the offensive until we put every category of crime on a downward trend in every American community.

To reach this goal we must continue to fight the battle on all fronts.

In our courts, we need judges who will help to strengthen the peace forces as against the criminal forces in this country. I have applied this principle in making appointments to the Supreme Court and to other Federal courts. As a result, our Constitution today is more secure; our freedoms are better protected.

. . .

The Federal role, however, is only a supportive one. As J. Edgar Hoover often used to tell me, it is our local police forces who are the real front-line soldiers in the war against crime. As President . . . , I have given all-out backing to our peace officers in their dedicated efforts to make all of us safer on the streets and more secure in our homes, and I shall continue to do so.

In three years we have provided States and localities with law enforcement assistance grants totaling $1.5 billion. That compares with only $22 million in grants during the final three years of the previous Administration.

In a single year, 1970, the Congress passed four landmark anti-crime bills which this Administration had recommended and fought for—an omnibus crime bill, a bill providing new tools to fight organized crime, a comprehensive reform of the drug abuse statutes and a new charter for courts and criminal procedures in the Nation's Capital.

The City of Washington had become the crime capital of the United States during the 1960s—but during our term of office we have cut the D.C. crime rate in half.

Let me turn now to the subject of drug abuse—America's public enemy number one.

The period 1965 to 1969, when drugs were widely glamorized and when Government was responding only feebly to this menace, brought America's narcotics problem to the epidemic stage. In that four-year period alone, the number of drug addicts doubled nationwide.

To turn this situation around, I declared total war against heroin and other illicit drugs. I personally shook up the bureaucracy and took steps to create two new Federal agencies to deal with narcotics-related crime and with addict treatment. The anti-drug funding which I have requested in the current budget is 11 times as great as the 1969 level.

We are winning this war. The raging heroin epidemic of the late 1960s has been stemmed.

Our domestic law enforcement operation has arrested twice as many pushers and has seized illicit drugs at four times the rate of the previous Administration. Our rehabilitation and treatment programs have created more federally funded drug treatment capacity in the last 12 months than in the 50 years before that.

Our international narcotics control work in 59 countries has achieved a doubling of global heroin and morphine base seizures in 1972 alone.

But the job is far from finished. A short time before Christmas last year, I received a heart-rending letter from a teenage boy in the Midwest. He told me in his letter how his brother, a college student of exceptional promise, after slipping deeper and deeper into drug experimentation, had gone over into the woods with a gun one day, completely without warning, and taken his own life.

Listen to the boy's letter: "If we can stop just one boy from doing what my brother did, his whole life will have been worthwhile . . . You can beat that drug, Mr. Nixon; you can destroy it before it destroys any more lives."

This is my answer to this letter: I cannot beat this problem by myself; but if all of us work together, we can and we will beat it.

To do so, we will need more clinics to treat addicts who need help. That is why I asked the Congress for speedy approval of funds to support additional drug treatment facilities.

We will need better cooperation abroad in apprehending the criminals who produce and smuggle heroin. That is why I have pledged the strictest compliance with the statute which requires a suspension of U.S. military and economic aid to countries which protect or participate in the movement of illegal drugs to this country.

We will need absolute assurance that convicted drug peddlers will go to jail and not back to the streets. The dangerous trend of light or suspended sentences meted out to convicted pushers by permissive judges must be halted. That is why I shall ask the next Congress to require stiff mandatory sentences for heroin traffickers, and to amend other Federal statutes so as to keep these peddlers of death off our streets after their arrest.

Wherever more money, more manpower or more teeth in the law are needed to maintain our momentum in the war against drugs and crime, I will do anything in my power to provide them.

My intention . . . is to continue and expand our massive Federal funding for helping to improve our local law enforcement.

I will propose to the new Congress a thorough-going revision of the entire Federal criminal code, aimed at better protection of life and property, human rights and the domestic peace.

I will move ahead with my comprehensive ten-year reform program for the Federal prison system . . .

I will continue to apply the criteria of strict constructionism and regard for the public safety in making appointments to the Supreme Court and other Federal courts.

I will ask the new Congress to move swiftly in enacting my proposals for Law Enforcement Special Revenue Sharing, to give States and cities greater decision-making power in meeting their own needs.

I will work unceasingly to halt the erosion of moral fiber in American life, and the denial of individual accountability for individual actions.

The increasingly urbanized, technological, crowded, pluralistic, affluent and leisure-oriented society which America has become in these final decades of the 20th century poses complex new dangers to our traditional concepts of personal safety, human dignity, and moral values.

Questions which were once the sole concern of novelists now intrude upon public policy. The endlessly drugged *Brave New World* which Huxley described could conceivably become our world a few years in the future.

Remote as such possibilities may seem, we cannot ignore them. We must shape our own vision for the 70's and the years ahead, a vision bright and clear and sharp, or one of the darker visions may begin to impose itself by default.

Government alone cannot determine the legal and moral tone of America's third century. Much depends on the character we build in our homes, our schools and our churches. Much depends on the values we exalt in our art, our literature, our culture.

Yet Government has an essential role, a role it must never abdicate. Government must never become so preoccupied with catering to the way-out wants of those who reject all respect for moral and legal values that it forgets the citizen's first civil right: the right to be free from domestic violence.

Government must never mistake license for liberty, amorality for tolerance, indulgence for charity or weakness for compassion.

Above all, Government must maintain that structure of ordered freedom, within which alone the human spirit can thrive and flourish.

The work of keeping the structure of freedom strong in the years ahead will not be easy and the price may sometimes be terribly high. It was terribly high for a young Federal narcotics agent in New York named Frank Tummillo.

I met Frank Tummillo last February when he and other agents came to the White House along with a group of professional athletes who have joined the fight against drugs. He was a fine young man—alert, dedicated, selfless. Just three nights ago—last Thursday—he was murdered by two hoodlums in the line of his duty, trying to break up a huge cocaine transaction.

He was only 25. He lived at home with his parents. The invitations recently went out for his wedding next month. Instead of that wedding, his funeral will be held tomorrow.

We cannot bring Frank Tummillo back again, any more than we can bring back the American soldiers who have given their lives in Vietnam. But in our war against crime and drugs, as in our war against aggression in Southeast Asia, we can resolve to redeem with honor the ultimate sacrifice which these brave men have made.

Together, and in their name, let us work to end the violence and the lawlessness against which they fought. Let us make the next four years a period of new respect for law, order and justice in America; a time of new hope in a land free of fear, and a world at peace.

Thank you and good afternoon.

SPEECHES AND MEETINGS: MISCELLANEOUS EXERCISES

1. Analyze 10 news stories from your local newspaper about speeches and meetings.

2. Compare several news stories written about the same speech or the same meeting. Send copies of the stories to the speakers or to the participants at the meetings and ask them to evaluate the stories.

3. Attend and report a speech or meeting held on your campus and in your community. Send a copy of each of your news stories to the speakers or to the participants at the meeting and ask them to evaluate it.

Interviews

Reporters often interview other persons (1) to obtain information about news events, (2) to discover individuals' reactions to news events and (3) to reveal the personalities of newsworthy individuals. You must prepare for an interview, obtaining as much information as possible beforehand so that you can ask intelligent questions. Prepare questions ahead of time, but listen carefully to your source's responses. If the source fails to provide the information you need, you may have to repeat or rephrase your questions. Moreover, sources often make interesting statements unexpectedly. You must listen for such statements and be ready to deviate from your list of questions to pursue them.

Your questions should be specific and brief. Avoid asking too many questions that can be answered "Yes" or "No." Ask your source to explain "Yes" or "No" responses. Do not hesitate to raise controversial issues or to ask difficult questions if they are essential to your story. But begin by asking easy questions that the source will answer readily. Ask your most difficult questions at the end of the interview. Then, if your source terminates the interview, you will already have gathered enough information for a news story.

Take extensive notes during an interview to avoid making factual errors and forgetting important responses. Taking notes will also enable you to use direct quotations in your story. Knowledge of shorthand is useful, but it is more important that you learn to recognize and record important statements. If necessary, ask your source to repeat key sentences. Some reporters use tape recorders, but they are impractical for most stories, since newspaper reporters must usually write their stories in a few minutes or hours; you can reread your notes more quickly than you can replay a tape recording of an entire interview.

In your lead, you may use a quotation that briefly summarizes the story, or you may summarize the story in your own words. If a story concerns a number of topics, the paragraphs immediately following the lead might briefly summarize those topics, and later paragraphs might discuss them in depth, one by one. If a story concerns a single idea, the paragraphs immediately following the lead might summarize the most important points about that idea. Then, after ensuring that you have captured your readers' interest, you can go on to discuss those points in more detail.

Use a varied style of writing. Do not rely entirely on long summaries. Use quotations to break up your summaries, to emphasize important points, to provide color, to explain complexities and to provide examples. Describe your source and his or her surroundings. Clearly attribute your information, and provide additional attribution each time you shift to a new idea. You may have to delete profane or libelous statements made by your source. And, to develop a well-rounded story, you should consult more than one source, particularly when you are dealing with controversial topics.

Remember that you are dealing with other individuals, and you have an obligation to be fair. Do not embarrass someone just for the sake of a sensational lead or a "good" story. Be objective. Even when you disagree with the persons you interview, you have a responsibility to report their ideas fully and accurately. You are seldom justified in concealing your identity or attempting to intimidate sources. On the other hand, you should not allow your sources to dictate what is included in news stories and what is omitted. It may sometimes be necessary to conceal a source's identity; in such cases, you can identify the source only by an initial, a first name, a fictitious name or a descriptive phrase instead of a name.

INTERVIEWS: EXERCISE 1

INSTRUCTIONS: Write a news story based on the following interview. "Q" stands for the reporter's questions, "A" for the respondent's answers.

Q. I'm a reporter for the local newspaper. Could you tell me what happened?
A. Sure. I was painting this house with two other guys and our scaffold collapsed.

Q. Could you tell me the names of everyone involved?
A. My name is John Klassar, and the other two are Mike Heckmann and Gary Gibson.

Q. What's your address?
A. Mike and I share an apartment. The address is 1043 E. Broadway. John lives at the Quality Trailer Court.

Q. Could you tell me exactly what happened?
A. Sure. We'd just started painting this house. We've been working on it two days, and I thought we'd finish the thing today. Anyway, we only have this one side left, and we put the scaffolding up to the very top. Mike and Gary got up there and were scraping the old paint away while I mixed the batch of paint we're going to use on this side; it's a real goofy yellow. Then the whole thing fell down. I didn't really see it. I was bending over the paint with my back to it. I still can't figure out why, but the scaffolding just tipped backwards and fell to the ground. It's all smashed up.

Q. Were the other two men hurt?
A. Mike wasn't. He's over there talking with the police now. He told me he had one hand on the rain gutter, and when the scaffolding collapsed he just hung on. He was dangling there for a couple of minutes until I ran and got another ladder and put it up to him so he could climb down. But Gary fell, and I think he's hurt bad. I ran to him as soon as I got Mike down, and he couldn't even talk. Just groaned. So I called an ambulance and they took him to the hospital. I'm afraid he may have broke his back. And I think his arm is busted, his right arm.

Q. Do you know why the scaffold collapsed?
A. Hell no! Could be any number of things. Maybe one of the legs slipped into some soft dirt. Or something could have broken. Or maybe it just wasn't set up right.

Q. Do you know who owns the house and what the address is?
A. Some old biddy. I don't know her name. She keeps fussing around, always looking over our shoulders to make sure we don't mess anything up. The address is 48 Parr Ave.

Q. Was anyone else here when the accident occurred?
A. The house was empty, so I had to bust a window and climb in to use the telephone. But there was a whole crowd of people waiting for a bus right there across the street. Those bastards just stood there. No one even offered to help. Then their bus came along and everyone got on it and rode off.

INTERVIEWS: EXERCISE 2

INSTRUCTIONS: Write a news story based on the following interview with Harrison R. Ostle, chairman of the county's United Negro College Fund Drive.

Q. I'm not acquainted with the United Negro College Fund. Could you tell me exactly what it is?

A. Certainly. We're a national organization, and this year we're trying to raise $10 million across the country. The fund supports more than 41,000 students in approximately 40 colleges. It's an annual campaign. The first one was conducted way back in 1944, and we've been helping a few more schools every year. Last year I think we had 37.

Q. How much are you trying to raise in this county?

A. We're hoping to get $20,000.

Q. How long will the campaign continue?

A. Six weeks. It officially opened with a banquet last night, and it will end in precisely six weeks. We never run over that deadline. It's always a six-week campaign. We feel if we run longer than that, we may alienate some donors. Also, we just don't have the facilities to sustain a longer campaign.

Q. How do you plan to raise the money?

A. One of the problems we've had in the past is that we've been a narrow fund. We've had fewer than 1,000 contributors at the end of the campaign. We've stressed corporate and foundation donations in the past, but I hope to broaden our base this year. So we'll really employ two methods. First, we'll campaign on a face-to-face basis on the corporate level. Corporations have been extremely generous in the past, and we'll actually send someone to talk to the corporation executives who've helped us in the past. Then we'll rely upon a mail campaign to reach other persons in the community that we think'll be receptive.

Q. Do you anticipate any trouble in reaching your goal?

A. No, not really. Last year we had a goal of $18,000, and we raised that amount, plus an extra $100, so I'm hopeful that we'll be able to reach our goal again this year. Our biggest problem every year is publicity, and that's where you can help us. I also anticipate appearing on several radio and television shows, and that always seems to help. Our mail really picks up after we get any publicity like that, and we always get a big batch of letters that begin by saying, "I saw you on television yesterday." I should add that we've got a statewide goal of $160,000, so if we go over our quota here we can help make up for deficits in other areas of the state.

Q. How much of the money is used to help residents of this county?

A. I really don't know offhand. I haven't seen any figures on that. I could check, but it'd take a couple days.

Q. Thank you.

INTERVIEWS: EXERCISE 3

INSTRUCTIONS: Write a news story based on the following interview by members of your class with Franklin J. Thomas, editor of a local newspaper.

Q. Mr. Thomas, most of us are going to graduate in a few years, and we want to get a job with a newspaper or a radio or television station. What should we be doing now?

A. Now I may be a bit different than other editors, but when I hire a new reporter I look for two things. First, experience; I want someone really interested in journalism, someone who knows what he's doing. So I look for someone who's worked for the student newspaper or spent a summer working for a paper. Second, I like someone who knows what he's writing about. If a student wants to review movies, I look to see if he's had a couple courses about movies. And if someone else wants to work the police beat, I look to see if he's had any courses in law enforcement.

Q. Do you hire any reporters without a college degree?

A. Sometimes. We've got two or three reporters on our staff right now that don't have a degree. But they all started working on smaller papers, and when they joined my staff they had a lot of good experience and had proved they were good.

Q. What about salaries? I've heard they're pretty low.

A. I'm not sure about how we compare with other fields. We start a new reporter off at somewhere between $125 and $150 a week, depending on his experience. That's for someone right out of college. After a reporter gets a couple years' experience, we pay them up to about $200, maybe $240 a week. Our editors get more than that. And a lot of our reporters pick up some extra money by working overtime and freelancing for magazines and things like that. It pretty much depends on how good you are.

Q. Who writes your newspaper's editorials?

A. I do that myself. Sometimes I ask a reporter for help if he knows more about the topic. And once in awhile a reporter comes to me and wants to write about something he's really interested in. But I imagine I write 95 per cent of them myself.

Q. The newspaper always seems terribly grim. I've stopped reading it because it's full of gore. Does it have to be that way?

A. A lot of critics say newspapers devote too much space to crime and violence, but everytime someone really studies newspapers, he finds that just isn't so. The last study I saw showed that only 10 per cent of the stories in newspapers concern crime and violence. But even if the percentage is higher than that, I'm not sure that's bad. We try to show the world as it is. And it isn't perfect. So you really should be criticizing society, not us, and perhaps working to improve society.

Q. Why don't you have any blacks on your staff?

A. We'd like to. We've been looking for people from various minority groups for years, but we just haven't found any who are really qualified. Look around here. There's not one black or Indian or Puerto Rican in your class. You find a black person with a college degree and who knows how to write and who wants to work for a newspaper and we'll hire him. We've been looking but just haven't been able to find any.

INTERVIEWS: EXERCISE 4

INSTRUCTIONS: Write a news story based on the following interview with Sheriff Melvin Jacobs, who recently announced his intention to resign.

Q. Sheriff, could you tell me why you're resigning?

A. Now that's a dumb question. You've been around here for a couple years now. You know what's going on. I keep asking for a new jail and those damn taxpayers keep saying "No." They don't know what the hell they're doing, and you can quote me on that.

Q. Why do you need a new jail?

A. Just look around. You can see for yourself. You're not blind. This place was built 90 years ago, and it's falling apart. The walls are limestone and it's just crumbling apart. Besides that, the place is overcrowded. As far as I can tell it was built to hold 20 prisoners. Instead of building a new jail those stupid politicians in the courthouse keep remodeling what we've got. It's cheaper, but now they expect me to squeeze 80 prisoners into this place.

Q. How many cells are there?

A. Twenty-two. I try to keep two for juveniles, but I usually have about 60 prisoners squeezed into the other 20 cells. There are only two cots in each cell, so that means someone has to sleep on a mat on the floor. I just can't keep them cooped up in those cells all day. So I just don't lock their cells and let them use the hallway and dining room during the day. We've got a TV set and some games to keep them busy, but not much else. There's usually a card game, but I try to ignore it. They've got to have something to do. It's really inhuman.

Q. Is that the reason for all the trouble you've been having?

A. You're damned right it is. Any one of those prisoners could break out of here any time he wanted to. All he'd have to do is chip away at the limestone around the bars in his cell or the locks on some of the doors. I've been sheriff here for seven years now, and there've been 17 escapes. There's just no way to stop it. The public thinks it's saving money, but when some of these men get loose they're just going to rob and kill some more. Some men are just bad, but there's no real safe way to lock them up in here. But that's not the worst part.

Q. What are the other problems?

A. First, the overcrowding. Then the food. I'm supposed to feed each prisoner on 87 cents a day. Now you tell me what kind of food I can give them when I can't spend more than 30 cents a meal. The stuff they get is slop. Most people wouldn't feed it to their dogs. But the worst part is having to put a lot of young kids in these places. Sometimes it does 'em good, really shakes 'em up to spend a couple days in here. But other kids have gotten mixed up with some really rough characters. There's no way to keep them apart. And then there's just no way to avoid the homosexual problem in a jail like this, where everyone is together. I don't know how many times I've charged someone with sodomy after a young kid got raped. I try to keep the juveniles separate, but even some 20-year-olds run into trouble, and there's just no way I can protect them.

Q. Can't anything be done?

A. I've tried. I've tried for seven years now, and I'm giving up. I've talked and must have told a hundred groups about the jail. I've talked to every civic group that would listen to me. But to tell you the truth, the county's not interested in spending any money on jailbirds. And that's exactly what the public seems to think, too.

INTERVIEWS: EXERCISE 5

INSTRUCTIONS: Write a news story based on the following interview with Dr. Richard Nybald, an assistant professor in the Department of Psychology and chairman of the Curriculum Committee for the Faculty Senate.

Q. Prof. Nybald, I understand your committee is studying a college program that would enable students to graduate in three years.

A. Well, that's not quite correct. We're trying to find some way to help qualified students graduate more quickly. But the programs we're recommending would not apply to every student. And they wouldn't necessarily reduce college programs to three years. They might enable some students to graduate in three years, but other students might graduate only one or two quarters early, not a full year.

Q. Exactly where are you now? Has your committee finished its report?

A. Yes, the committee's been meeting for the last six months, and we approved a list of eight recommendations last week.

Q. What will happen to the recommendations?

A. We're going to present them at the next meeting of the full Faculty Senate. My secretary has already mailed copies of the recommendations to every member of the senate, so I hope we'll be able to discuss them and perhaps even vote on them at the next meeting. I think the meeting is scheduled for the 14th of next month.

Q. Will the recommendations go into effect if the senate approves them?

A. No. The senate serves as an advisory board for the school's administrators. If the full senate approves the recommendations, the president of the senate will give them to the university president, and he's the one who will have to set the school's policies. I understand that an administrative committee is also investigating the matter, but it hasn't issued its recommendations so far.

Q. What specifically did your committee recommend?

A. First, we recommend that every student still be required to earn 180 quarter-hour or 120 semester-hour credits for graduation. We aren't recommending any changes there. We considered reducing the number but rejected that idea. We believe that a bachelor's degree reflects the attainment of a certain amount of knowledge and that the level of that knowledge should not be allowed to deteriorate. The committee agreed that reducing the number of credits would have an adverse effect on the knowledge and level of maturation that students achieve in college.

Q. Could you describe some of the other recommendations in the report?

A. We suggest that the college develop an early admissions policy so qualified high school students can enroll in college courses during the summers following their junior and senior years. We also recommend that exceptional high school students be encouraged to skip their senior year of high school and enroll in college one year early.

Q. But is that new? I know a girl that skipped her senior year of high school. She's a freshman here now.

A. No. It's not entirely new. The university has admitted some students early, but on an individual basis. It hasn't formulated any clear guidelines and hasn't publicized the program. I'm sure there are hundreds of students that could take advantage of the program—if they knew about it.

Q. You mentioned eight recommendations. What are the other five?

A. We recommend that advisers encourage capable students to take heavier than normal course loads. We also recommend that students be encouraged to attend summer sessions. Again, that's already being done to some extent. Besides that, a lot of the students here are veterans, and we recommend that they be given credit for courses they took while serving in the military.

Q. My editor said I should ask you about the CLEP exams.

A. That's another part of our recommendations. Incoming freshmen can take advantage of the College Level Examination Program. If they take the program's general exams and get a score of 550 or above, they'll receive up to 17 credits from the university without having to take any courses.

Q. What does a score of 550 represent?

A. A score of 550 represents the 70th percentile for students who have completed two years of college. I guess I should add that we've got a pretty high standard here. Some other schools award students up to 60 credits on the basis of the CLEP exams, and a lot of schools don't require a score anywhere near as high as 550.

Q. There's one more recommendation, isn't there?

A. One more big one: credit by examination. My committee recommended that each department at the college offer as many courses by examination as possible, and that the departments compile a list of the courses for which examinations are available. We want to make this just as easy as possible for students. One of the big problems now is that a lot of these programs already exist, but no one knows about them. So part of our recommendation is that every department be required to list all the courses for which examinations are available and to explain why they excluded any courses from the list.

Q. Do you think the Faculty Senate will approve the report?

A. I'm not sure. I think we may have a 50-50 chance. A lot of departments, particularly the hard sciences, feel they already have a hard time squeezing in all the required courses. They're not too happy about the idea of pushing students through their programs faster. But the committee deliberately tried to shape our guidelines so each department can establish its own policies, and that should help. Some departments may do quite a bit more than others.

INTERVIEWS: EXERCISE 6

INSTRUCTIONS: Write a news story based on the following transcript of a press conference held by Vice President Spiro Agnew. The press conference took place at Andrews Air Force Base in Maryland on July 22, 1972, the day after President Richard Nixon announced that Agnew would once again be his running mate.

A. Good afternoon, ladies and gentlemen. Let me say first, I'm tremendously gratified at the President's announcement that he wants me to be a part of the Republican ticket in 1972. It seems as though speculation on this subject began about 10 days after the inauguration in 1969. In any event, I have tried very hard during the period of controversy to not put any pressure on the President by attempting to build support in a constituency because as I've said many times I wanted him to make this decision in a cold, hard, pragmatic political fashion, deciding to go with whomever he thought could do him the most good. He's apparently made that decision. Personally I'm delighted to be a part of the ticket. I think the President's programs in foreign policy, in economic policy, in the domestic areas have been extremely effective for the country. I'm delighted to see how the foreign policies have brought about a change, a diminution in world tensions. I'm glad to see the economic news is tremendously favorable this morning—I understand from most analysts, the best in a decade. And I'm certain that the American people will opt for four more years of the same. Now I'll take your questions.

Q. Mr. Agnew, sir, the President's staff has indicated that he's not going to campaign actively, he'll just do a good job at the White House. Do you intend to actively campaign?
A. Yes, I intend to campaign across the country in a most affirmative fashion on the issues and not on personalities. I intend to carry the President's record to the country in every state.

Q. Mr. Vice President, do you know what Mr. Connally's new assignment might be?
A. I have no indication of Mr. Connally's exact activity in the campaign but I would expect that will be announced by the President sometime soon.

Q. Mr. Vice President, what do you intend to do if Senator McGovern, as he did Thursday, makes a personal attack on the President? Like he said the President then was trying to bear down the faces of the poor. Do you intend to take that sort of thing?
A. Well, I'm going to try to keep my campaigning on the issue level. If the rhetoric from the other side gets a little inflammatory, I certainly feel that it's incumbent on me, as the campaigner in the field, to respond to that. I'm going to respond to it only in the sense of setting the record straight and I'm not going to dwell on a continuation of any name calling in the campaign.

Q. Mr. Vice President, will you keep your options open for a possible race for the presidency in 1976?
A. Well it's a little premature to think about 1976. We've got our hands full for 1972 and that's as far as I'm thinking at the moment. I'm going to put every bit of energy and effort I can into this coming campaign to re-elect a great President.

Q. Mr. Vice President, now that the President has chosen his running mate, what do you think will be the main issues of the GOP convention? It seems like there's nothing left.
A. Well, the issues of the convention are to write the kind of platform that's descriptive of the Nixon position and to make certain that not only the Republican party and the Republicans around the country understand these positions, but to make certain that the silent majority in the United States and all of the Democrats that find it impossible to endorse the positions of Senator McGovern—many of whom have spoken out already— are assured of the President's exact posture on all of the important issues. We're going to urge them to join us in this effort to re-elect the President.

Q. Mr. Vice President, you say that you sought not to put pressure on the President in his deciding to keep you on the ticket, but the fact of the matter is there are many conservatives in the country who were quite adamant about your being on the ticket. Do you think that was a form of pressure on the President?

A. I don't think the President felt any pressure on him about naming one person or another for the vice presidential slot. I think the President is secure enough in his knowledge that the country is with him in his policies to believe that the Republican convention and the people in the United States would have gone along with him so long as he made any intelligent selection for the vice presidency.

Q. Mr. Vice President, could you tell us why independents and Democrats should support you and the President?

A. Well, I'd have to say that the McGovern positions don't represent the thinking and the feelings of the people in the United States. I can quote the statement of Senator Jackson, who referred to those positions as the "new extremism." It seems as though the Democratic party is presently controlled by an ideological elite, and that these people in their articulation of the positions they have McGovern following—positions which call, for example, for the regulation of marijuana in the same way that alcohol is regulated; for unconditional amnesty; for the $1,000-a-year give-away, the cost of which is going to be taken out of the earnings of the hard-working wage earners of this country; the foreign policy attitude that we should beg Hanoi for our prisoners. These things are repugnant to the working man in the United States.

Q. Mr. Vice President, what about you and the news media? What kind of campaign will you run in relation to us?

A. I intend to make the issues in the campaign the subject of my effort and not any argument with the news media. I don't intend to look for problems with the news media. On the other hand, when the news media attack the Administration, or when I see bias prevalent in the news media. I intend to exercise my right of free speech to call attention to it, not because I want to repress or intimidate the media, but because I think the people of the United States have a right to hear both sides of the question.

Q. Mr. Vice President, with the polls showing your ticket far ahead, do you believe you're going to have to wage a strong campaign, or is it going to be an easy fight?

A. There's no such thing as an easy presidential campaign. History tells us that the separation of candidates in the polls at this stage is a very transitory thing. It's an illusory lead that can disappear unless the candidate and his surrogates keep a very active posture in the field. And I'm not going to campaign with any complacent attitude. I'm going out as though this were a last ditch fight, and I'm going to treat it that way through the campaign.

Q. Mr. Vice President, can you tell us anything in any detail at all about your meeting with the President yesterday? How you were told about this? And did you discuss the campaign when you met with him?

A. I don't think it would be proper for me to go into details of what we discussed, but I can only say that during our discussion we obviously did have things to say about campaign strategy. Also he told me, as I indicated, that he's made a final decision and was going to announce it; that he was going to inform other members of the Republican party in key leadership positions of his decision.

Q. What did you say to him?

A. I simply said, "Mr. President, I am delighted to have the chance to serve again with you, and I will do everything I can to see that we are re-elected."

Q. Mr. Vice President, was there ever a time when you didn't think you were going to get it?

A. Well, I guess everybody has moments of insecurity from time to time, but I never did really feel that I was in deep trouble, you might say, as far as the selection was concerned. But I think the important thing for me to emphasize here is that, had I not been selected, I was very serious and sincere when I said that I would still do everything I could to assist the re-election of the President. I am not the kind of person who goes into politics purely from a point of his own interests in holding elective office. I regard it as a service.

. . .

Q. This, Mr. Vice President, pretty much eliminates any suspense for the Republicans in Miami, doesn't it?

A. Well, conventions, in my judgment, are not for the purpose of providing a spectator sport for the public. They're there to get the job done—the serious business of defining the issues so that the intelligent selection of an American president can take place in the fall. And if our convention appears to be a little dull by reason of the fact that we don't have quite the same degree of suspense that the Democrats had at their convention, I guess we'll just have to live with being a little dull this year.

Q. Is this western trip your opening campaign salvo?

A. Well, my campaigning has really continued throughout my entire term of office, not on a steady basis but certainly I've made fund raising and campaign appearances during all of the years I've been vice president. So it will be more a matter of degree than it will anything else.

Q. Thank you, Mr. Vice President. Thank you very much.

INTERVIEWS: EXERCISE 7

INSTRUCTIONS: Write a news story based on your interviews with a minimum of 10 persons, about half men and half women. They may be students, professors, college employes or anyone else you encounter on your campus. Conduct your interviews separately, not simultaneously with other members of your class—if only because it is disconcerting to be approached by two or three people, all asking the same questions. Identify yourself, explain why you are taking the poll, then ask the question selected by your instructor or class—perhaps one of the following:

1. Do you believe that newspapers and radio and television stations in the United States report the news fairly and accurately?
2. Do you agree or disagree with the women's liberation movement and women's struggle for equality?
3. Do you think movies and television programs portray too much crime and violence?
4. Should the state or federal government limit the sale and possession of guns?
5. Are churches becoming irrelevant?
6. Should stricter laws be passed to curb environmental pollution, or are present laws enough? Have you done anything to clean up the environment?

Go beyond the superficial; for example, if the question is whether the person supports women's liberation, ask for more than a simple "Yes" or "No." Ask *why* the person favors or opposes women's liberation. If people refuse to answer your questions or refuse to identify themselves, ask them why they are reluctant to respond.

When you write the lead for your story, do not begin by saying, "Students at the school today were polled about women's liberation." Your lead should summarize the results of the poll—whether most people favored or opposed women's liberation, and why.

After the lead, summarize the other major findings in two or three paragraphs. Also report the wording of the question asked each person. Identify each person you interviewed. In addition to their names, identify students by major and year in school, faculty members by rank and department and college employes by job. Try to add some color to your story. Describe the persons you interviewed—their appearance, their reactions and so on. Use direct quotes, when appropriate. Be sure to stress the answers to your questions, not the questions themselves.

Organize the answers you receive in a meaningful pattern. Do not simply quote people in the order in which you interviewed them. For example, you might first quote persons who favor women's liberation, then persons who oppose it. Provide transitions between various segments of your story.

Your instructor may tell you to conduct your interviews and submit your completed story within one class period, or he may tell you to complete the assignment outside class.

Statistical Material 12

When you are given a mass of figures and asked to write a news story about them, look for and emphasize the most significant and interesting figures. Translate as many of the numbers as possible into words, since readers can understand words more easily.

Go beyond the superficial. For example, if you are writing up the results of a city election, do more than report who won and the number of votes the candidates received. Report overall trends: for example, did the incumbents (or women or blacks or young candidates) tend to win or lose? Emphasize the unusual: Did any candidates win by unusually large or small margins? Compare the number of votes cast in different wards. Look for significant changes from one year or election to the next. When you make such inferences from statistics, be careful to do so accurately and objectively; do not slant the data to support a previously formulated conclusion.

When you do report numbers, report them as simply as possible. Avoid a series of long paragraphs that contain nothing but figures. Use transitions, explanations and commentary to break up strings of numbers and to retain the interest of readers.

STATISTICAL MATERIAL: EXERCISE 1

INSTRUCTIONS: Write a news story based on the following statistics, which were released by Chief of Police Ralph O'Brien at a news conference in his office today.

	Last Year	Previous Year
Total Number of Accidents Reported in the City	741	682
1. Accidents resulting in injuries	143	126
2. Total number of injuries	221	189
3. Accidents resulting in deaths	14	12
4. Total number of deaths	21	22
5. Accidents involving a single vehicle	247	284
6. Accidents involving two vehicles	421	329
7. Accidents involving three or more vehicles	73	69

Causes of the Accidents
(*Note:* More than one factor contributed to a number of the accidents.)

	Last Year	Previous Year
1. Use of alcohol	231	214
2. Traveling at excessive speeds	224	217
3. Failure to yield right of way	168	162
4. Improper passing	102	91
5. Improper turning	84	82
6. Improper backing	34	34
7. Use of drugs	32	8
8. Reckless driving	31	56
9. Mechanical failures	27	14
10. Miscellaneous	27	42

	Last Year	Previous Year
Total Number of Tickets Issued	30,923	31,660
1. Moving violations	3,281	3,487
2. Convictions for moving violations	2,888	3,042
3. Parking violations	27,642	28,173
4. Convictions for parking violations	27,401	27,862

STATISTICAL MATERIAL: EXERCISE 2

INSTRUCTIONS: Write a news story based on the following statistics, which were issued today by the County Welfare Department as part of its annual report. The figures show the total number of persons the department helped during the past three years.

Program	Number of Individuals		
	Last Year	2 Years Ago	3 Years Ago
Old age assistance	1,971	2,093	2,297
Aid to families with dependent children	12,075	10,788	9,850
Aid to the blind	122	134	149
Aid to the disabled	1,178	986	690
General relief	4,372	4,435	4,933
Blind rehabilitation services	92	94	83
Mentally ill	675	576	493
Mentally retarded	1,688	1,534	1,529
Unmarried mothers (85% do not receive direct financial aid)	858	734	764
Illegitimate children (85% do not receive direct financial aid)	1,791	1,594	1,441
Foster day care	681	622	508
Children cared for in boarding homes	759	706	684
Adoptive home studies	210	168	203
Totals	26,472	24,464	23,624

STATISTICAL MATERIAL: EXERCISE 3

INSTRUCTIONS: Write a news story based on the following comparison of prices in five local supermarkets.

Item	Size	Supermarket				
		Saver's Mart	*Mayfair*	*Jerry's*	*G&O*	*Samuelson's*
Food Products						
Mayonnaise	1 qt.	.49	.45	.59	.49	.47
Folger's coffee	1 lb.	.79	.79	.85	.76	.83
Eggs	1 doz.	.49	.52	.55	.35	.49
Apples	1 doz.	.69	.59	.69	.45	.65
Bananas	1 lb.	.10	.10	.12	.09	.10
Celery	1 bunch	.23	.22	.29	.19	.24
Crackers	1 lb.	.43	.47	.49	.39	.39
Tuna	4 oz.	.29	.32	.35	.27	.27
Sugar	5 lb.	.88	.79	.99	.85	.89
Potato chips	9 oz.	.49	.39	.49	.45	.47
Welch's jelly	32 oz.	.67	.69	.69	.67	.69
Potatoes	10 lb.	.59	.59	.69	.55	.54
Butter	1 lb.	.89	.76	.95	.84	.87
Ice cream	2 qt.	.99	.79	.95	.69	.76
Apple juice	32 oz.	.39	.39	.35	.36	.45
Kraft caramels	14 oz.	.45	.49	.47	.45	.49
Bread	1 lb.	.36	.33	.39	.35	.36
Total		9.22	8.68	9.90	8.20	8.97
Meat						
Sirloin steak	1 lb.	1.19	1.15	1.39	1.24	1.29
T-bone steak	1 lb.	1.49	1.35	1.79	1.59	1.39
Smoked ham	1 lb.	.63	.69	.88	.65	.59
Sliced ham	12 oz.	1.39	1.19	1.47	1.49	1.39
Rib roast	1 lb.	1.28	1.29	1.45	1.19	1.24
Ground round	1 lb.	1.28	1.19	1.29	1.29	1.28
Sliced bacon	1 lb.	.79	.76	.92	.69	.69
Wieners	12 oz.	.59	.52	.74	.64	.59
Bologna	1 lb.	.69	.69	.76	.65	.72
Hamburger	1 lb.	.63	.59	.69	.57	.59
Frying chicken	1 lb.	.33	.29	.36	.29	.31
Cube steak	1 lb.	1.18	1.09	1.19	1.09	.99
Corned beef	1 lb.	.78	.95	.99	.89	.86
Total		12.25	11.75	13.92	12.27	11.93

(Continued)

Item	Size		Supermarket			
		Saver's Mart	Mayfair	Jerry's	G&O	Samuelson's
Miscellaneous Products						
Busch beer	6-pack	.99	1.05	1.19	.95	.99
Aluminum foil	25 ft.	.43	.39	.45	.41	.39
Bayer aspirin	100 tablets	.88	.79	.98	.89	.95
Crest toothpaste	7 oz.	.88	.89	.96	.83	.89
Spray starch	22 oz.	.61	.59	.69	.57	.63
Charcoal	20 lb.	.89	.87	1.19	.87	.85
Listerine	7 oz.	.69	.69	.78	.67	.75
Hair spray	13 oz.	.49	.59	.59	.54	.56
Purina Dog Chow	10 lb.	1.59	1.39	1.79	1.49	1.55
Almaden wine	1 qt.	1.55	1.59	1.85	1.59	1.65
Aerowax	27 oz.	.89	.84	.95	.86	.87
Fab	49 oz.	.83	.92	.98	.79	.82
Total		10.72	10.60	12.40	10.47	10.90
Grand Total		$32.19	$31.03	$36.22	$30.94	$31.80

STATISTICAL MATERIAL: EXERCISE 4

INSTRUCTIONS: Write a news story based on the following returns from the municipal elections that were held yesterday in the neighboring town of Roseville. "I" stands for "incumbent," "U" means the candidate ran unopposed and "W" indicates a write-in candidate.

Office	Ward 1	Ward 2	Ward 3	Ward 4	Ward 5	Totals
Mayor						
Alfred Bingston	7,891	3,911	11,824	7,787	9,123	40,536
Thomas Field (I)	6,041	5,886	9,348	4,016	9,007	34,298
Stephen Hamilton (W)	438	521	147	21	86	1,213
City Attorney						
George McCartney	11,121	6,780	9,987	9,987	12,067	49,942
Louis Swanson	3,041	4,844	10,711	1,641	5,291	25,528
City Treasurer						
Joseph Alvito (I,U)	12,942	9,041	21,431	10,039	16,441	69,894
City Clerk						
Henry Wong (I,U)	12,734	9,119	21,402	10,114	16,434	69,803
Superintendent of Schools						
Walter Pfaff	8,824	6,779	13,466	6,004	11,612	46,685
Peter Wilke (I)	5,129	3,412	7,854	4,387	8,941	29,696
Municipal Court Judge						
Frederick Cole	3,824	2,711	6,409	2,878	4,731	20,553
Richard Kernan (I)	9,743	7,443	14,385	8,562	13,862	53,995
Alderman, First Ward						
Mary Hyatt	5,014					
Robert Isaac (I)	8,279					
George Reynolds (W)	482					
Alderman, Second Ward						
Paul Putnam (I)		4,003				
Luis Ramirez		4,019				
Norman Shumate (W)		46				
Alderman, Third Ward						
Alan Kline			10,831			
Jerome Mack			10,176			
Alderman, Fourth Ward						
Howard Elton (I)				8,260		
Leonard Pollard				3,642		
Alderman, Fifth Ward						
Jerry Crum					7,469	
Michael Kelly (I)					8,944	

STATISTICAL MATERIAL: EXERCISE 5

INSTRUCTIONS: Write a news story based on the following news release by the Office of Education of the Department of Health, Education and Welfare. The announcement was made in 1972, but in your story assume that the figures are for the current year.

Urban and rural school districts serving the highest concentrations of children from low-income families in 46 States and the District of Columbia will receive an additional $24.8 million in Federal assistance under grant allotments announced today by HEW's Office of Education.

The awards are being made under a recent amendment to Title I of the Elementary and Secondary Education Act. The amendment provides special additional grants to eligible urban and rural school districts. The funds will be used to help defray the costs of compensatory education programs and are in addition to nearly $1.6 billion in Title I grants previously awarded school systems for this school year.

Largest of all Federal aid-to-education programs, Title I serves nearly 7.2 million educationally deprived children in 15,300 school districts. Projects are designed to meet pupil needs for remedial reading, language development, mathematics, and other instructional programs and services.

The extra Title I money allotted under the Urban and Rural Grant program will be used during this school year. It will help support new or expanded projects for preschoolers and youngsters in elementary school. Under special circumstances, the funds may also be used for high school programs—when there is an exceptionally high dropout rate in a school, for example, or if local employment opportunities exist for which educationally deprived high school students could be trained.

To be eligible for a grant under the Urban and Rural program, a school district must have 20 per cent of its school-age population drawn from low-income families, or 5,000 such children who comprise 5 per cent or more of the total school-age population. The amount each school district receives under the special program is limited by the district's basic Title I grant and the total funds available for the fiscal year.

(NOTE TO EDITORS: A listing of the total value of grants allocated under the Urban and Rural Grant program in each State follows.)

Alabama	$1,013,618	Maine	$ 34,208	Oregon	$ 70,652
Alaska	31,991	Maryland	313,046	Pennsylvania	1,065,900
Arizona	95,202	Massachusetts	276,505	Rhode Island	54,942
Arkansas	561,250	Michigan	626,591	South Carolina	831,193
California	1,798,072	Minnesota	341,945	South Dakota	21,942
Colorado	119,467	Mississippi	1,109,298	Tennessee	855,245
Connecticut	144,993	Missouri	467,279	Texas	1,373,437
Florida	492,671	Montana	4,479	Utah	21,287
Georgia	902,310	Nebraska	67,546	Vermont	11,893
Hawaii	88,039	New Hampshire	1,026	Virginia	664,118
Illinois	1,107,348	New Jersey	813,054	Washington	142,761
Indiana	99,720	New Mexico	173,918	West Virginia	413,592
Iowa	63,978	New York	4,197,892	Wisconsin	140,145
Kansas	102,522	North Carolina	1,259,588	Wyoming	2,174
Kentucky	860,849	Ohio	615,941	District of Columbia	221,740
Louisiana	738,944	Oklahoma	389,742		
				National Total:	$24,804,053

Community Reporting 13

To promote efficiency, newspapers assign reporters to gather news on regular "beats." A beat consists of a specific building (such as the police station, city hall, courthouse or federal building), a geographical area (such as a specific neighborhood or suburb) or a particular subject (such as education, religion or the arts).

On a typical day, the reporter assigned to cover, say, city hall for a medium-sized daily newspaper will begin work at 7 or 8 a.m. and may spend the first hour at his desk, writing minor stories left from the previous day, reading other newspapers published in the area or rewriting publicity releases. The reporter is likely to go to the city hall at 8 or 9 a.m. after conferring with his editor about any major stories expected to develop during the day. The reporter will stop at all the important offices in the city hall during the next two or three hours, particularly the offices of the mayor, aldermen, city clerk, city treasurer, city attorney and city planner. The mayor is the most newsworthy individual in most communities and may schedule a press conference in his office at the same time each morning to disseminate information about current developments—and to generate favorable publicity for himself. The reporter will probably return to his office by 11 a.m. to write his stories in time to meet the deadline, which for most afternoon newspapers falls between 11:30 a.m. and 2 p.m. Other reporters, meanwhile, will have been gathering information from the remaining beats; for example, the reporter covering the federal building will have seen the postmaster, local FBI agents, federal marshal, federal court officials, county agricultural agent, Internal Revenue Service employes and recruiters for the armed forces.

This section will emphasize the police beat, to which new reporters are often assigned because it requires less expertise than other areas. Police officers must write reports about every case they investigate, and most police departments let journalists inspect the reports. Some departments also provide a special room for the press and equip it with typewriters, telephones and a police radio. When a reporter reaches the police station each morning, he quickly pages through all the reports filed during the past 24 hours and takes notes on the most newsworthy cases. He may also ask the officers on duty whether any major crimes or accidents are being investigated at that moment. In most cases, all the information necessary for a news story has already been gathered for the reporter. He does not have to drive to the scene of a crime nor interview the victims; all the information he needs can be taken from the police report.

Most newsrooms contain a police radio, and the reporter will listen to it when he returns to his office and begins to write the news stories. If a major story develops late in the morning, the reporter will have to cover it himself; he cannot wait for the police report, since the police are not likely to investigate the incident and file their report before the newspaper's earliest deadline. To save time, the reporter will try to cover late stories by telephone. If a store is robbed, he may call the clerk and ask him or her to describe the robbery. If a child is injured, he may call the child's parents and ask them to describe the accident. The reporter will go to the scene only if the story is unusually important and impossible to cover by telephone.

This method of police coverage is not ideal, but it is efficient. Law enforcement officials complain that newspapers use the police beat as a training ground, and that police officers are forced to deal with a succession of novices. The police are reluctant to trust new reporters who have not proven that they are competent and reliable. (New reporters often do not understand how the police operate and tend to sensationalize in an effort to obtain a "big" story.) With some justification, critics also believe that newspapers report the "official" version of events because they get the information for news stories from public officials. As a result, stories tend to protect rather than criticize officials and their policies..

Like police reports, legal documents—wills, bankruptcy petitions, divorce petitions and so on—can serve as bases for news stories. Examples of such documents and sample police reports are reprinted on the following pages. Assume that the police reports were prepared by police officers who investigated the incidents in your community, and that the legal documents, with the exception of the bankruptcy petition, were filed in your county courthouse. After reviewing the libel laws in your state, write news stories based on the information the documents contain. (Note: The wording of the legal documents has been altered slightly for inclusion in this workbook.)

POLICE DEPARTMENT

MISSING PERSON

171

2. Date & Time Subject Last Seen		11. CR No. 14	12. Zone 3	5. Day	6. Disp.	7. Arr. 10:48 p.m.	8. In Ser. 11:15 p.m.	3. Date Yesterday

6. Located Missing Before: ☐ Adult ☒ Juvenile — Previous Case No. _____

☐ Yes ☒ No

107. Located Previously At:

2. Case No. 148824   1. Command No. 1

7. Missing Person — **Brenda Dunkle**

Age - Sex - Race: **14, F, White**   Res. Address: **936 Sonata Lane**   Res. Phone: **277-0626**   99. School Attending: **North High**   Grade: **Freshman**   Phone: **267-8880**

5. Reported by — **Mother**

Res. Phone: **277-0626**   Bus. Address: **None**   Bus. Phone:

9. Last Person Seeing Subject:

Brother, James — Age - Sex - Race: **11, M, White**   Res. Address: **936 Sonata Lane**   **277-0626**   **Greer Elementary**   **6th**   **267-0678**

1. Relative or Friends:

(a) **Janet Drake** — **13, F, White**   **Unknown**   **North High**   **Freshman**   **267-8880**

(b) **Anne Rhodes** — **14, F, White**   **932 Sonata Lane**   **277-8142**   **North High**   **Freshman**   **267-8880**

0. Parent or Guardian: (a) **Deborah Dunkle** — **39, F, White**   Relationship: **Mother**   Address (Give Name & Address of Business if Res. is same as 87.)

(b)

8. Date & Time Subject Left Home: **Last night, 7:30 p.m.**   94. Locality Last Seen: **Home**   101. Probable Destination: **North High School**

7. Birth Date _____ Place **City**   100. Former Address of Subject: **None**   63. Occupation: **Student**   Bus. Address:

3. Personal Habits: **Studious, hard worker, "normal teenager"**   102. Mental Condition ☐ **Good**   104. Religion: **Catholic**   96. Marital Status: **Single**

5. Jewelry, Papers, Etc. Carried: **Gold bracelet on left wrist**   93. Alias or Maiden Name   41. Person or Unit Notified: **All units**   47. Storage Receipt ☒ Yes ☐ No   Desc. Form

0. Vehicle Used: Model   Make   Year   Body Style   53. Color   52. License   State   Year   55. Ident. Marks

None

3. Remarks: **Brenda's mother says she left home at 7:30 p.m. last night to go to a high school play, but her friends say she never got there, and several of her friends stopped at the Dunkle house after the play last night to see where she was. Her mother called the police at that time. Mrs. Dunkle says Brenda never misbehaved and wouldn't go anywhere by herself. She's afraid the girl may have been hurt or forced off but doesn't have any idea who would do it. Teachers confirmed the fact she's a good student and quite stable and isn't likely to have run off. She had no known interest in any boys. (NOTE TO NEWSMEN: We would appreciate your help in appealing to the public for any possible information concerning the girl's whereabouts at this time.)**

0. Reporting Officer's Signature: (a) **Andrew Hirsch**   Badge No. **482**   87. District **1**   19. Approved By **JK**   21. Person Reporting Crime

   22. State TWX Msg. No. _____

   23. Local TWX Msg. No. _____

(b)   Referred To   Signature   27. Recorded **Yes**   25. Indexed **Yes**   29. Statistics **Yes**

0. Disposition — Assigned To: **Detective Bureau**   Supervisor

0. Disposition — ☐ Cleared by Arrest   ☐ Unfounded   Date

0. Disposition — ☐ Exceptionally Cleared   ☐ Pending   Date

POLICE DEPARTMENT

MISSING PERSON

2. Date & Time Subject Last Seen **7:15 a.m.**	11. CR No **182**	1. Command No. **1**
	12. Zone **3**	
6. Located Missing Before:		
☒ Adult ☐ Juvenile	5. Day **Today**	2. Case No. **1448825**
6. Located Missing Before:	6. Disp.	7. Arr. **7:20 a.m.** 8. In Ser. **7:27 a.m.**
☒ Yes ☐ No ——— Previous Case No. **431721**		3. Date
7. Missing Person	Age - Sex - Race	99. School Attending	Grade	Phone
Donald F. Causeaux	**87, M, White**	Res. Address **539 Sheridan Blvd.**	Res. Phone **424-5706**	Bus. Phone
5. Reported by		Res. Phone **424-5706**	Bus. Address	
Exel Nursing Home	**539 Sheridan Blvd.**			
9. Last Person Seeing Subject:				
Unknown	104. Religion **Lutheran**	96. Marital Status **Widower**		
1. Relative or Friends:				
(a) **None known outside home**				
(b)				
0. Parent or Guardian	Relationship	Address (Give Name & Address of Business if Res. is same as 87.)		
(a) **Atty. Vincent Dawson**	**Guardian**	**112 Main St.**		**522-5685**
(b)				
8. Date & Time Subject Left Home:	94. Locality Last Seen	107. Located Previously At: **Belks Restaurant**		
Early today	**Breakfast at nursing home**			
7. Birth Date	Place	101. Probable Destination		
	100. Former Address of Subject **1537 Hillcrest Ave.**	63. Occupation **Retired Fireman**	Bus. Address	
3. Personal Habits	102. Mental Condition ☐	104.		
None				
Very quiet, forgetful, loves children	93. Alias or Maiden Name ☒ **Senile**	41. Person or Unit Notified **All Units**		
5. Jewelry, Papers, Etc., Carried	53. Color	52. License	55. Ident. Marks	47. Storage Receipt
None				Desc. Form ☒ Yes ☐ No
0. Vehicle Used: Model	Make	Year	Body Style	State Year

3. Remarks:

The manager of the nursing home says Causeaux is quite senile and has wandered off before. She says he's got a history of heart trouble and is on medication and may have a relapse if he doesn't get his regular medication within the next 48 hours. They think he's wearing an old white shirt, green bowtie and blue slacks. There doesn't seem to be any pattern to his wanderings. The last time he walked off he was found at Belks. Before that, he was found down near the river and at a fire station.

0. Reporting Officer's Signature	Badge No. **74**	87. District **14**	19. Approved By **RB**	21. Person Reporting Crime
Daniel Cortez				22. State TWX Msg. No.
				23. Local TWX Msg. No.
0. Disposition	Referred To	Signature	27. Recorded **Yes**	29. Statistics **Yes**
(a)			25. Indexed **Yes**	
(b)				
0. Disposition		Assigned To— **Detective Bureau**		
☐ Cleared by Arrest ☐ Unfounded		Supervisor—		Date—
☐ Exceptionally Cleared ☐ Pending				Date—

POLICE DEPARTMENT

MISSING PERSON

| 11. CR No. 182 | 12. | Zone 3 | 5. Day Today | 6. Disp. | 7. Arr. 7:14 a.m. | 8. In Ser. 7:29 a.m. |
| | | | | | 2. Case No. | 3. Date |

2. Date & Time Subject Last Seen

6. Located Missing Before: ☒ Yes ☐ No ——— Previous Case No.

7. Missing Person
☒ Adult ☐ Juvenile

107. Located Previously At:

| | Age - Sex - Race | Res. Address | Res. Phone | 99. School Attending | Grade Phone |
| **Donald Grantz** | 37, M, white | 203 Lucerne Circle | 376-0905 | | |

5. Reported by

| | | | Res. Phone | Bus. Address | Bus. Phone |
| **Lani Grantz** | 34, F, white | 203 Lucerne Circle | 376-0905 | | |

9. Last Person Seeing Subject:

1. Relative or Friends:

| (a) **Victor Greene** | M, white | Unknown | | 806 Lyndell Drive | 376-0905 |
| | | Relationship | Address (Give Name & Address of Business if Res. is same as 87.) | | |

0. Parent or Guardian

| (a) | | | | |

(b)

(b)

8. Date & Time Subject Left Home: 5 p.m. Saturday

| 94. Locality Last Seen **Corner Lounge 8th St. & Garner Ave.** | 101. Probable Destination **Unknown** | |

7. Birth Date

| Place **Atlanta, Ga.** | 100. Former Address of Subject **4312 Kasper Drive, Apt. 408** | 102. Mental Condition ☐ **Mad at wife** | 63. Occupation **Salesman** |
| | | 104. Religion **None** | 96. Marital Status **Married** | Bus. Address **2717 Rogan Road** |

3. Personal Habits

| **Likes to bowl. Frequents bars** | 93. Alias or Maiden Name | 41. Person or Unit Notified **All units** | | Desc. Form ☒ Yes ☐ No |

5. Jewelry, Papers, Etc., Carried

| **Silver watch and wedding ring** | 52. License | 55. State Year | 55. Ident. Marks | 47. Storage Receipt |

0. Vehicle Used:

| Model | Make **VW** | Year **1971** | Body Style **Sedan** | 53. Color **Red** | 52. License **Not yet determined** | 55. Ident. Marks **Smashed left fender** | |

3. Remarks: The subject's wife said they had a fight Saturday night about one of her old boy friends who called her, and her husband went storming out the door. She thinks he went to a bar and got drunk. She says he's done it before, but always came back home in a couple hours. Now he's been gone since Saturday and she's afraid something may be wrong—that he got hurt or was in an accident. She insists he'd never leave her. The bartender at the Corner Lounge says Grantz was there from about 8 until closing time Saturday and left with one or two other men he didn't know. He says they had been drinking heavily. Greene says he hasn't seen Grantz in weeks and doesn't expect to see him again because Grantz owes him $100.

0. Reporting Officer's Signature

(a) **Hirsh**	Badge No. 482	87. District 1	19. Approved By JK	21. Person Reporting Crime	25. Indexed Yes
				22. State TWX Msg. No.	29. Statistics Yes
(b)	Signature		27. Recorded Yes	23. Local TWX Msg. No.	

0. Disposition — Assigned To— **Detective Bureau** Date

0. Disposition — Supervisor— Date

0. Disposition ☐ Cleared by Arrest ☐ Unfounded
☐ Exceptionally Cleared ☐ Pending

173

POLICE DEPARTMENT

CRIME — GENERAL

4A. Offense	Vandalism
10. Address of Occurrence	1420 Elmwood Dr.
14. Victim's Name	
12. Zone	3
9. Occurred	
4. U.C.R. Classification	548.72.2a
5. Day	Today
11. CR. No. lo.	71
1. Command No.	19
2. Case No.	148831
6. Disp.	
7. Arr.	7:14 a.m.
8. In Ser.	7:43 a.m.
3. Date	

No.	Name	Age-Sex-Race	Res. Address	Res. Phone	Bus. Address	Bus. Phone
15. Reported by	Ruth Ewald	28, F, Negro	1309 Temple Drive	647-1331	Grant Junior High School	671-2739
16. Discovered By	Frank Gerald	47, M, White	682 Lakemont Ave.	831-4461	Grant Junior High School	671-2739
17. Witnessed By						

49. Owner: City

63. Victim's Occupation (14)

42. Type of Premises	Junior High School
129. Protect. Dev.	None
38. Exact Location of Victim or Property	School office, classrooms, hallways

35. Tool-Weapon or Means Used — Serial No.: Paint, blunt instrument

34. Method Used to Commit Crime	General Vandalism
37. General Type of Property Taken	None known of

45. Trade Mark or Unusual Event (Modus Operendi)	Probably children; Vandals entered small window, nothing taken	64. Weather	Cloudy, some rain

130. Value of Property: $12,000

68. What Did Offenders Say

50. Vehicle Used	Make: Unknown	Model	Year	Body Style	53. Color	52. License	State	55. Year	Ident. Marks	47. Storage Receipt

31. ☐ Subject ☐ Suspect	Juv. ☐	Age-Sex-Race	Res. Address	Incarcerated ☐ Yes ☐ No	Where	Occupation

131. Kind of Property Recovered	132. Value	48. Property Recovered ☐ Yes ☐ No	41. Person or Unit Notified — Time

	19. Approved By AC	21. Person Reporting Crime
		22. State TWX Msg. No.
		23. Local TWX Msg. No.

33. Remarks:

Gerald noticed the damage when he unlocked the building at 7 a.m. this morning. He estimates damage at around $12,000. Office files were torn and scattered over the floor and smeared with paint. Refrigerator doors in the school cafeteria were left open and school officials say large quantities of food will have to be thrown out. Several classrooms were entered and papers, books and other materials thrown about. The vandals urinated and defecated on rug floors in several locations and scrawled obscene remarks on the walls. Several interior windows were broken.

20. Reporting Officer's Signature (a)	Ben Roth	Badge No. 88	District 4
(b)			

30. Disposition	☐ Cleared by Arrest ☐ Unfounded ☐ Exceptionally Cleared ☐ Pending	Referred To	Signature

Recorded	Yes	Assigned To	Detective Bureau
Supervisor		Date	

29. Statistics	Yes
Indexed	Yes
Date	

POLICE DEPARTMENT

CRIME — GENERAL

11. CR No. lo. 519	1. Command No. 6
	2. Case No. 148833
	3. Date

4A. Offense
Burglary

4. U.C.R. Classification
847.01a

10. Address of Occurrence
818 Garner Ave.

| 12. Zone 1 | 9. Occurred Between 1 & 10 a.m. | 5. Day Today | 6. Disp. | 7. Arr. 10:14 | 8. In Ser. 10:54 a.m. |

14. Victim's Name
Tom Parker

| Age-Sex-Race 51, M, White | Res. Address 3040 Aloma Ave. | Res. Phone 647-3639 | Bus. Address Corner Lounge | Bus. Phone 647-3326 |

15. Reported by
Same as above

16. Discovered By
Same as above

17. Witnessed By
None

49. Owner
Same as above

63. Victim's Occupation (14)
Bar Keeper

42. Type of Premises
Tavern

| 129. Protect. Dev. None | 38. Exact Location of Victim or Property 8th St. and Garner Ave. |

35. Tool-Weapon or Means Used — Serial No.
Back door forced open

| 34. Method Used to Commit Crime Cash register, drawer pried open | 37. General Type of Property Taken Money and alcoholic beverages |

45. Trade Mark or Unusual Event (Modus Operendi)

130. Value of Property
$1,550

50. Vehicle Used By Offenders:

| Make | Model | Year Unknown | Body Style | 53. Color | 52. License | State | Year | 55. Ident. Marks | 47. Storage Receipt |

| | | | | | | | | 64. Weather | |

68. What Did Offenders Say

| 131. Kind of Property Recovered | 132. Value | 48. Property Receipt ☐ Yes ☐ No | 41. Person or Unit Notified — Time | |

31. ☐ Subject ☐ Suspect

| Juv. ☐ | Age-Sex-Race | Res. Address | | Incarcerated ☐ Yes ☐ No | Where | Occupation |

33. Remarks: Parker said when he opened the bar at 10 this morning he found the cash register and a cash drawer behind the bar had been pried open. He claims that $50 in change was taken from the cash register and $500 from the drawer. Several vending machines also were looted and an unknown amount of change taken. Parker says that several cases of liquor seem to be missing and he's taking an inventory to determine his exact losses. He estimates the losses at about $1,000. Entry was gained by cutting through a lock and prying open a rear door that opens onto an alley.

| 21. Person Reporting Crime | | 22. State TWX Msg. No. | | 23. Local TWX Msg. No. | | 29. Statistics Yes |

20. Reporting Officer's Signature
Cecil Roehl

| Badge No. 104 | District 7 | 19. Approved By RW | Recorded Yes | Indexed Yes |

(b)

Referred To | Signature | Assigned To Detective Bureau | Supervisor

30. Disposition
☐ Cleared by Arrest   ☐ Unfounded
☐ Exceptionally Cleared   ☐ Pending

Date _____   Date _____

175

POLICE DEPARTMENT

CRIME — GENERAL

4A. Offense Larceny			4. U.C.R. Classification 314.87	11. CR No. lo. 482	1. Command No. 7	2. Case No. 148832

10. Address of Occurrence
828 Geele Ave.

| 12. Zone
2 | 9. Occurred
9:35 a.m. | 5. Day
Today | 6. Disp. | 7. Arr.
10:40 a.m. | 8. In Ser.
11:32 a.m. | 3. Date |

14. Victim's Name
Mrs. Alice Kuchle

| Age-Sex-Race
67, F, White | Res. Address
828 Geele Ave. | Res. Phone
827-5828 | Bus. Address
None | | Bus. Phone |

15. Reported by
Same as above

16. Discovered By

17. Witnessed By

49. Owner

63. Victim's Occupation (14)
Retired

| 42. Type of Premises
Private home | 129. Protect. Dev.
None | 38. Exact Location of Victim or Property |

35. Tool-Weapon or Means Used — Serial No.
None

| 34. Method Used to Commit Crime
Fast Talk | 37. General Type of Property Taken
Money | 64. Weather
Raining |

130. Value of Property
$6,000

| 45. Trade Mark or Unusual Event (Modus Operendi)
None (same old swindle) | | | | |

50. Vehicle Used

| Make | Model | Year | Body Style
53. Color | 52. License | State | Year | 55. Ident. Marks
47. Storage Receipt |

68. What Did Offenders Say
By Offenders: Victim never saw vehicle

31. ☐ Subject ☐ Suspect

| Juv. ☐ | Age-Sex-Race | Res. Address | | Incarcerated
☐ Yes ☐ No | Where | Occupation |

131. Kind of Property Recovered

| 132. Value | 48. Property Receipt
☐ Yes ☐ No | 41. Person or Unit Notified — Time |

33. Remarks: Mrs. Kuchle said two men came to her door just after nine this morning and said they were auditors at her bank and suspected she might have been robbed. They suggested that she check the balance in her bank account. She did and determined that the amount credited to her was correct. The men then asked her to help them check the honesty of a cashier by withdrawing some money—they suggested the sum of $6,000. She did and the men later came back to her house and thanked her and said they would return the money to the bank for her. They then took her money. Mrs. Kuchle said she called her daughter and her daughter told her to call us. The bank has confirmed the fact it was a swindle. (Newsmen: Mrs. Kuchle doesn't want her name in the paper.)

20. Reporting Officer's Signature
(a) Ben Roth

(b)

| Badge No.
88 | District
4 | 19. Approved By
RB | 21. Person Reporting Crime | |

30. Disposition

| | | | | Referred To | Signature | Recorded
Yes | 22. State TWX Msg. No.
23. Local TWX Msg. No. |

| ☐ Cleared by Arrest | ☐ Unfounded |
| ☐ Exceptionally Cleared | ☐ Pending |

	Indexed Yes	29. Statistics Yes
Assigned To Detective Bureau		Date
Supervisor		Date

176

POLICE DEPARTMENT

MOTOR VEHICLE

177

4A. Offense	Stolen Car
4. U.C.R. Classification	937.14.3
11. CR No.	813
1. Command No.	3
2. Case No.	148835
10. Address of Occurrence	North High School
12. Zone	2
9. Occurred	Between 8 a.m. & 4 p.m. Yesterday
5. Day	Yesterday
6. Disp.	
7. Arr.	4:14 p.m.
8. In Ser.	4:37 p.m.
3. Date	
50. Vehicle:	Auto
Model	Impala
Make	Chevy
Year	1971
Body Style	Sedan
53. Color	Blue
52. License	F62481
State	Current
Year	51. Motor or Serial No. #841726928
57. Doors Locked	X Yes ☐ No
46. Registered Owner	
56. Ignition Locked	☐ Yes X No
58. Keys in Ignition	☐ Yes X No
44. Date Last Payment	1st of this month
135. Sobriety of Complainant	X Sober ☐ H.B.D. ☐ Intox
62. Person Last Driving Vehicle	Michael Chakey
Age-Sex-Race	39, M, White
Res. Address	1004 Esplanda Way
Res. Phone	843-9817
Bus. Address	North High School
Bus. Phone	647-2395
17. Witnessed By	Same as above
39. Name of Insurance Co.	Allstate
None	
Address	Plaza Shopping Center
Phone	647-0419
130. Value	$2,600
54. Title Holder	First National Bank, 804 Main St.
Phone	647-8313
32. Mileage when Stolen	About 34,000
45. Trade Mark or Unusual Event (Modus Operandi)	Professional. Very fast, unnoticed.
55. Ident. Marks (Accessories)	None
64. Weather	Clear
66. Personal Articles in Vehicle	Raincoat, flashlight, 2 blankets
61. Where Recovered	City dump
32. Mileage (Recovered)	34,317
34. Method of Theft (Jump Wires, Tinfoil, etc.)	Jump Wires
43. Evidence of Stripping	X Yes ☐ No
132. Recovered Value	$50
48. Property Receipt	X Yes ☐ No
47. Storage Receipt	☐ Yes X No
59. Vehicle Stored At	City garage
31. ☐ Subject ☐ Suspect	Juv. ☐	Age-Sex-Race	Res. Address		Incarcerated ☐ Yes ☐ No	Where	Occupation

33. Remarks: When the car was found this morning it had been stripped of everything of value--the motor, tires, air conditioner, radio, seats, etc. An employe at the city dump called at 6:15. He was suspicious because he said the car seemed new and the body was in good condition. He couldn't understand why anyone would get rid of it. He said someone must have dropped it off last night, because it wasn't there yesterday. A further investigation uncovered three additional stolen cars abandoned in various parts of the dump. All three also were stripped, and some apparently had been there for several weeks.

20. Reporting Officer's Signature (a)	Cecil Roehl
Badge No.	104
District	7
19. Approved By	RW
21. Person Reporting Crime	
(b)		Signature	Recorded	Indexed Yes	29. Statistics Yes
			22. State TWX Msg. No.		
			23. Local TWX Msg. No.		
30. Disposition	Referred To	Recorded Yes	Assigned To Detective Bureau Supervisor	
☐ Cleared by Arrest	☐ Unfounded			Date
☐ Exceptionally Cleared	☐ Pending			Date

POLICE DEPARTMENT

CRIME AGAINST PERSON

4A. Offense			4. U.C.R. Classification 283.47T	II. CR No. lo. 812	1. Command No. 4	
						2. Case No. 148830

10. Address of Occurrence	Mugging	12. Zone	9. Occurred	5. Day	6. Disp.	7. Arr.	8. In Ser.	3. Date
1600 Iowa Ave.		1	9:15 a.m.	Today		9:22 a.m.	9:51 a.m.	

14. Victim's Name
Mrs. Ellen Pfantz

Age-Sex-Race	Res. Address	Res. Phone	Bus. Address	Bus. Phone
F, White	2102 Jacobs Place	322-8045	None	

15. Reported by
Rev. James Williams

16. Discovered By

	41, M, Negro	539 N. Jackson Ave.	627-8093	St. Marks Lutheran Church 322-1433

17. Witnessed By
Rev. James Williams

90. Parent (If 14. Juvenile)

	Same as above	

63. Victim's Occupation (14)
Retired

35. Weapon or Means of Attack — Serial No.

42. Type of Premises	86. Next of Kin notified	38. Exact Location of Victim
Bus stop	☒ Yes ☐ No	

136. No. of Offenders
One

65. Nature of Injuries (Location on Body)	34. Method Used to Commit Crime	67. Hospital	69. Pronounced By — Time	95. Condition
Shock. Broken right arm	See remarks below	Memorial		Good

50. Vehicle Used
By Offenders:
None

Model	Make	Year	Body Style	53. Color	52. License	State	Year	55. Ident. Marks	47. Storage Receipt

68. What Did Offenders Say
Nothing

72. How Offender Approached — Flight		64. Weather Overcast	

31. ☐ Subject ☐ Suspect

Juv. ☐	Age-Sex-Race	Res. Address		Incarcerated ☐ Yes ☐ No	Where	Occupation

70. Will Victim Prefer

Charge ☐ Yes ☐ No	Referred To	48. Property Receipt ☐ Yes ☐ No	41. Person or Unit Notified — Time
	71.		

33. Remarks:

Miss Pfantz must be around 80 but refused to tell anyone her exact age. She said she was waiting for a bus when someone knocked her down from behind and grabbed her purse. She broke her right arm when she fell and was taken by ambulance to Memorial Hospital. She said she didn't see her assailant. Williams was driving past and said a youth, about 16 to 18 years old took her purse and then ran behind a grocery store at 1640 Iowa Ave. Williams said he didn't try to chase the youth because he thought Mrs. Pfantz needed help. He said the assailant was a white and wore a white jacket and blue pants and white sneakers. We cruised the area but didn't see anything.

20. Reporting Officer's Signature
(a) **Manuel Cortez**

(b)

Badge No. 74	87. District 14	19. Approved By RB	21. Person Reporting Crime

30. Disposition

	Referred To	Signature	27. Recorded Yes	25. Indexed Yes	29. Statistics Yes
☐ Cleared by Arrest ☐ Exceptionally Cleared	☐ Unfounded ☐ Pending	Assigned To Detective Bureau Supervisor		22. State TWX Msg.	Date
				23. Local TWX Msg.	Date

POLICE DEPARTMENT

CRIME AGAINST PERSON

4A. Offense		4. U.C.R. Classification	11. CR No. lo.	1. Command No.	2. Case No.
Aggravated Assault		142.73c	821	1	148828

10. Address of Occurrence		12. Zone	9. Occurred	5. Day	6. Disp.	7. Arr.	8. In Ser.	3. Date
2410 Main St.		3	1:20 a.m.	Today		1:27 a.m.	1:53 a.m.	

14. Victim's Name	Age-Sex-Race	Res. Address	Res. Phone	Bus. Address	Bus. Phone
Dennis Hodgins	37, M, Negro	1002 Indian River Road	267-9203	3608 N. Westmorland Rd.	767-3240

15. Reported by
Same as above

16. Discovered By

17. Witnessed By

90. Parent (If 14. Juvenile)
None

63. Victim's Occupation (14)	42. Type of Premises	86. Next of Kin notified	38. Exact Location of Victim
Insurance Salesman	Parking lot	☐ Yes ☐ No	

35. Weapon or Means of Attack — Serial No.	34. Method Used to Commit Crime	67. Hospital	69. Pronounced By — Time	95. Condition
Knife	See remarks below ☒ Yes ☐ No	Memorial		Fair

136. No. of Offenders	65. Nature of Injuries (Location on Body)	64. Weather
Two	Knife wounds to chest and lower abdomen	Cold, clear

50. Vehicle Used	Make	Model	Year	Body Style	53. Color	52. License	State	Year	55. Ident. Marks	47. Storage Receipt

68. What Did Offenders Say
By Offenders: **Unknown**

72. How Offender Approached — Flight

31. ☐ Subject ☐ Suspect	Juv. ☐	Age-Sex-Race	Res. Address	41. Person or Unit Notified — Time

70. Will Victim Prefer	71.		48. Property Receipt	Incarcerated	Where	Occupation
Charge ☐ Yes ☐ No	Referred To		☐ Yes ☐ No	☐ Yes ☐ No		

33. Remarks: Hodgins said he had just left Shiek's Restaurant and was getting his car which was parked in the restaurant parking lot when two men suddenly came up behind him and said they'd cut him up if he didn't give them his wallet. Hodgins said he didn't see a knife and tried to slug the closest man and the other started sticking a knife into him. Then they grabbed his wallet and fled to the south, toward Simmons Ave. Hodgins didn't see any car. He said he stumbled back into the restaurant to get help. He said both of the men were white; one was about 40, 6' 200 pounds and was wearing a pair of dark jeans and a jacket. The other was about 25, medium build, 5' 10" and wearing pants and an olive shirt. Hodgins said he had about $14 left in his wallet.

30. Disposition		Referred To	Signature		19. Approved By	21. Person Reporting Crime
☐ Cleared by Arrest	☐ Unfounded				BW	
☐ Exceptionally Cleared	☐ Pending					

20. Reporting Officer's Signature
(a) **Cecil Roehl**

Badge No.	87. District	27. Recorded	25. Indexed
104	7	Yes	Yes

(b)

	22. State TWX Msg.	29. Statistics
Detective Bureau	23. Local TWX Msg.	Yes

Assigned To _____ Date _____
Supervisor _____ Date _____

POLICE DEPARTMENT

CRIME AGAINST PERSON

4A. Offense		4. U.C.R. Classification		11. CR.No. lo.	1. Command No.	2. Case No.
Suicide		642.73.2		481	3	148829

10. Address of Occurrence		12. Zone	9. Occurred	5. Day	6. Disp.	7. Arr.	8. In Ser.	3. Date
2035 Holland Ave.		4	Last Night			8:14 a.m.	10:30 a.m.	

14. Victim's Name	Age-Sex-Race	Res. Address	Res. Phone	Bus. Address	Bus. Phone
Rudi Jensen	57, M, White	2035 Holland Ave.	855-4563	1740 Grimell Ave.	647-8080

15. Reported by **Steven Coyle**

16. Discovered By **Same as above** / Howell Apts., #47 / 855-1886 / 1740 Grimell Ave. / 647-8080

17. Witnessed By

90. Parent (if 14. Juvenile)

63. Victim's Occupation (14)	42. Type of Premises	86. Next of Kin notified	38. Exact Location of Victim	67. Hospital	95. Condition
Butcher	Apartment	☒ Yes ☐ No	Kitchen floor	Memorial	DOA

35. Weapon or Means of Attack — Serial No. **Shotgun #14328474**

34. Method Used to Commit Crime **Placed gun barrel in mouth**

69. Pronounced By — Time **Coroner 9:32 a.m.**

136. No. of Offenders	65. Nature of Injuries (Location on Body)	
One	Severe gunshot wound to head	

50. Vehicle Used | Model | Make | Year | Body Style | 53. Color | 52. License | State | 55. Year | 55. Ident. Marks | 47. Storage Receipt

68. What Did Offenders Say | By Offenders: **None**

72. How Offender Approached — Flight

31. ☐ Subject ☐ Suspect	Juv. ☐	Age-Sex-Race	Res. Address			64. Weather

Incarcerated ☐ Yes ☐ No | Where | Occupation

70. Will Victim Prefer Charge ☐ Yes ☐ No | Referred To | 71. | 48. Property Receipt ☐ Yes ☐ No

41. Person or Unit Notified — Time

33. Remarks:

Coyle is assistant manager of the supermarket where Jensen works and said he had been worry about Jensen for some time, and when Jensen didn't come in for work this morning he tried calling him but didn't get an answer, so he drove to Jensen's apartment. The apt. manager let him in Jensen's apartment, and he found the body on the kitchen floor. The top of his head was blown off and the shotgun was on the floor next to the body. Coyle said he knows its Jensen's gun because he's been hunting with him a couple times. He said Jensen's been real depressed because he's divorced and lonely and has been sick.

20. Reporting Officer's Signature	Badge No.	87. District	19. Approved By	21. Person Reporting Crime
(a) Cecil Roehl	104	7	RW	

(b) | | | 22. State TWX Msg. | 23. Local TWX Msg.

30. Disposition	Referred To	Signature	27. Recorded	25. Indexed	29. Statistics
☐ Cleared by Arrest ☐ Exceptionally Cleared			Yes	Yes	Yes
☐ Unfounded ☐ Pending					

Assigned To — **Detective Bureau** / Supervisor

180

POLICE DEPARTMENT

ROBBERY

4A. Offense **Armed Robbery**	4. U.C.R. Classification **414.73a**	II. CR No. **894**	I. Command No. **4**	2. Case No. **148834**

| 10. Address of Occurrence **2640 Howell Road** | 12. Zone **3** | 9. Occurred **10:40 a.m.** | 5. Day **Today** | 6. Disp. | 7. Arr. **10:44** | 8. In Ser. **11:28 a.m.** | 3. Date |

14. Victim's Name **Mildred Trevor** — Age-Sex-Race **34, F, White** — Res. Address **635 Poplar Road** — Res. Phone **645-3039** — Bus. Address **2640 Howell Road** — Bus. Phone **671-2138**

15. Reported by

17. Witnessed By **Earl Inez Jr.** **46, M, Negro 2541 Bahama Ave.** **671,2565 2640 Howell Road** **671-2138**

49. Owner **Jiffy Loans, Inc.**

63. Victim's Occupation (14) **Cashier** — 42. Type of Premises **Loan company** — 129. Protect. Dev. **Silent alarm**

35. Weapon or Means Used — Serial No. **Revolver** — 34. Method Used to Commit Crime **See remarks below**

45. Trade Mark or Unusual Event (Modus Operendi)

135. Sobriety of Victim Sober **XX** H.B.D. ☐ Intox. ☐ — 37. General Type of Property Taken **Money** — 64. Weather **Sunny** — 130. Value **$700**

Lone gunman went directly to cashier, displayed weapon, told her to give him all her money.

50. Vehicle Used — Make — Model **Fury Plymouth** — Year **1973** — Body Style **4-door** — 53. Color **Blue** — 52. License **Unknown** — State — Year — 55. Ident. Marks — 136. No. of Offenders **Two** — 47. Storage Receipt

68. What Did Offenders Say **Just keep cool and give me all the money you've got. You try anything and I'll kill you.**

31. ☐ Subject ☐ Suspect — Juv. ☐ — 72. Sex-Race-Age — Res. Address — Incarcerated ☐ Yes ☐ No — Where — Occupation

138. Disguises

131. Kind of Property Recovered — 132. Value — 48. Property Receipt ☐ Yes ☐ No — 41. Person or Unit Notified — Time — 67. Hospital (14) — 95. Condition

33. Remarks: **Miss Trevor said she hit the silent alarm as soon as she saw the gun, but the suspect was gone before we reached the scene. Inez, the manager, got a partial description of the getaway vehicle. He said a woman was driving but he didn't get a good look at her and couldn't describe her. He and Miss Trevor agreed the gunman was black, about 60, had a moustache and was almost entirely bald. They said he was about 6 feet tall and very thin, maybe 140 pounds. He was wearing gray pants and shirt and a green nylon jacket. We cruised the area looking for the suspects' vehicle but were unable to locate it. Inez says he thinks he saw the man before but doesn't remember where.**

20. Reporting Officer's Signature (a) **Cecil Roehl** — Badge No. **104** — 87. District **7** — 19. Approved By **RW** — 21. Person Reporting Crime

(b) — Referred To — Signature — 27. Recorded **Yes** — 25. Indexed **Yes** — 22. State TWX Msg. No. — 23. Local TWX Msg. No. — 29. Statistics **Yes**

30. Disposition ☐ Cleared by Arrest ☐ Exceptionally Cleared ☐ Unfounded ☐ Pending — Referred To — Assigned To **Detective Bureau** — Supervisor — Date — Date

DOG BITE REPORT

Victim Arthur Heath   Age 7   D.O.B. Unknown   Phone 831-2712

Address 534 Ridgewood Ave.

Reported by Mrs. Ruth Heath   Address 534 Ridgewood Ave.   Phone 831-2712

Received by Sgt. Phelps   Phone 821-8000

Address where bitten Evergreen Park   Date Today   Time 9:20 a.m.

Part of Body where Bitten

Leg   ( )   Arm   (X)
Upper   ( )   Upper   ( )
Lower   ( )   Lower   (X)
Right   ( )   Right   (x)
Left   ( )   Left   ( )

Other part of body bitten None

Owner of Dog Denise Gaul   Address 1220 Roberta Ave.   Phone 796-2873

Was owner of dog notified to keep dog confined?

Yes (X)   No ( )

Where In pen at owner's home   Doctor treating victim Beeker

Type of dog   Large (X)   Short Hair ( )   Color Brown
                   Small ( )   Long Hair (X)   Breed Mixed

Dog Tag: Yes (X)   No ( )
Rabies Tag: Yes ( )   No (X)

Doctor Treating Dog Not yet determined   Address

Phone Notification   City Health Department: Yes (X)   No ( )

Remarks Miss Gaul said the youth put out his hand to pet the dog and the dog
snapped at it. The boy required 12 stitches since his skin was torn when
he tried to pull away. Miss Gaul said she just bought the dog a month ago
and doesn't know whether it's had any rabies shots or not but will check.

Officer Julivets
Date Today   Time 10:10 a.m.

182

TRAFFIC ACCIDENT REPORT
MAIL TO: ACCIDENT RECORDS BUREAU, DEPT. OF HIGHWAY SAFETY & MOTOR VEHICLES

TIME & LOCATION

DATE OF ACCIDENT	DAY OF WEEK	TIME OF DAY	
Today		1:55	A. M

COUNTY	CITY, TOWN OR COMMUNITY
(Yours)	(Yours)

IF ACCIDENT WAS OUTSIDE CITY LIMITS, INDICATE DISTANCE FROM NEAREST TOWN: **12** — ☐ Feet ☒ Miles — N S E ☒ W — Of **(Yours)** City, Village or Township

ROAD ON WHICH ACCIDENT OCCURRED: **U.S. 50** — ☐ Ext Ramp ☐ Entrance R. — ☐ At its intersection with ☐ Influenced by intersection — Use State or County Road Number or Name — Highway Number or Name of Intersecting Street

IF NOT AT INTERSECTION: **3** — ☐ Feet ☒ Miles — N S E W ☒ — Of **Alfaya Trail** — Show nearest milepost, intersecting street or highway, bridge, RR crossing, underpass or curve

IS ENGINEERING STUDY NEEDED (If so explain)

DO NOT WRITE IN SPACE ABOVE

TYPE MOTOR VEHICLE ACCIDENT

OVERTURNING **XXXXXXXXX**	OTHER NONCOLLISION	PEDESTRIAN	MV IN TRANSPORT	MV ON OTHER ROADWAY	HIT AND RUN
PARKED MV	RAILWAY TRAIN	PEDALCYCLIST	ANIMAL	FIXED OBJECT	OTHER OBJECT	NON-CONTACT

VEHICLE 1

TOTAL NO. VEH. INVOLVED: **1**

YEAR	MAKE	TYPE (Sedan, Truck, Bus, etc.)	VEHICLE LICENSE PLATE NO.	STATE	YEAR	VEHICLE IDENTIFICATION NO.
1971	Ford	Sedan	S23149	Yes	Current	#272811347

| Area of Vehicle Damage | 15 | | | | Damage Scale | 3 | Damage Severity | 3 | AMOUNT (Approximate) $2,800 | Safety Equipment | No | VEHICLE REMOVED BY Alco Towing |

NAME OF INSURANCE (Liability Only): **Farmer's Mutual** — POLICY NO. **#74-16599-3** — Owner ☒ Driver ☒ — ☐ Owner's Request ☐ Other (Explain) — ☒ Rotation List

OWNER (Print or type FULL name): **Lawrence T. Hansbrough** — ADDRESS (Number and street) **2324 Lea Road** — CITY and STATE

DRIVER (Exactly as on driver's license): **Same as above** — ADDRESS (Number and street) — CITY and STATE

OCCUPATION	Driver's License Type	DRIVER'S LICENSE NUMBER	STATE	DATE (Month, Day, Year) OF BIRTH	RACE	SEX	Safety E.	Eject.	Injury
Farmer	F	J37349126	Yes	3/11/31	W	M	0	0	Yes

OCCUPANTS	Name	ADDRESS - Number and Street	City and State	AGE	RACE	SEX	Safety E.	Eject.	Injury
Front center									
Front right									
Rear left									
Rear center									
Rear right									

VEHICLE 2 or PEDESTRIAN

YEAR	MAKE	TYPE (Sedan, Truck, Bus, etc.)	VEHICLE LICENSE PLATE NO.	STATE	YEAR	VEHICLE IDENTIFICATION NO.

| Area of Vehicle Damage | | | | | Damage Scale | | Damage Severity | | AMOUNT (Approximate) | Safety Equipment | | VEHICLE REMOVED BY |

NAME OF INSURANCE (Liability Only): — POLICY NO. — Owner ☐ Driver ☐ — ☐ Owner's Request ☐ Other (Explain) — ☐ Rotation List

OWNER (Print or type FULL name): — ADDRESS (Number and street) — CITY and STATE

DRIVER (Exactly as on driver's license): — ADDRESS (Number and street) — CITY and STATE

OCCUPATION	Driver's License Type	DRIVER'S LICENSE NUMBER	STATE	DATE (Month, Day, Year) OF BIRTH	RACE	SEX	Safety E.	Eject.	Injury

OCCUPANTS	Name	ADDRESS - (Number and Street)	City and State	AGE	RACE	SEX	Safety E.	Eject.	Injury
Front center									
Front right									
Rear left									
Rear center									
Rear right									

PROPERTY DAMAGED—Other than vehicles: **Fence** — AMOUNT **$50** — OWNER – Name **Undetermined** — ADDRESS - Number and Street — CITY and STATE

INVESTIGATOR – Name and rank (Signature): **Pvt. Paul Harrold** — BADGE NO. **1428** — I.D. NO. **H227** — DEPARTMENT **Sheriff** — ☐ F.H.P. ☐ C.P.D. ☐ S.O. ☐ Other — DATE OF REPORT **Today**

FHP – 3 Revised 1-1-72

SHEET **1** OF **2** SHEETS

DIAGRAM WHAT HAPPENED – (Number each vehicle and show direction of travel by arrow)

↑
INDICATE NORTH
WITH ARROW

U.S. 50

Vehicle #1

X Overturned

POINT OF IMPACT

	1	2	
	☐	☐	Front
	☐	☐	Right front
	☐	☐	Left front
	☐	☐	Right side
	☐	☐	Left side
	☐	☐	Rear
	☐	☐	Right rear
	☐	☐	Left rear

DESCRIBE WHAT HAPPENED – (Refer to vehicles by number)

Two deputies discovered the car at 1:55 a.m. while patrolling U.S. 50 east of the city and stopped to investigate after the headlights of their patrol car illuminated pieces of the wreckage. They found the victim still in his car, unconscious and unable to tell what happened. He smelled heavily of alcohol. He apparently suffered a severe concussion, both legs broken and internal injuries. He's reported in critical condition at the hospital. We'd estimate the accident occurred at about midnight.

WHAT VEHICLES WERE DOING BEFORE ACCIDENT

VEHICLE No. 1 was traveling ☐ ☐ ☒ ☐ On U.S. 50 at 70 M.P.H.
VEHICLE No. 2 was traveling ☐ ☐ ☐ ☐ On _____ at _____ M.P.H.
                                N S E W

	1	2			1	2			1	2			1	2	
	☐	☐	Going straight ahead		☐	☐	Making right turn		☐	☐	Slowing or Stopping		☐	☐	Starting from parked position
	☐	☐	Overtaking		☒	☐	Making left turn		☐	☐	Changing lanes		☐	☐	Stopped or parked
													☐	☐	Other (explain above)

WHAT PEDESTRIAN WAS DOING

PEDESTRIAN was going ☐ ☐ ☐ ☐   ☐ Along   ☐ Across or into   from _____ to _____   Color of Clothing ☐ Dark ☐ Light
                      N S E W

☐ Crossing at Intersection	☐ Stepped into path of Vehicle	☐ Getting on or off Vehicle	☐ Playing in roadway
☐ Crossing not at Intersection	☐ Standing in roadway	☐ Hitching on Vehicle	☐ Other roadway
☐ Walking in roadway – with traffic	☐ Standing in safety zone	☐ Pushing or working on Vehicle	☐ Not in roadway
☐ Walking in roadway – against traffic	☐ Lying or Sitting on roadway	☐ Other working in roadway	☐ Other (explain above)

DRIVERS AND VEHICLES

	VEHICLE 1	VEHICLE 2
PHYSICAL DEFECTS (Driver)		
VEHICLE DEFECTS	NONE	
CONTRIBUTING CIRCUMSTANCES		

ACCIDENT Characteristics

LIGHTING CONDITION	Dark	ROAD DEFECTS	None	TRAFFICWAY CHARACTER	Level	CLASS OF TRAFFICWAYS	State
WEATHER	Cloudy	TRAFFIC CONTROL	None	TRAFFICWAY LANES	2	TYPE TRAFFICWAY	3
ROAD SURFACE	Dry	TYPE LOCATION	Curve	VISION OBSCURED	Yes		

WITNESSES other than occupants

| NAME | ADDRESS – Number and street | City and State |
| None | | |

FIRST AID GIVEN BY

☐ Doctor or Nurse   ☐ Cert. First Aider
☐ Cert. First Aider (Police)   ☐ Other (Explain)

CHEMICAL TEST: TEST RESULTS:
YES NO
Driver No. 1 ☒ ☐   Drunk
Driver No. 2 ☐ ☐

INJURED TAKEN TO Memorial Hospital   BY:
☒ Priv. Ambulance   ☐ Other (Explain)
☐ Gov't. Ambulance

ARREST

NAME	CHARGE	Citation No.	PHOTOGRAPHS TAKEN
Lawrence Hansbrough	Drunk Driving		☐ Yes ☒ No
NAME	CHARGE	Citation No.	☐ Agency
			☐ Other (Explain)

| TIME NOTIFIED OF ACCIDENT | TIME ARRIVED AT SCENE | WAS INVESTIGATION MADE AT SCENE (If not where) | IS INVESTIGATION COMPLETE (If not why) |
| 19__ 1:55 A M | 1:55 A M | Yes | Yes |

TRAFFIC ACCIDENT REPORT

MAIL TO: ACCIDENT RECORDS BUREAU, DEPT. OF HIGHWAY SAFETY & MOTOR VEHICLES

TIME & LOCATION

DATE OF ACCIDENT	DAY OF WEEK	TIME OF DAY
Today		8:20 a.m. M

COUNTY	CITY, TOWN OR COMMUNITY
(Yours)	(Yours)

IF ACCIDENT WAS OUTSIDE CITY LIMITS, INDICATE DISTANCE FROM NEAREST TOWN _____ ☐ Feet ☐ Miles ☐☐☐☐ N S E W Of _____ City, Village or Township

ROAD ON WHICH ACCIDENT OCCURRED **State Hwy. 436** Use State or County Road Number or Name ☐ Exit Ramp ☐ Entrance R. ☐ At its intersection with ☐ Influenced by intersection _____ Highway Number or Name of Intersecting Street

IF NOT AT INTER-SECTION **1/2** ☐ Feet ☒ Miles ☒☐☐☐ N S E W Of **Carter Expressway** Show nearest milepost, intersecting street or highway, bridge, RR crossing, underpass or curve

IS ENGINEERING STUDY NEEDED (If so explain)

DO NOT WRITE IN SPACE ABOVE

TYPE MOTOR VEHICLE ACCIDENT

OVERTURNING	OTHER NONCOLLISION	PEDESTRIAN XXXXXX	MV IN TRANSPORT	MV ON OTHER ROADWAY	HIT AND RUN XXXXX
PARKED MV	RAILWAY TRAIN / PEDALCYCLIST	ANIMAL	FIXED OBJECT	OTHER OBJECT	NON-CONTACT

VEHICLE 1

TOTAL NO. VEH. IN-VOLVED

YEAR	MAKE	TYPE (Sedan, Truck, Bus, etc.)	VEHICLE LICENSE PLATE NO.	STATE	YEAR	VEHICLE IDENTIFICATION NO.
1971	Chevrolet	Pickup	Not visible			

Area of Vehicle Damage | Damage Scale | Damage Severity | AMOUNT (Approximate) | Safety Equipment | VEHICLE REMOVED BY

NAME OF INSURANCE (Liability Only) | POLICY NO. | Owner ☐ Driver ☐ | Owner's Request ☐ Other (Explain) ☐ | Rotation List ☐

OWNER (Print or type FULL name) **Unknown** | ADDRESS (Number and street) | CITY and STATE

DRIVER (Exactly as on driver's license) | ADDRESS (Number and street) | CITY and STATE

OCCUPATION	Driver's License Type	DRIVER'S LICENSE NUMBER	STATE	DATE (Month, Day, Year) OF BIRTH	RACE	SEX	Safety E.	Eject.	Injury

OCCUPANTS	Name	ADDRESS – Number and Street	City and State	AGE	RACE	SEX	Safety E.	Eject.	Injury
Front center									
Front right									
Rear left									
Rear center									
Rear right									

VEHICLE 2 or PEDESTRIAN

YEAR	MAKE	TYPE (Sedan, Truck, Bus, etc.)	VEHICLE LICENSE PLATE NO.	STATE	YEAR	VEHICLE IDENTIFICATION NO.

Area of Vehicle Damage | Damage Scale | Damage Severity | AMOUNT (Approximate) | Safety Equipment | VEHICLE REMOVED BY

NAME OF INSURANCE (Liability Only) | POLICY NO. | Owner ☐ Driver ☐ | Owner's Request ☐ Other (Explain) ☐ | Rotation List ☐

OWNER (Print or type FULL name) | ADDRESS (Number and street) | CITY and STATE

DRIVER (Exactly as on driver's license) **Pedestrian: Rosemary Harrell, 1408 Winn Ave.** | ADDRESS (Number and street) | CITY and STATE

OCCUPATION	Driver's License Type	DRIVER'S LICENSE NUMBER	STATE	DATE (Month, Day, Year) OF BIRTH	RACE	SEX	Safety E.	Eject.	Injury
Student	None			2/7/61	Negro				

OCCUPANTS	Name	ADDRESS – (Number and Street)	City and State	AGE	RACE	SEX	Safety E.	Eject.	Injury
Front center									
Front right									
Rear left									
Rear center									
Rear right									

PROPERTY DAMAGED–Other than vehicles **No** | AMOUNT | OWNER - Name | ADDRESS - Number and Street | CITY and STATE

INVESTIGATOR – Name and rank (Signature)	BADGE NO.	I.D. NO.	DEPARTMENT		DATE OF REPORT
Sgt. Phelps	907	2331	City Police ☐ F.H.P. ☐ C.P.D. ☐ S.O. ☐ Other		Today

FHP 3 Revised 1-1-72   SHEET **1** OF **2** SHEETS

INDICATE NORTH
WITH ARROW

State Highway 436

Vehicle #1

Pedestrian
Point of impact

POINT OF IMPACT

	1	2	
	☐	☐	Front
	☐	☐	Right front
	XX	☐	Left front
	☐	☐	Right side
	☐	☐	Left side
	☐	☐	Rear
	☐	☐	Right rear
	☐	☐	Left rear

DESCRIBE WHAT HAPPENED – (Refer to vehicles by number)

Witnesses agreed Miss Harrell started to cross the roadway on foot, hesitated apparently when she saw the approaching vehicle, then panicked and began to run across the road. The left front fender of the hit-and-run vehicle struck her, throwing her into a ditch. Witnesses said the truck driver braked just before impact, almost came to a stop, then suddenly speeded up again and continued down the road. The victim was pronounced Dead On Arrival at Memorial Hospital.

*WHAT VEHICLES WERE DOING BEFORE ACCIDENT

VEHICLE No. 1 was traveling ☒☐☐☐ On State Hwy. 436 at 65 M.P.H.

VEHICLE No. 2 was traveling ☐☐☐☐ On .... at .... M.P.H.

N S E W

1	2		1	2		1	2		1	2	
☒	☐	Going straight ahead	☐	☐	Making right turn	☐	☐	Slowing or Stopping	☐	☐	Stopped or parked
☐	☐	Overtaking	☐	☐	Making left turn	☐	☐	Changing lanes	☐	☐	Other (explain above)

☐ Starting from parked position

*WHAT PEDESTRIAN WAS DOING

PEDESTRIAN was going ☐☐☐☒ ☐ Along / ☒ Across or into Hwy. 436 from East to West

N S E W

Color of Clothing ☒ Dark ☐ Light

☐	Crossing at Intersection	☐	Stepped into path of Vehicle	☐	Getting on or off Vehicle	☐	Playing in roadway
☒	Crossing not at Intersection	☐	Standing in roadway	☐	Hitching on Vehicle	☐	Other roadway
☐	Walking in roadway – with traffic	☐	Standing in safety zone	☐	Pushing or working on Vehicle	☐	Not in roadway
☐	Walking in roadway – against traffic	☐	Lying or Sitting on roadway	☐	Other working in roadway	☐	Other (explain above)

DRIVERS AND VEHICLES

	VEHICLE 1	VEHICLE 2
PHYSICAL DEFECTS (Driver)	UNKNOWN	
VEHICLE DEFECTS		
CONTRIBUTING		
CIRCUMSTANCES		

ACCIDENT Characteristics	LIGHTING CONDITION	Daylite	DEFECTS	None	TRAFFICWAY CHARACTER	Level	CLASS OF TRAFFICWAYS	State
	WEATHER	Clear	TRAFFIC CONTROL	None	TRAFFICWAY LANES	4	TYPE TRAFFICWAY	4
	ROAD SURFACE	Dry	TYPE LOCATION	Open	VISION OBSCURED	No		

WITNESSES other than occupants

NAME Still checking   ADDRESS – Number and street   City and State

FIRST AID GIVEN BY

☐ Doctor or Nurse ☐ Cert. First Aider
☐ Cert. First Aider (Police) ☐ Other (Explain)

CHEMICAL TEST: TEST RESULTS:
YES NO
Driver No. 1 ☐ ☐
Driver No. 2 ☐ ☐

INJURED TAKEN TO Memorial Hospital   BY: ☒ Priv. Ambulance ☐ Other (Explain)   ☐ Gov't. Ambulance

ARREST

NAME   CHARGE   Citation No.

NAME   CHARGE   Citation No.

PHOTOGRAPHS TAKEN
☒ Yes ☐ No
☒ Agency
☐ Other (Explain)

TIME NOTIFIED OF ACCIDENT	TIME ARRIVED AT SCENE	WAS INVESTIGATION MADE AT SCENE (If not where)	IS INVESTIGATION COMPLETE (If not why)
19 8:20 A.M	8:26 A. M	Yes	No. Searching for driver

TRAFFIC ACCIDENT REPORT

MAIL TO: ACCIDENT RECORDS BUREAU, DEPT. OF HIGHWAY SAFETY & MOTOR VEHICLES

TIME & LOCATION

DATE OF ACCIDENT **Yesterday**	DAY OF WEEK	TIME OF DAY **7:45** P.M

COUNTY (Yours) *Orange* CITY, TOWN OR COMMUNITY (Yours) *Chapel Hill*

IF ACCIDENT WAS OUTSIDE CITY LIMITS, INDICATE DISTANCE FROM NEAREST TOWN: ☐ Feet ☐ Miles N S E W Of ___ City, Village or Township

ROAD ON WHICH ACCIDENT OCCURRED **Aloma Ave.** Use State or County Road Number or Name
☐ Exit Ramp ☐ Entrance R. ☒ At its intersection with ☐ Influenced by intersection **Semoran Boulevard** Highway Number or Name of Intersecting Street

IF NOT AT INTERSECTION: ☐ Feet ☐ Miles N S E W Of ___ Show nearest milepost, intersecting street or highway, bridge, RR crossing, underpass or curve

IS ENGINEERING STUDY NEEDED (If so explain) **No**

DO NOT WRITE IN SPACE ABOVE

TYPE MOTOR VEHICLE ACCIDENT

| OVERTURNING | OTHER NONCOLLISION | PEDESTRIAN | MV IN TRANSPORT | MV ON OTHER ROADWAY XXXXXXX | HIT AND RUN |
| PARKED MV | RAILWAY TRAIN | PEDALCYCLIST | ANIMAL | FIXED OBJECT | OTHER OBJECT | NON-CONTACT |

VEHICLE 1

TOTAL NO. VEH. INVOLVED **2**

YEAR	MAKE	TYPE (Sedan, Truck, Bus, etc.)	VEHICLE LICENSE PLATE NO.	STATE	YEAR	VEHICLE IDENTIFICATION NO.
1971	Toyota	Sedan	B84190	Yes	Current	#8417623494

Area of Vehicle Damage **2 3 4 5 6** | Damage Scale **3** | Damage Severity **3** | AMOUNT (Approximate) **$2,000** | Safety Equipment **1** | VEHICLE REMOVED BY **Ray's Shell**

NAME OF INSURANCE (Liability Only) **State Farm** POLICY NO. **# 82-17428-11**
Owner ☐ Driver ☒ ☐ Owner's Request ☐ Other (Explain) ☒☒ Rotation List

OWNER (Print or type FULL name) **Alfred Caseo** ADDRESS **1627 Mizell Ave.** CITY and STATE

DRIVER (Exactly as on driver's license) **Same as above** ADDRESS CITY and STATE

OCCUPATION **truck driver** | Driver's Type **R** | DRIVER'S LICENSE NUMBER **LB4721982** | STATE **Yes** | DATE OF BIRTH **8/4/40** *34 yr.* | RACE **W** | SEX **M** | Safety E. **1** | Eject. **0** | Injury **Yes**

OCCUPANTS	Name	ADDRESS - Number and Street	City and State	AGE	RACE	SEX	Safety E.	Eject.	Injury
Front center									
Front right	Anna Caseo, 1627 Mizell Ave. *(killed)*			28	W	F	2	2	Yes
Rear left	Sandra Caseo " *kids (injured)*			6	W	F	1	0	Yes
Rear center	Charles Caseo "			3	W	M	0	0	Yes
Rear right	Martha Caseo "			5	W	F	0	0	Yes

VEHICLE 2 or PEDESTRIAN

YEAR	MAKE	TYPE (Sedan, Truck, Bus, etc.)	VEHICLE LICENSE PLATE NO.	STATE	YEAR	VEHICLE IDENTIFICATION NO.
1973	VW	Van	B 842	Yes	Current	#1418294761

Area of Vehicle Damage **1 2 12** | Damage Scale **3** | Damage Severity **3** | AMOUNT (Approximate) **$1,000** | Safety Equipment | VEHICLE REMOVED BY **Ray's Shell**

NAME OF INSURANCE (Liability Only) **Uninsured** POLICY NO.
Owner ☐ Driver ☐ ☐ Owner's Request ☐ Other (Explain) ☒☒ Rotation List

OWNER (Print or type FULL name) **Fred Johansen** ADDRESS **1576 Harris Circle** CITY and STATE

DRIVER (Exactly as on driver's license) **Fred Johansen** ADDRESS **1576 Harris Circle** *18 yr. old* CITY and STATE

OCCUPATION **Student** | Driver's License Type **S** | DRIVER'S LICENSE NUMBER **L8971428** | STATE **Yes** | DATE OF BIRTH **6/2/56** | RACE **W** | SEX **M** | Safety E. **0** | Eject. **0** | Injury **Yes**

OCCUPANTS	Name	ADDRESS - Number and Street	City and State	AGE	RACE	SEX	Safety E.	Eject.	Injury
Front center	Elsie Perrin, 1576 Harris Circle			18	W	F	0	0	Yes
Front right									
Rear left	*Both dead*								
Rear center									
Rear right									

PROPERTY DAMAGED - Other than vehicles **None** | AMOUNT | OWNER - Name | ADDRESS - Number and Street | CITY and STATE

INVESTIGATOR - Name and rank (Signature) **Sgt. Phelps** | BADGE NO. **907** | I.D. NO. **2331** | DEPARTMENT **City Police** | ☐ F.H.P. ☐ C.P.D. ☐ S.O. ☐ Other | DATE OF REPORT

FHP - 3 Revised 1-1-72   SHEET **1** OF **2** SHEETS

Semoran
Avenue

Aloma Ave.
Vehicle #1 →

Vehicle #2

INDICATE NORTH
WITH ARROW

POINT OF IMPACT

	1	2	
	☐	☒	Front
	☐	☐	Right front
	☐	☐	Left front
	☒	☒	Right side
	☐	☐	Left side
	☐	☐	Rear
	☐	☐	Right rear
	☐	☐	Left rear

DESCRIBE WHAT HAPPENED – (Refer to vehicles by number)

Vehicle #1 was proceeding east on Aloma when Vehicle #2 failed to heed a stop sign and entered the intersection, striking Vehicle #1 on the passenger side. Vehicle #1 then continued on into a ditch. Both subjects in Vehicle #2 were killed. Mrs. Caseo, who was thrown from Vehicle #1, also was killed.

All 4 other occupants of Vehicle #1 were taken to Memorial Hospital with serious injuries. Both vehicles were totally demolished.

*WHAT VEHICLES WERE DOING BEFORE ACCIDENT

VEHICLE No. 1 was traveling ☐ ☐ ☒ ☐ On Aloma   at 45 M.P.H.
VEHICLE No. 2 was traveling ☒ ☐ ☐ ☐ On Semoran at 50 M.P.H.
N S E W

	1	2			1	2			1	2			1	2	
	☒	☒	Going straight ahead		☐	☐	Making right turn		☐	☐	Slowing or Stopping		☐	☐	Starting from parked position
	☐	☐	Overtaking		☐	☐	Making left turn		☐	☐	Changing lanes		☐	☐	Stopped or parked
													☐	☐	Other (explain above)

*WHAT PEDESTRIAN WAS DOING

PEDESTRIAN was going ☐ ☐ ☐ ☐   ☐ Along   Color of Clothing
N S E W   ☐ Across or into .... from .... to ....   Dark   Light

☐ Crossing at Intersection	☐ Stepped into path of Vehicle	☐ Getting on or off Vehicle	☐ Playing in roadway
☐ Crossing not at Intersection	☐ Standing in roadway	☐ Hitching on Vehicle	☐ Other roadway
☐ Walking in roadway – with traffic	☐ Standing in safety zone	☐ Pushing or working on Vehicle	☐ Not in roadway
☐ Walking in roadway – against traffic	☐ Lying or Sitting on roadway	☐ Other working in roadway	☐ Other (explain above)

DRIVERS AND VEHICLES

	VEHICLE 1	VEHICLE 2
PHYSICAL DEFECTS (Driver)		
	NONE	
VEHICLE DEFECTS		
CONTRIBUTING CIRCUMSTANCES		

ACCIDENT Characteristics	LIGHTING CONDITION	Dusk	ROAD DEFECTS	None	TRAFFICWAY CHARACTER	Level	CLASS OF TRAFFICWAYS	Local
	WEATHER	Clear	TRAFFIC CONTROL	Stop sign	TRAFFICWAY LANES	4	TYPE TRAFFICWAY	Undivi
	ROAD SURFACE	Dry	TYPE LOCATION	6	VISION OBSCURED	No		

WITNESSES other than occupants

NAME None   ADDRESS – Number and street   City and State

FIRST AID GIVEN BY   ☐ Doctor or Nurse   ☐ Cert. First Aider
                                       ☐ Cert. First Aider (Police)   ☐ Other (Explain)

CHEMICAL TEST:		TEST RESULTS:
	YES NO	
Driver No. 1	☐ ☐	
Driver No. 2	☐ ☐	

INJURED TAKEN TO Memorial Hospital   BY: ☒ Priv. Ambulance ☐ Other (Explain)
                                              ☐ Gov't. Ambulance

ARREST

NAME Fred Johansen   CHARGE Failure to stop for stop sign   Citation No. #641832
NAME   CHARGE   Citation No.

PHOTOGRAPHS TAKEN
☒ Yes ☐ No
☒ Agency
☐ Other (Explain)

TIME NOTIFIED OF ACCIDENT	TIME ARRIVED AT SCENE	WAS INVESTIGATION MADE AT SCENE (If not where)	IS INVESTIGATION COMPLETE (If not why)
197:48 P.M	7:53 P.M	Yes	Yes

LAST WILL AND TESTAMENT
OF
JONATHAN WILBURT CULBERTSON

I, Jonathan Wilburt Culbertson, being of sound and disposing mind and memory, do hereby make, publish, and declare this instrument to be my Last Will and Testament, hereby revoking any and all previous Wills and Codicils which may have been executed by me.

1. I direct that my Executor, the law firm of Green, Dawson and Genik, pay all my legal obligations as soon after my demise as may conveniently be done.

2. My loving wife, Marsha, shall be given full title to our home and two automobiles. She also shall receive all my personal property and the entire amount contained in our savings account at the First National Bank, an amount in the sum of approximately $80,000.

3. Further, upon my death, my property, consisting of the Blackhawk Hotel and the Jonathan Motor Inn, shall be sold to the highest bidder, and all but $100,000 of the proceeds shall be invested in bonds issued by the United States Government. The interest from these bonds shall go directly to my wife, Marsha.

4. I direct that $50,000 of the sum set aside from the sale of my property be given to my secretary for these past twenty years, Sally Wiscoff, with any and all inheritance taxes on the aforementioned sum paid by my estate. Further, my executor is to give Miss Wiscoff any help and advice she requests in investing the money.

5. Another $50,000 shall be given to Robert J. Rawle, with the understanding that he diligently care for my two hunting dogs for the remainder of their lives and provide them with (a) weekly grooming, (b) twice yearly physical examinations from my regular veterinarian, (c) freedom to roam his farm at will and (d) whatever diet and medical treatment are prescribed by the veterinarian.

6. The sum of $1 shall be left to my only child, Jonathan Wilburt Culbertson, Junior, who has proven on occasions too numerous to mention that he is incapable of handling any larger amount wisely.

7. Upon the death of my wife, or if she precedes me in death, the sum of $25,000 shall be given to each of my nieces and nephews alive at that moment, and the residue of my estate shall be placed in trust with the State, and the interest earned upon it every year shall be used as a scholarship fund for worthy students who were born and raised in this State and who plan to continue their studies at any state-run college, university or junior college within this State.

IN WITNESS WHEREOF, I have hereunto set my hand and seal, this 6th day of August, 1964.

Jonathan Wilburt Culbertson
Jonathan Wilburt Culbertson

LAST WILL AND TESTAMENT
OF
PAUL HALSTON TAYLOR

I, Paul Halston Taylor, being of sound and disposing mind and memory, do hereby make, publish and declare this instrument to be my Last Will and Testament, hereby revoking any and all previous Wills and Codicils which may have been executed by me.

1. I direct that my Executor, hereinafter named, pay all my legal obligations as soon after my demise as may conveniently be done.

2. I give, devise and bequeath unto my only living relative, my wife, Suzanne, the sum of $250,000, our home, our automobile and all such personal belongings as she may want to keep.

3. The interest from the aforementioned sum, and income from other sources, being adequate to sustain her for the remainder of her life, I direct that the remainder of my estate, which consists of approximately $400,000 in cash and bonds, be given to the Boy Scouts of America, provided the organization meet the following stipulations.

   (a) The money shall be used to buy land and to construct a Boy Scout camp within the boundaries of this State.

   (b) The Boy Scouts of America must purchase the land within two years and complete construction of the camp within five years. Should the Boy Scouts of America fail to do so, the money will revert to the estate and I direct my Executor to give the money to the city for the purchase of a park, to be known as "Taylor Park."

   (c) The camp shall be known as "Taylor Camp."

   (d) At least $25,000 shall be set aside in a special fund, to be administered by the First National Bank, and interest derived from the fund shall be used to provide scholarships to enable needy youths to attend the camp.

   (e) Should the Boy Scouts of America ever cease to use the camp, the land shall be sold and the proceeds from the sale (1) be used to purchase land for a comparable 'camp or (2) be given to the city for the creation of a park, to be known as "Taylor Park."

4. I nominate my wife, Suzanne Taylor, as Executor of this, my Last Will and Testament, and direct that no security be required on her official bond as such Executor, or upon any additional bond given for sale of property or for any other purpose in the course of the administration of my estate.

IN WITNESS WHEREOF, I have hereunto set my hand and seal, this 14th day of September, 1973.

Paul Halston Taylor
Paul Halston Taylor

Jay R. Ralston
    Office: 691 Apple Boulevard
    Telephone: 879-2662

Attorney for Plaintiff

Mary Ellen Wycoff,
                    Plaintiff,

            vs.

Andrew Ernest Wycoff,
                    Defendant.

COMPLAINT FOR DIVORCE

Plaintiff alleges:

I

Plaintiff and defendant intermarried on June 1, 1963, and ever since have been and now are husband and wife.

II

Plaintiff is, and has been, a resident of the State for more than one year, and of the County therein for more than three months, next preceding the commencement of this action.

III

The statistical facts required by section 426a of the State Code of Civil Procedure and other facts alleged for the purpose of this Complaint are:
1. Place of marriage: San Francisco, California.
2. Date of marriage: June 1, 1963.
3. Date of separation: January 3 of this year.
4. Number of children from said marriage: six.

IV

Since the marriage of the parties hereto, defendant has treated plaintiff with extreme cruelty and has wrongfully inflicted on plaintiff grievous mental suffering.

V

WHEREFORE, plaintiff prays:

1. That plaintiff be granted a divorce from defendant.
2. The plaintiff be granted custody of their six children.
3. That plaintiff be granted full title to the family residence at 923 Riverview Drive.
4. That plaintiff be granted the immediate sum of $500,000 for her interests in the Wycoff Corporation, a manufacturer of plastics jointly owned heretofore by plaintiff and defendant.
5. That, so plaintiff may continue the style of life to which she has grown accustomed, said plaintiff be granted alimony in the amount of $2,500 each month; child support in the amount of $200 for each child per month; salary for the payment of the family housekeeper in the amount of $350 per month; and monies for the livery of the family's horses in the amount of $60 per month.
6. That plaintiff also be granted full title to a new Buick automobile, used exclusively by her heretofore.

7. For such other and further relief as this court may deem proper and equitable.

By   *J. R Ralston*
                Jay R. Ralston
                Attorney for Plaintiff

VERIFICATION

I am a party to the above-entitled matter; the foregoing document is true of my own knowledge, except as to the matters which are therein stated on my information or belief, and as to those matters I believe to be true.

I declare under penalty of perjury that the foregoing is true and correct.

Mary Ellen Wycoff

Mary Ellen Wycoff
Plaintiff

First National Bank,	
	Plaintiff,
vs.	
Ralph John Fritz,	
	Defendant.

COMPLAINT

File #18462833

Plaintiff, for its complaint, alleges:

FIRST: At all times hereinafter mentioned, plaintiff was and still is a domestic banking corporation.

SECOND: On or about March 14, 1969, defendant, in order to induce the plaintiff to loan money and extend credit to him, gave plaintiff a written statement of his then financial condition.

THIRD: In said written statement, defendant stated and represented that he was not obligated to any other creditors.

FOURTH: Said financial statement and the representations contained therein were false, were known by defendant to be false and were made with the knowledge that plaintiff would rely on them, with the intent to deceive and defraud plaintiff and to induce plaintiff to loan money to defendant.

FIFTH: In truth, at the time such statement was given and such representations were made to plaintiff, defendant was obligated to other creditors in a large amount.

SIXTH: Plaintiff, at the time of receiving said statement made by defendant, did not know the truth, but believed said statement and representations to be true, relied upon them, and was thereby induced to loan money and extend credit to defendant on March 14, 1969, in the sum of $8,000.

SEVENTH: No part of said sum or interest thereon has been paid, although duly demanded, and there is now due and owing to plaintiff the sum of $8,000 with interest from March 14, 1969.

WHEREFORE, Plaintiff demands judgment against defendant in the sum of $8,000, with interest from March 14, 1969, together with costs and disbursements of this action, a total as of this date of $9,781.

Paul Baylor

Paul Baylor
Attorney for Plaintiff
691 Apple Boulevard
Telephone: 879-2662

```
-------------------------------------------------
Roger C. Hulick,

            Plaintiff,

      vs.

Richard Wiese,

            Defendant.
-------------------------------------------------
```

Case No. 84428

PLAINTIFF DEMANDS JURY TRIAL

COMPLAINT AT LAW

NOW COMES THE PLAINTIFF by Albert Green, his attorney, and complains of the defendant as follows:

1. On February 13, 1973, plaintiff purchased a home located at the address of 4213 Blueberry Lane from the defendant. Plaintiff paid the defendant the sum of $42,800 for the property.

2. Plaintiff made the aforementioned payment in the belief that certain representations made by the defendant were true and accurate and, in the absence of such representations, would have refrained from purchasing said property.

3. Plaintiff subsequently has determined that certain of the representations made by defendant to the effect that the house was in good condition and fully habitable were untrue and false.

4. Plaintiff further declares that:
   (a) Plaintiff was told that the house was three years old, whereas evidence now in his possession conclusively proves that the house actually is fourteen years old.
   (b) Land surrounding the house is zoned G4 (light industrial), not R2 (single-family residential) as represented by defendant at the time of the transaction.
   (c) Rugs, drapes, stove, refrigerator, as well as certain shrubs and other garden plants, were absent when plaintiff occupied the house, despite promises by defendant to include said items with the purchase.
   (d) Further, bills incurred by defendant to prepare the home for sale have not yet been paid, and painting and construction companies have placed liens in the total amount of $1,487.15 against the house.

WHEREFORE, due to such calculated and deliberate misrepresentations, plaintiff Roger C. Hulick asks the court to declare the contract transferring the property from defendant Richard Wiese to himself be declared null and void; that defendant be ordered to return the entire $42,800 paid for the property; and that defendant be ordered to award plaintiff an additional $20,000 due to the anguish and inconvenience caused by the misrepresentations.

Albert Green
Albert Green
Attorney for Plaintiff
841 Hollydale Lane
Telephone: 871-9438

Mildred Anne Talbot,
              Plaintiff,

    vs.

George Raymond Hebert,
              Defendant.

Case No. 84429

PLAINTIFF DEMANDS JURY TRIAL

COMPLAINT AT LAW

NOW COMES THE PLAINTIFF by Paul Baylor, her attorney, and complains of the defendant as follows:

1. On November 23 of last year, plaintiff was driving her automobile south along Main Street in a safe and cautious manner, fully obeying all laws concerning use of said vehicle.

2. On said date, plaintiff stopped for a red semaphore at the intersection of Main Street and Georgia Avenue, then proceeded forward in a cautious and responsible manner when the light turned green.

3. At said time and place defendant:

   (a) With a conscious indifference to surrounding circumstances and conditions, willfully and wantonly drove his said motor vehicle.

   (b) Failed to yield the right-of-way and proceeded into the intersection, failing to heed a semaphore which was red.

   (c) Drove his vehicle into the side of the motor vehicle driven by plaintiff.

4. That by reason of the foregoing, plaintiff suffered serious and permanent injuries that have caused her terrible pain and suffering. It is further stated that:

   (a) Plaintiff has lost all sight in her left eye.

   (b) Because of injuries suffered in the accident, plaintiff's left leg has been shortened by two inches, and she must walk with a permanent limp and with the aid of mechanical devices.

   (c) Plaintiff remained confined to a hospital for a period of eighty-four days directly as a result of the accident.

   (d) Plaintiff suffered grievous pain and incurred bills in excess of $10,000 and antici- pates that medical expenses will continue throughout her life.

WHEREFORE, plaintiff Mildred Anne Talbot asks judgment against defendant George Raymond Hebert for Three Hundred Thousand Dollars ($300,000).

Paul Baylor
_____
Paul Baylor
Attorney for Plaintiff
691 Apple Boulevard
Telephone: 879-2662

GENERAL RELEASE

KNOW ALL MEN BY THESE PRESENTS, THAT _____Mildred Anne Talbot_____

for and in consideration of the sum of _— —Eighty-two Thousand and no/100ths_____

Dollars ($82,000) in lawful money of the United States of America paid to

_____her_____ by __Safeco Insurance Company_____

on behalf of George Raymond Hebert

has remised, released and forever discharged, and, by these Presents, does, for _____

_____herself_____, _____her_____ heirs, executors

and administrators, remise, release and forever discharge the said _____

Safeco Insurance Company representing George Raymond Hebert

of and from all manner of actions, cause and causes of action, suits, debts, sums of money, accounts, reckonings, bonds, bills, specialties, covenants, controversies, agreements, promises, variances, trespasses, damages, judgments, executions, claims and demands whatsoever in law or in equity, and particularly without limiting the generality of the foregoing, for personal injury arising out of accident occurring at the corner of Main Street and Georgia Avenue on November 23 of last year,

which _____she_____ now has _____against it_____ or ever had, or which _____her_____ heirs, executors or administrators, hereafter can, shall or may have, for, upon or by reason of any matter, cause or thing, whatsoever, at any time prior to the date of these Presents.

Mildred Anne Talbot

Mildred Anne Talbot

VOLUNTARY PETITION IN BANKRUPTCY

To The Honorable Judges of the Southern District Court of the United States

THE PETITION of Arthur Robert Stein of 3241 Broadway, engaged by occupation as a teacher, and employed by the City.

RESPECTFULLY REPRESENTS:

I

That petitioner has not been known nor has he conducted business under any assumed, trade or other name or designation other than as above set forth, within six years next preceding the filing of this petition in bankruptcy.

II

That he has had his principal place of residence at 3241 Broadway within said Judicial District for the longer portion of the six months immediately preceding the filing of this petition, than in any other Judicial District. That he owes debts and is willing to surrender all his property for the benefit of his creditors except such as is exempt by law, and desires to obtain the benefit of the Bankruptcy Act.

III

That the schedule hereto annexed, marked A, and verified by your petitioner's oath, contains a full and true statement of all his debts, and the names and residences or places of business of all his creditors, and such further statements concerning said debts as are required by the provisions of said Act.

That the schedule hereto annexed, marked B, and verified by your petitioner's oath, contains an accurate inventory of all his property, both real and personal, and such further statements concerning said property as are required by the provisions of said Act.

WHEREFORE, your petitioner prays that he may be adjudged by the Court to be a bankrupt within the purview of said Act.

_____
Arthur Robert Stein
Petitioner

Albert Green
Attorney for Petitioner
841 Hollydale Lane
Telephone: 871-9438

_____
Attorney for Petitioner

FINANCIAL SCHEDULE

A.

DESCRIPTION OF ASSETS AND LOCATION OF PHYSICAL ASSETS

1. Cash in the amount of $14.91 in a checking account at Security National Bank, 892 Main Street.
2. Cash in the amount of $2.14 in a savings account at the Security National Bank, 892 Main Street.
3. A 1968 Ford automobile valued at $400 being held at Bryant Ford, 5800 North Cleveland Avenue.
4. Miscellaneous furniture and other household items valued at $250 in an apartment located at 3241 Broadway.

Total Assets: $667.05

B.

LIST OF CREDITORS

1. King Loan Company, 432 Alton Street, an unsecured loan of $300.
2. County Educators' Credit Union, an unsecured loan of $550.
3. Jiffy Loans, an unsecured loan of $800.
4. Bryant Ford, 5800 North Cleveland Avenue, $210.
5. Memorial Hospital, 3100 Eisenhower Drive, $3,146.19.
6. Dr. Alton Smythe, 1032 Eisenhower Drive, $419.12.
7. Dr. Earl Bruhn, 4832 Jamestown Drive, $147.
8. Medical Supply House, 434 Main Street, $82.99.
9. Jansen's Drug Store, 48 Smith Court, $73.11.
10. Meadowglory Milk, 2914 Nela Avenue, $282.05.
11. Empire Gas Co., 2115 Central Boulevard, $38.64.
12. Bell Telephone Company, 703 Broadway, $23.86.
13. Semoran Apartments, $125.00.
14. Emery's Department Store, 973 Main Street, $839.87.
15. Snell Boats, 8413 Riverview Drive, $3,645 (boat has been repossessed).
16. Sonny's Television, 4 Dillard Street, $423.10.
17. Quality Stereo, 325 South Highland Boulevard, $382.19.

Total Debts: $11,488.12

Feature Stories

As we have seen, news stories *inform* readers about *new* topics (often events) that occur in *their* communities and that are *important, unusual* and *relevant* to readers' lives. Feature stories, on the other hand, need only interest or entertain readers. They may describe a person, place or idea rather than an event. Their topics may be old, distant, insignificant and not directly relevant to readers' lives, rather than new, local, important and relevant. So, though feature stories involve an infinite variety of topics and styles of writing, they do have one common characteristic: they must interest readers. For that reason, they are also known as "human interest stories."

In addition, feature stories share two characteristics with news stories: they must be factual and original. Feature stories are not a form of fiction, they must be based on facts. Moreover, reporters must personally gather the facts for their feature stories. They cannot merely rewrite stories that have already been published elsewhere. Those who do so may be guilty of plagiarism.

Often the same set of facts can be used to write either a news story or a feature story; the reporter must then decide which type of story is more appropriate. The following stories are written as both news stories and feature stories. The news stories begin with a summary lead, are more concise and are perhaps easier to write. The feature stories rely more on quotation and description; the writing is more informal, subjective and experimental. Essentially, the news stories inform; the feature stories entertain.

News Story

Two cars suffered extensive damage yesterday when a young girl misunderstood some instructions and rammed her car into the back of another vehicle at 30 m.p.h.

The incident occurred when a motorist on State Route 72 signaled for help after his car stalled on the highway.

When the girl stopped and asked

Feature Story

"Can I help?" the young girl asked.

"You sure can," the man replied. His new car had stalled amid the heavy traffic on State Route 72 yesterday afternoon. He struggled for 45 minutes to restart his car's engine. Then, tired and disgusted, he tied a white hankerchief to the car door and waited for someone to stop and help.

A girl driving a faded blue sedan drove up moments later.

"What can I do?" she asked. "Want me to get a tow truck?"

whether she could help, the motorist asked her to push his car at about 30 m.p.h. to restart its engine.

The girl backed up, then sped forward at precisely 30 m.p.h. and drove into the rear of the stalled vehicle.

Neither driver was injured, but both cars had to be towed away.

"No, this has happened before. The car should start if you'll push it at about 30 m.p.h.," the motorist replied.

"OK, I'll do that," the girl nodded. She waited for other traffic to pass, then carefully backed up on the shoulder of the road for about 100 yards.

Shifting into drive, she stepped on the gas until she was going precisely 30 m.p.h. and drove into the rear of the stalled vehicle.

Neither driver was injured, but both cars had to be towed away.

News Story

The telephone directory contains two listings for "S. Claus," and both Claus families receive dozens of calls each year from children who want to talk to Santa.

Mrs. Sidney Claus of 2102 Erie Ave. and Mrs. Samuel Claus of 341 Jamestown Drive say they usually listen to young children whom they believe are sincere, but are bothered when older children call them as a joke.

Young children usually ask whether they can speak to Santa, then tell him what they want for Christmas.

If their husbands are not home, the women say Santa is out feeding his reindeer or working in his toy factory.

The Claus children also enjoy answering the telephone. They tell callers they are Santa's elves.

Feature Story

"I'm sorry, but Santa is out feeding his reindeer," Mrs. Claus of 2102 Erie Ave. told a young boy who called her home last night.

Mrs. Claus of 341 Jamestown Drive recently told another boy that her husband was busy working in his toy factory.

The boy then asked whether she was Mrs. Claus. When she replied "Yes," he began to question her.

"Do you have any snow there?" he asked. "How's Rudolph? Will Rudolph pull the sleigh again this year? My mother says I can leave some carrots for him."

Two families named "S. Claus" are listed in the telephone directory, and both have received dozens of telephone calls from children who want to talk to Santa.

Mrs. Sidney Claus of 2102 Erie Ave. said she and her husband talk to the children "if we can tell by their voices that they're small." She explained, "The trouble is, older children sometimes call, and they make a mockery of it."

She said most children just want to know if Santa is there. If her husband isn't home, Mrs. Claus tells children he is out feeding his reindeer.

Mrs. Samuel Claus of 341 Jamestown Drive said she receives several calls every December.

She added, "At first I just told the children this wasn't Santa's house and then hung up, but later I thought it would be fun to go along with them just to hear what they'd say. It's surprising how some of them will just keep talking.

"They usually ask whether they can speak to Santa, and then I'll get my husband. They tell him everything they want for Christmas.

"Our three children are all teenagers, and sometimes they answer the telephone and say they're Santa's elves. They love to listen and find out what the callers want."

Selecting an appropriate topic is the most crucial aspect of writing a good feature story. If a reporter selects a bad topic, he or she must work twice as hard to make the story interesting. Ideally, a feature story should be dramatic, humorous or fresh enough to interest every reader. You may, of course, write a feature story about a topic that has been written about before, but you must then approach the topic from a new point of view or emphasize new developments or angles. The most common types of feature stories are described below.

Profiles

Profiles describe interesting, colorful and unusual persons. Subjects might be persons who have overcome a handicap, achieved success, pursued an unusual career or become prominent. A good profile must do more than list a person's achievements; it must quote the person and describe him and his environment. A profile should be so revealing that readers should feel as if they actually know the subject. Reporters can obtain information for a profile by interviewing not only the subject but also relatives, friends, business associates and other acquaintances of the subject.

Adventure Stories

An adventure story describes an unusual or exciting experience. It might report the experiences of someone who survived an airplane crash, climbed a mountain, sailed around the world, joined the Peace Corps or moved to Sweden to evade the draft. In this type of feature story, too, quotes and descriptions are especially important.

Historical Stories

Newspapers publish historical feature stories about the anniversary of a famous person's birth or death, about persons celebrating their 50th wedding anniversaries or 100th birthdays or about some other noteworthy and presumably interesting date. A historical story might also commemorate the date of an important event, such as the attack on Pearl Harbor, the bombing of Hiroshima or the assassination of President John F. Kennedy. A sample introduction to a historical story is the following, which was distributed by the North American Newspaper Alliance:

> The project was so supersecret that the trim fighter plane had a dummy propeller fastened to its nose so spies wouldn't suspect that America was developing a new aircraft propulsion system.
> This was the Bell P59A Airacomet, first jet-propelled airplane ever built in the United States.
> . . . Only 30 years ago today, Bell test pilot Robert Stanley climbed into the ship and made the first jet flight in America.

Historical features can be tied to current events that generate interest in their topics. If a tornado, flood or earthquake struck your community, the local newspaper might publish a feature story about earlier disasters. When President Kennedy was assassinated, newspapers published stories about the assassinations of Presidents Lincoln and McKinley. When American prisoners returned from North Vietnam, newspapers published feature stories about the prisoners who returned after World War II and the Korean War.

Topics for historical features abound on college campuses. For example, if a professor retires after 30 years, you might ask him to describe changes in the campus and its students during his teaching career. Other historical features might examine what effect the end of American troop involvement in Vietnam and the end of the draft have had on enrollment in your college, whether 18-year-olds are exercising the right to vote and how the Supreme Court ruling on abortion has affected your college and community.

Seasonal Stories

Reporters are often assigned to write feature stories about Christmas, Easter, St. Patrick's Day, Friday the 13th, the first day of spring and other holidays and seasons. Such stories are difficult to write because in order to make them interesting, reporters must come up with a fresh angle that has not been used before.

Explanatory Stories

Explanatory stories may examine almost any topic of widespread interest. They are sometimes called "local situation" or "interpretive" stories. They may explain a particular organization, activity, trend or idea. For example, an explanatory feature might go beyond a superficial story about a demonstration by a political or racial group and describe the group in detail: its members, goals, activities and significance. Other explanatory features might examine the changing role of downtown business districts, the impact of growth on the community, new trends in education, the effects of rising prices and the use of mass transport systems.

Sidebars

Reporters occasionally write feature stories to supplement news stories about the same topic. Such features are called "sidebars" or "color stories." In essence, a sidebar provides more color and description than the related news story. Often it describes the scene of an event or the role and reactions of an individual involved in the news. For example, if an airplane crashed into an apartment complex, newspapers would immediately publish a news story reporting the cause of the accident, the number of persons killed and the amount of damage, and might also publish a separate color story describing the scene of the accident: burning wreckage, shattered building, rescue operations and fascinated crowd. For a later sidebar, a reporter might interview survivors and ask them to describe themselves, the flight, the crash, the turmoil aboard the airplane and their rescue.

How-to-Do-It Stories

How-to-do-it stories tell readers how to perform some task: buy a house, get a date, tour Europe, obtain an abortion, succeed in college, save money and so on. Such stories are often shorter than other types of features and are difficult to write clearly and concisely. Inexperienced reporters tend to preach or dictate to readers in lieu of consulting expert sources and providing detailed, factual advice.

You can find appropriate topics for feature stories by being observant: by carefully listening, looking and thinking. For example, one student majoring in home economics became intrigued by the use of soybean products as an inexpensive substitute for meat, and she wrote an excellent feature story about it. The topic was ideal because it involved two subjects that affect every reader: food and money. Moreover, the topic was new; the media had not yet reported it in detail. Another student noticed several blind students on his campus and wrote a feature story about their problems. Other students have written about thefts from their campus library, abortions, drugs, millionaires, elderly persons, unwed fathers and venereal diseases.

Because people are most interested in reading about other people, you should stress the involvement of people in your stories. You should name, quote and describe people and show how your topic affects people or how people affect your topic.

After selecting a topic, you must limit it; you must decide what single individual, theme or episode is most important and focus on it. For example, a profile should be limited to one aspect of the subject's life: one experience, one trait or one success. If you do not limit your topic to a single aspect, your story will lack unity. Readers will be unable to determine the meaning and purpose of the story. It will meander from one point to the next without clarifying each point's significance and relationship to the whole.

You should consult at least four or five sources of information in order to obtain a well-rounded, detailed picture of your topic. Before you begin to write, you should gather at least twice as much information as you need for the story; you can then select the most interesting and colorful details from this material.

The lead is a critical segment of a feature story. It must immediately capture the attention of readers and make them want to continue reading the story. It must also reveal the story's theme and suggest how that theme will be treated. It should not exaggerate, mislead or sensationalize. Feature stories, like most news stories, may begin with a summary lead. They may also begin with a quotation, an anecdote, a question, an action, a description, a shocking fact or a combination of these. Following are examples of the various types of feature story leads.

Summaries

Twenty youths plan their own curriculum and live and work at Freedom House School. The students are all from welfare families and most have police records.

Soviet-born Raisa Kisilnikova, who defected to Mexico while working for the Soviet embassy in Mexico City, has found happiness as a secretary in an advertising agency.
(Reprinted by permission of United Press International)

Quotations

"My husband died of a heart attack," said Mrs. H. "I don't know what was wrong with me after that. I lost a few years of my life somewhere. I can't remember. Maybe I don't want to."

"When it hit me, I was unconscious for three days, and when I came to I couldn't remember a thing. I asked my boy what happened, and he told me, 'You were hit by lightning.' "
(Orlando, Fla., "Sentinel Star")

Anecdotes

Dr. Thomas Strewl seems more enthusiastic about England—its tradition and its heritage—than any other person on campus. For example, his secretary said, "Whenever he goes over to England, he sends us a card addressed to 'The Colonies' and not the 'United States.' "

The firemen said few women are prepared to fight fires in their homes. When grease began to burn in a skillet, one woman picked up the skillet and ran toward the front door. She fell in the living room, spilling the burning liquid over the rug and furniture.

What is cable television?

What happens to letters that mailmen are unable to deliver?

Action

The Japanese airplanes dropped their first bombs just forward of the bridge, shattering the U.S. gunboat's only anti-aircraft gun and sending shrapnel into its radio room.

Visibility was unlimited as the single-engine Cessna sped westward, climbing to 10,500 feet as it approached the snow-capped Sierra, a rugged mountain range that separates Nevada and California.

Then the airplane's motor stopped: suddenly, completely, without warning.

"After all these years of flying I'm going to crash," the pilot thought. "And it's going to happen at the worst spot in the United States and at the worst time of year—midwinter in the High Sierra."

Description

Pancho is a short, dark-skinned, curly-haired 20-year-old with flashing black eyes, a bouncing step and a Spanish accent.

Neighbors say the frail and gray-haired woman rarely goes out of the house and sometimes refuses to come to the door or answer the telephone.

Occasionally, struggling with a garden hose, she waters her yellow-green lawn on one of Southern California's hot summer days. Once in awhile she beats out a rug on the porch.

But mostly she sits alone inside the old white frame two-story house, her only fellowship the company of two of her five bachelor sons.

One of her sons is Sirhan B. Sirhan, 28, under life sentence at San Quentin Prison for assassinating Sen. Robert F. Kennedy. (The Associated Press)

Shockers

Within the lifetime of today's people, humans may be in touch with beings on other worlds. ("The Christian Science Monitor")

Some personal secrets can kill you.

Therefore many people are making them public. They include such personages as Andy Devine, actor; Joan Fontaine and Dorothy Malone, actresses; Peter Nero, pianist; Dan Rowan, television performer; Billy Casper, golfer; Billy Talbert, tennis star. (The Associated Press)

(The story went on to explain that all these people wear Medic-Alert bracelets or necklaces that warn of serious medical problems.)

They leave at the rate of 40 per day. Who are they? They are the dissatisfied, disappointed and disillusioned employes at Walt Disney World.

She is 86 years old, but she doesn't like to admit it. "It's like admitting defeat," Martha says. She wonders, "Why does growing old have to be such a hardship?"

Like the lead, the body of a feature story can take a number of forms. The inverted pyramid style may be most appropriate for some stories, and chronological order for others. In still other cases, the writer may find it best to state the main theme, then offer facts to support and explain that theme. Regardless of the form you decide on and the style of writing you adopt, your feature story must be coherent. All the facts must fit together smoothly and logically. Transitions must guide readers from one segment of the story to the next and clearly reveal the relationship between those segments. You should also make your feature stories detailed and colorful by using quotations, dialogue, anecdotes, descriptions and examples.

Quotations and dialogue provide more color than a flat summary of the facts. They can also be used to introduce new characters, to break up long factual passages and to support generalizations. For example, instead of merely stating that "President Calvin Coolidge was a taciturn man," it would be better to reveal that fact by quoting Coolidge himself:

A woman meeting President Coolidge for the first time said to him, "My friends bet that I couldn't get you to say three words."
The President replied, "You lose."

Dialogue can also be used to reveal such important elements as time, place, circumstances and theme:

"Hi, Charley! How many days do you have left?" a woman asked as she entered the small grocery store at 2636 Brady St.
"Until Jan. 1. We're selling out, you know," replied Charles Foss, who started selling groceries 56 years ago.

Description—what the reporter sees, feels, smells and tastes, as well as what he hears—is an equally valuable means of providing color and detail.

Anecdotes are short and, often, humorous stories. Like quotations, they can illustrate a point, reveal character or supply interesting details. They also help sustain readers' interest in the story. To be most effective, anecdotes should be specific, mentioning names, times and places.

You should use examples to illustrate statistics and abstract ideas; otherwise, you may bore and confuse readers. If actual examples are not available or are too complex, you may use hypothetical examples, but you must clearly indicate that they are hypothetical.

You can use examples, anecdotes, quotations and dialogue to indicate that a previously stated generalization is accurate, or you may present them first, then draw a conclusion from them. In either case, the generalization becomes more credible when it is accompanied by solid evidence.

You should not attempt to persuade or advocate in a feature story, but you can report your own emotions and impressions and make reasonable judgments, as in the following feature leads:

Julie is a 19-year-old college student. Two years ago she made a decision that could haunt her for the rest of her life: she had an abortion.

He packs a stainless steel .25 caliber pistol in the pocket of his judicial robes and stalks to the bench in pointed-toe cowboy boots.
Policemen generally adore him, defense attorneys generally hate him and defendants both fear and admire him.

> Judge Robert L. Hamilton, 31, has been Municipal Court judge for less than five
> months, but he has carved a reputation as a flamboyant and fearsome judge.
>
> (Orlando, Fla., "Sentinel Star")

These leads do more than report facts; they draw certain conclusions about those facts. The conclusions are reasonable, supported by evidence presented later in the stories.

News stories are usually written in the third person, with the reporter as a neutral observer or outsider. Feature stories, however, can be written in the first person, with the reporter himself appearing in the story, and in the second person, with the reporter addressing readers directly. At times the styles can be extremely effective. Note the following lead for a feature story in which a young woman describes the attempt of herself and her three companions to swim ashore after their boat sank in a storm about two miles from the coast of California:

> It felt like an endless battle. I paddled as hard as I could but thought we'd never
> reach shore. My arms ached and Jip's legs were numb. All I wanted was to be warm again.
> Every time a wave splashed over us the chill ran through our bodies.
>   It was horrible, not really knowing if we were going to make it to shore or if we
> should stop trying because we were going to drown anyway.

It is tempting to write about your own experiences because it seems easy: you do not have to interview anyone, dig for information or do any other research. But you should use the first person cautiously in your first feature stories. When describing your own experiences, you run a greater risk of selecting poor topics and dwelling upon insignificant, dull and vague generalities, as in the following feature leads:

> The clock read 6:30. I was already 30 minutes late for the fishing date. Waking up
> will never be easy for me, especially when I am to go fishing.
>   I have never been enthusiastic about fishing. The aversion probably began when I
> was a boy and every vacation was spent in the same fishing camp. I had decided to give
> the sport one more chance, however.

> When I entered the university library for the first time, I wanted to go to the card
> catalogue. After finally finding it on the third floor, I again was confused. It is divided
> into three sections instead of one conglomerate catalogue.

> During the summer, 20 ardent cyclists (I among them) biked through 300 miles of
> the Canadian Rockies. In the course of our journey, we encountered many exciting ex-
> periences.

As for the conclusion of a feature story, some writers say that features should end like news stories, by reporting the last solid chunk of information. Other writers, particularly those who work for magazines rather than newspapers, say that a feature story should end with a conclusion that "satisfies" readers, perhaps with a quote or an anecdote or a key word or phrase that is repeated in some surprising or meaningful way. In any case, you should avoid ending a feature story with a summary. Summary endings are almost always flat, boring and obvious.

You should slant your feature stories for particular newspapers or magazines and submit them to those publications. If the stories are accepted, you will receive your first professional byline and perhaps your first check. You will probably find it easiest to sell your stories to newspapers, particularly Sunday supplements, and to small magazines, which do not receive as many manuscripts and may be less demanding. A useful guide is "Writer's Market," which is published annually and describes the types of stories sought by most magazines and Sunday newspapers in the United States.

FEATURE STORIES: EXERCISE 1

INSTRUCTIONS: Evaluate the following feature leads. Are they effective? Why or why not? (If they are not, your instructor may ask you to rewrite them.)

1. David, 44, was learning to write his name. Karen, 7, repeatedly practiced buttoning her sweater. Despite the difference in their ages, they have a common plight. Both are mentally retarded.

2. Sgt. David Blaren's first and favorite assignment was at Fort Meade, Md., where he was a member of the color guard at all Washington Redskins home football games. Between Fort Meade and his current assignment were 11 busy years in the U.S. Army.
   The 5-foot-11 Blaren, now 28, enlisted at the age of 17.

3. It's a typical small town. For kicks, people go to the carwash to watch the chrome rust. When the carwash is closed, they tramp out to the fields to watch rabbits race.

4. In the past few months a new service has become available in this area. That service is cable television.

5. A group of Californians, hoping to reduce the number of suicides, which some experts believe claim more lives than automobile accidents, is offering "love, concern and a sympathetic audience" for persons intent on destroying themselves.

6. Almost 18,600 students are enrolled in the city's public schools, but 26 of them never leave home.
   The 26 students are unable to attend school because of accidents and illnesses. They are tutored by three teachers from the school system's Home Instruction Department.

7. He is a college student, a composer and an accomplished guitarist. He is also a good conversationalist.

8. Few college students today seem to be concerned with the old adage, "You are what you eat."

9. The advent of modern refrigeration systems has all but eliminated the ice delivery man of 30 years ago from the American scene.

10. The concept of "night watchman" has been redefined.

11. An alcoholic doesn't want to drink, but he cannot help himself. What can he do? Who can he turn to?

12. "As I passed the Statue of Liberty, I got a cold chill. For the first time I felt I was really alone."
    Henry H. Sleczkowski, 60, came to the United States in 1930 to start a new life. He had no idea he would be so successful.

13. A 19-year-old coed has an interesting, if not unusual job.

14. "Mommy, am I an American boy now?" a 4-year-old Cuban child asked yesterday.
    Julio Lopez and his twin brother, José, were among 31 persons who became American citizens during ceremonies in U.S. District Court.

15. Garbage, garbage everywhere, and not an end in sight.

16. Last Thursday marked the first anniversary of the "Turn in a Pusher" (TIP) program. TIP was established by the Chamber of Commerce to aid local law enforcement agencies in the control of hard drugs.

17.　　Twenty-two-year-old Ralph Stimpson said, "I'll try anything once." And he proved it—first by taking drugs and then by turning to Christ.

18.　　Tractors filled the yard as dozens of farmers, most dressed in light denim jackets and trousers, helped harvest 155 acres of corn on the Victor Stalling farm 18 miles northwest of here.
　　"This is the custom around here," explained one of the farmers. "If somebody dies or has an accident, everyone pitches in to help."
　　Stalling, 47, died of a heart attack 10 days ago.

19.　　The County Health Department has adopted a new approach in its fight against venereal disease.

20.　　One might scoff at the idea of anyone being cured of serious illness without medical help, but Christian Scientists claim it happens often. And they are quick to point out that they are not in the same class as quacks, frauds and charlatans.

FEATURE STORIES: EXERCISE 2

INSTRUCTIONS: First, write a straight news lead for each of the following stories. The lead should concisely summarize each story. Second, write a complete feature story for each set of facts. Be particularly careful to develop a strong feature lead.

1. An armored truck was traveling down Orange Avenue during this morning's rush hour. The truck hit a particularly bad bump, and the back door of the vehicle flew open. The truck contained approximately $5,000 in change the city had collected from parking meters. The money fell to the pavement. Several bags burst open. Police halted traffic. City workers summoned to the scene used brooms to sweep up the coins, then shoveled them back into the truck. But, before the police and other city employes arrived at the scene, hundreds of other motorists and bystanders offered to help gather the coins. When city officials later counted the money retrieved by the workers, they found they had exactly $3,810.71. The remainder apparently was stolen.

2. Manuel Dominguez is 75 years old and married. Three days ago he was admitted to Memorial Hospital. He was taken to the hospital after suffering a major heart seizure. Because he did not seem to have any money, he was placed in a charity ward. His wife was not notified of his illness and location for three days. Later, she said, "I lived in fear. I knew something was wrong but not what it was."
   The couple resides in Chicago, Illinois, and was visiting friends here. Mrs. Dominguez had remained in a motel while her husband went to a department store to buy a shirt. He suffered the heart seizure in the store's parking lot. Firemen administered artificial resuscitation, then took him to the hospital. A fire department spokesman said it was the responsibility of the police or hospital to notify Mrs. Dominguez. A police spokesman blamed the hospital and the fire department. A spokesman at the hospital said the hospital never notifies the next of kin in emergency-room cases.
   Mrs. Dominguez learned of her husband's plight when a security officer from the store contacted her and asked when somebody was going to pick up her husband's car.

3. Mrs. Kate Smyth lives at 1319 W. Princeton St. She has a granddaughter who lives in Roseville, which is 14 miles from her home. Her granddaughter is 5 years old. She mailed a pumpkin to her granddaughter for Halloween, but did not wrap it. Mrs. Smyth explained, "You can mail anything as long as it's got the right postage on it. I wanted my granddaughter to have that particular pumpkin, and I know she loves to get things in the mail, just as all children do." So she pasted four 50-cent stamps to the pumpkin and a label bearing her granddaughter's address to the pumpkin. It arrived, intact, two days later.

4. Firemen received a call at 11:24 a.m. today. The call came from a service station at the corner of Geele Avenue and Pastle Road. Persons in the area had noticed a cat in a tree two days ago. It was still there today. At about 11 a.m. a 14-year-old boy climbed the tree to rescue the cat. When the boy approached the cat, the cat quickly climbed down the tree and fled. But the boy was unable to get down, and firemen were summoned to help him. To prevent any further embarrassment, firemen did not identify the youth.

5. The police in this municipality received a call at 3:45 yesterday afternoon. A woman shouted at the sergeant who answered the telephone. She said, "My son's been beaten. His teacher whipped him again this afternoon. He says she only used her hand, but he's all red where she paddled him. Can teachers do that? I want her arrested. This is the second time it's happened this month." Two police officers were sent to the home. They questioned the boy. He is 7 years old. At his mother's insistence, the police officers also inspected the boy's reported injuries. They reported, "We couldn't tell that the boy had been paddled. His fanny didn't look red to us. But we did note that his pants were wet and muddy. As we talked to the boy, it became apparent that he was lying. He finally admitted that he played in some water on the way home from school, forgot the time and got home late. He told his mother the teacher had spanked him and kept him after school. His mother was there with us and heard the whole story. She said she'd take

care of the situation, and we're quite sure that she will, as she was very embarrassed. In fact, we could hear her giving the kid a real paddling as we left."

6. Thomas J. Serle works for Parker Bros. Circus, which is in town this week. Performances are scheduled at 2 p.m. and 7:30 p.m. every day, through Sunday. Serle, who maintains a home in Fort Lauderdale, Fla., is a laborer who helps care for the animals at the circus, including 10 elephants. During a conversation with a reporter, he said, "Some people look on work with a circus as a glamorous job. It ain't. But I been doing it all my life, and it's too late for me to change. I'll be 60 next year. I was born into it. Both my folks were circus people. I started out as an acrobat until I fell and busted a leg. It never healed quite right, so they offered me this job, and I took it. What else could I do? There's all kinds of myths about circuses, like about these elephants here. Some people say they're afraid of mice, but that's a lie. When we pen the elephants up for the winter there's always mice gets in their hay, and it don't bother them none. The elephants never try to run away or kill 'em or anything. They share the same pen all winter. And then some people say elephants got a good memory. Hell, some of the ones we got can't even remember a simple trick from one year to the next."

7. The police received a call at 6:41 a.m. today. A woman had spotted a pig trotting along Iowa St. Two police officers sent to look for it were unable to find it. Two hours later, someone else spotted a pig at 800 Pershing Ave. Two officers again were sent to catch it before it caused any harm. They reported, "It was a black and white porker weighing approximately 120 pounds. We chased it west toward Brady St. and cornered it near North High School. We moved in for the capture, but the pig ran past us. Officer Roehl tried a flying tackle and knocked the pig off its feet, but it got loose again. Officer Roehl hit it with another flying tackle. This time he got a better grip on it and was able to hold on. However, he tore his jacket and trousers and bruised his elbow in the scuffle. No medical attention was required. But in view of the trouble he had capturing the pig and the price of bacon, would it be all right if he kept the pig if no one else claims it?"

FEATURE STORIES: MISCELLANEOUS EXERCISES

1. Clip 10 feature stories from newspapers and evaluate each story's topic, lead and general style of writing, particularly its organization and development of color.

2. Rewrite the introductory paragraphs of 10 news stories as feature leads.

3. Rewrite the introductory paragraphs of 10 feature stories as news leads.

4. Read and report on a magazine article or a chapter in a book that discusses free-lance writing.

5. Outline three feature stories that you might write.
   a. Explain why each topic is newsworthy.
   b. Using "Writer's Market," identify three publications that might publish each story and explain why.
   c. List at least five sources of information for each story.
   d. Describe your major themes and the methods you would use to develop those themes.
   e. Discuss the three outlines with your instructor and the other members of your class, then write the feature story they believe is most promising.
   f. Send a letter to the publication you believe is most likely to publish your story. Describe the story and ask whether the editor would like to look at it. If he reacts negatively, mail a similar letter to the second publication, and then to the third.
   g. Write up your second feature story outline and submit it for publication.

City Directory

Abbreviations

adm	administration		dispr	dispatcher
adv	advertising		dist	district
aldm	alderman		dr	drive, driver
am	American		ele	elementary
apt	apartment		eng	engineer
asst	assistant		h	home
atty	attorney		hospt	hospital
av	avenue		inc	incorporated
bd	board		ins	insurance
bkpr	bookkeeper		insptr	inspector
blvd	boulevard		jr	junior
bros	brothers		jtr	janitor
bur	bureau		la	lane
capt	captain		libr	library
ch	church		lt	lieutenant
Cir	Circle		mach	machine, machinist
clk	clerk		mech	mechanic
clns	cleaners		mgr	manager
co	company		muncp	municipal
collr	collector		ofc	office
const	construction		opr	operator
ct	court		pcpl	principal
ctr	center		phys	physician
cty	county		pkwy	parkway
D	divorced		pl	place
dent	dental, dentist		pres	president
dept	department		pstr	pastor
dir	director			

ptlm	patrolman	st	saint, street
ptr	painter	stk	steak
rd	road	studt	student
rel	relations	supvr	supervisor
retd	retired	tchr	teacher
rr	rural route	ter	terrace
schl	school	treas	treasurer
sec	secretary	vp	vice president
secy	security	w	wife
serv	service	watr	waiter
sgt	sergeant	watrs	waitress
slsm	salesman	wid	widow
soc	social	widr	widower
sr	senior	wkr	worker

Adler, Stuart (w Shela) pstr Ch of Christ, h4008 Kasper Av

Ahl, Fritz, dr Carl's Clns, h907 Romana Av

Allenson, Harold (w Dorothy) retd, h550 Central Av

Alson, George, studt, h3225 Palmer St

Alston, Samuel (w Beth) asst dist atty, h1029 Cypress Av

Andersen, Ray (w Priscilla) cty health insptr, h2418 Formosa Av

Bauer, Karen (wid Cecil) h2132 S 11th St

Baylor, Paul (w Ethel) atty, h636 Columbia St

Beeker, Ronald (w Susan) phys, h361 Lake Av

Blaren, David (w Mary) Army recruiter, h3613 Delaney Av Apt 204

Bruhn, Earl (w Marleah) phys, h3225 Palmer St

Cairns, Ronald R (w Anne) city aldm, h609 Church St

Cannon, Albert L, mgr Rexall Drugs, h711 Brockway Av

Carlson, Robert V (w Cora) pres Carlson Plastics, h1029 Cypress St

Carthey, Jim, fire marshal, h163 Lake St Apt 44

Carvel, Reba, tchr Colonial Ele Schl, h1338 Hope Ter

Caseo, Alfred (w Anna) dr Becker Trucking, h1627 Mizell Av

Cassata, Ralph (w Olla) jtr city schls, h531 Mariposa St

Causseaux, Donald F, retd, h539 Sheridan Blvd

Chakey, Michael, tchr North High Schl, h1004 Esplada Av

Chaney, Laurence (w Susan) baker Sunrise Bakery, h920 Stacy Dr

Cortez, Manuel (w Elena) city ptlm, h1519 Constantine St

Costello, Alan (w Rose) dr Branham Inc, h112 E Elmwood Av

Coyle, Stephen, asst mgr Econo Supermart, hHowell Apts, Apt 47

Cramer, Gladys (D) h1123 Hall La

" Melba (wid Herbert), h1123 Hall La

Culbertson, Jonathan Wilburt Sr (w Marsha) U.S. Congressman, 4th Dist, h841 S Broughton Dr

" Jonathan Wilburt Jr (D) artist, h892 S 14th St Apt 472

Dagget, Frederick (w Edith) mgr Sears Roebuck Co, h777 E Lancaster Rd

Dawsen, Vincent (w Katy) atty, h4817 Crescent Rd

Dawson, Roger (w Vivian) fire chief, h708 S Hampton Av

Dees, George (w Helen) supt of schls, h1122 Latta La

Doss, Karl (w Naomi) capt Fire Dept, h414 Sunset Dr

Drake, Phillip (w Mary) pres Drake Motor Co, h8812 Bell Av

Dunkle, Deborah (wid Roger T) mgr Aloma Stk House, h906 Sonata La

Emersen, Ralph A (w Marsha) vp for stud affairs State College, h1046 Citrus St

Ewald, Ruth, sec City Schl Bd, h1309 Temple Av

Failor, Edward (w Elaine) muncp ct judge, h1120 Latta La

Felton, Harry (w Grace) city tax collr, h1231 Vantage Dr

Fort, Lynda, clk Travelers Ins Co, h2713 Stacy Dr

Fritz, Ralph John (w Vivian) city aldm, h1007 Sunwood La

Gable, J. Nicholas (w Shirley) mgr OK SuperMart, h1701 Woodcrest Dr

Garner, Elmer F (w Dorothy) cty ct judge, h592 Ross Pl

Gaul, Denise, watrs Fred's Stk House, h1220
Roberta Av
Gerald, Franklin C (w Tessie) jtr city schls, h682
Lakemont Av
Gibson, Gary (D) ptr Mears Painting & Decorating,
hQuality Trailer Ct
Golinvaux, Paul (w Jean) city ptlm, h811
Ferndell Rd
Grantz, Donald (w Lorry) slsm Lando Screen &
Awning, h203 Lucern Cir
Green, Albert (w Julia) atty, h2502 E Jefferson St
Green, Victor (w Sandra) barber Vic's Barber
Shop, h2431 Stevenson Blvd
Greene, Ernest (w Julia) eng Lawton Bros,
h807 W Broadway
Greenstein, Merrill (w Bertha) city aldm, h2115
E Jefferson Av
Grimes, Herbert (w Mary) tchr Central High
Schl, h3613 Delaney Av Apt 803
Halvens, John (w Florence) slsm Wiese Realty,
h891 Emersen Av
Hansbrough, Lawrence T (w Jean) farmer,
h2342 Lea Rd
Harde, Salley M (D) tchr Colonial Ele Schl,
h430 Sunrise Ct
Harrell, Samuel (w Bertha) cty clerk, h1408
Winn Av
Harrold, Paul (w Carol) deputy Cty Sheriff's
Dept h842 E Harvard St
Hassard, Cole (w Estelle) adv dir Plaza Shopping
Ctr, h1708 Stryker St
Hawkins, Samuel L (w Marie) vp Am Life Ins
Co, h504 N Tampa Av
Hawsler, Joe (D) pres Teamsters Local 431,
h329 Virginia Dr Apt 9
Heath, Ruth (D) ofc mgr Cosmopolitan Const
Co, h534 Ridgewood Av
Hebert, George Raymond (w Florence) tchr
North High Schl, h2714 E Washington St
Heckmann, Michael, ptr Mears Painting &
Decorating, h1043 E Broadway
Helget, Maurice E (w Peggy) vp Statewide Title
Guaranty, h2147 E Jefferson St
Henley, Thomas K (D) city aldm, h2922 Hillcrest
St Apt 320
Herbert, Daniel (w Sarah) mgr Aloma Shell,
h1812 Garvin St
Hirsch, Andrew (w Suzanne) city ptlm, h511
E Concord St
Hodgins, Dennis (w Beatrice) slsm Aetna Life
Ins Co, h102 Indian River Rd
Hoffman, Samuel (w Helen) fireman, city aldm,
h908 Edgewater Dr

Horton, Robert J (w Winifred) city dist atty,
h2537 Vine St
Howland, Joseph (w Ruth) mech Kelly Chevrolet,
h1808 Gadsden Blvd
Hulich, Arlene, vp First National Bank, city aldm,
h8150 Charlin Pkwy
Hulick, Roger C (D) mach cty garage, h4213
Blueberry La
" Sarah J (D) clk Am Fire & Casualty, h502
Delaney St
Hunt, Reynold, fire insptr, h607 E Jackson Apt 30
Inez, Earl Jr, mgr Jiffy Loans Inc, h2541 Bahama Av
Ingalls, Arthur L, pstr St Mary's Catholic Ch,
h3847 Hargil Dr
Jacobs, Melvin (w Hazel) cty sheriff, h907 Harwood
St
Janvier, Janette, tchr Colonial Ele Schl, h1338
Hope Ter
Jenson, Rudi (D) butcher Econo Supermart,
h2035 Holland Av
Jepson, Thomas R (w Minnie) city ptlm, h5601
Larado Pl
Johansen, Fred, studt, h1576 Harris Cir Apt 99
Jones, Roger, studt, h330 Wymore Dr
Julivets, William (w Sylvia) city ptlm, h1338
Vantage Dr
Keel, Timothy (w Carolyn) tchr Central High Schl,
h1314 Griese Dr
Keele, Vernon (w Sylvia) pres Keele-Baldwin Corp,
h640 Clayton St
Kennedy, Lorrie, dispr A-1 Block, h1935 Colonial
Dr Apt D6
Kernan, Andrew, mech Falcon Aviation, h1432
Hillmore La
" David J (w Kathryn) pres Security Ins Co,
h815 Lawsona Blvd
" Harold (widr Judy) treas Falcon Aviation,
h1432 Hillmore La
Klasar, John (D) ptr Mears Painting & Decorating,
h1043 E Broadway
Kline, Bernard (w Dagny) mgr Kline's Shoe Store,
h525 Michigan Av
" Samuel J (w Martha) retd, h1493 James Av
Knight, George (w Violet) pres Knight Realty,
h1627 Lake Av
" Richard (w Fanny) pstr Redeemer Lutheran Ch,
h720 Bryn Mawr Rd
Knudson, Albert (w Audrey) mgr Radio Station
WRSL, h1307 Westmoreland Dr
Kohn, Andrew (D) private investigator h1731
Gurtler Ct Apt 2
Koleda, Gregory (widr Aurelia) mailman, h804
Delaney Park Dr

Kooster, Samuel J (w Ella) atty, h1722
    Virginia Dr
Kopp, Susanne (wid Carl) retd, hQuality Trailer Ct
Kramer, Raymond (w Doris) vp State Graphics
    Corp, h3614 Kasper Av
Kreps, T E (w Catherine) dent, h630 Lake Av
Kuchle, Alyce (wid Richard) retd, h828 Geele Av
LeMayy, Paul (w Rose) atty, h1409 Cole Rd
Lopez, José (w Teresa) mech Kelly Chevrolet,
    h1182 Melody La
Lowell, Lawrence G Jr (w Judy) pstr Azalea Park
    Methodist Ch, h222 S 8th St
Mahew, Arthur (w Laura) mgr Frische's Bowling
    Alley, h6470 Tifton Pl
Markle, George (w Mabel) mayor, h1431 Quailey St
McCaully, Melvin, asst mgr OK SuperMart,
    h540 Osceola Blvd
McGuire, Delbert R (w Sandra) retd, h191 N 7th St
Merritt, Marie A (D) dent asst T E Kreps, h301
    Wymore Dr
Mitchell, Fredric (w Marie) counselor Youth
    Opportunity Ctr, h2024 Concord St
Mornese, James (w Donna) secy guard Taylor
    Dept Store, h623 N 5th St
Murphy, Lyle (w Kathy) city aldm, h114 E
    Harvard St
Neff, Fred (D) mech Aloma Shell, h81 E Miller St
Netoe, Clarence (w Janice) city ptlm, 1415 E
    Livingston St
Niece, Richard R (w Virginia) cook Kentucky
    Fried Chicken, h438 S Daniels Av
Norbratten, Leo (w Vickie) tchr State College,
    h4956 Eastwind St
Nybald, Richard, tchr State College, h418 Lake Av
O'Brien, E J, phys, h321 Meadowlark Dr
" Ralph (w Sarah) police chief, h847 Olive Rd
Ortson, T J (w Martha) plant mgr NTR Corp,
    h810 N 14th St
Osburn, Ervin (widr Mildred) phys, city coroner,
    h4324 Canton St
Ostle, Harrison R (w Lucille) pcpl Greer Ele Schl,
    h1415 Falcon Dr
Page, Howard C (w Salley) retd, h6314 Ridge Ter
" Mary Anne, nurse Memorial Hospt, h6314
    Ridge Ter
Parker, Thomas, bartender Corner Lounge, h3040
    Aloma Av
Perin, Elsie, studt, h1576 Harris Cir
Pfantz, Ellen (wid Howard) retd, h2102 Jacobs Pl
Phelps, Raymond, sgt City Police Dept, h615
    W Amelia St
Plambeck, Emil (w Isabella) supt City Park
    Commission, h3221 Fitzgerald Dr

Platte, Henry (w Sylvia) mgr Soc Secy Adm,
    h1675 Edwin Blvd
Powers, Diana (D) tchr Greer Ele Schl, h4132
    Oakland Av
Ralston, Jay R, atty, h417 S Terry Av
Rauscher, Carrie (wid Marvin) retd, hRR3
Rawle, Robert J (w Clare) lt City Police Dept,
    h110 N Alder Dr
Ray, Lucille R (wid Fred) retd, hJamison's Nursing
    Home, 1822 St Claire Av
Raye, William D (w Beth) pres Alder's Real Estate
    Co, h112 Riverview Dr
Reeder, Albert (w Charlotte) slsm Blue Cross &
    Blue Shield, h427 Summerlin Av
Reedy, Jerome (w Leila) lt·Cty Sheriff's Dept,
    h4510 Fontana St
" Richard (w Beverly) mach Gibs Bros, h1906
    Center Av
Rhodes, Cecil (w Lucille) bus dr, City Transit Co,
    h932 Sontana La
Richards, Wilfred (w Velma) const wkr Cosmopolitan
    Const Co, h817 N Atlantic Av
Rielly, Thomas (w Betty) watr Sizzlin' Stks, h1432
    Center Av Apt 6
Roehl, Cecil (D) city ptlm, h739 Plaza Ct Apt 814
Roth, Benjamin (D) city ptlm, h739 Plaza Ct
    Apt 814
Rue, Wesley (w Margarita) phys, hAloma Apartments,
    4713 Bell Av Apt 5A
Schmidt, Michael (D) mach opr Gibs Bros, h120
    E Miller St Apt 6
Schwartz, Gerald (widr Marie) supvr City Glass Co,
    h517 Harfield Av
Sheppard, Raymond R (w Nell) dr Jay's Furniture,
    h850 Maury Rd
Shorey, Wilson (w Melody) pres Shorey Const Co,
    h811 Lime Av
Sleczkowski, Henry (w Alma) pres Best Shoe Stores,
    h1206 S Terry Av
Small, Louis (w Gloria) parts dept Heintzel Ford,
    h532 DeWitt Dr
Smythe, Alton (w Kate) phys, h1319 W Princeton St
Souder, Steven (w Claudia) art coordinator city
    schls, h2137 Atlanta Av
Stein, Arthur R, tchr North High Schl, h3241
    Broadway
Stimson, Ralph, carpenter, h892 S 14th St Apt 706
Talbertsen, Sara Ann, sec Knight Realty, h3214
    Riverview Dr
Talbot, Mildred Anne (D) watrs Sizzlin' Stks,
    h2003 Stanley St
Taylor, Paul H (w Suzanne) pres Taylor's Dept
    Store, h806 San Luis Dr

Thomas, Franklin J (w Carlynn) editor Daily
    Newspaper, h3005 Concord St
" Alice (D) ofc mgr City Electric Co, h404
    Athertan St
Thompson, Mark (w Nell) studt, h1513 S 4th St
    Apt 1
Tigue, Phillip (w Marian) phys, h8241 Oaklando Dr
Tiller, Julius (w Betty) city ptlm, h534 Calloway Dr
Tipton, Kenneth (w Patricia) window washer
    Office Maintenance Co, h428 N 7th St
Tousel, Frederick W (widr Olive) retd, h1651
    Knollwood Cir
Trever, Mildred, cashier Jiffy Loans Inc, h635
    Poplar Rd
Troxell, Mildred (D) dir pub rel City Libr,
    hCarver Ct Apt 14
Turner, Gladies, sec First National Bank, h411
    Main St
" Homer (widr Patricia) retd, hJamison's Nursing
    Home, 1822 St Claire Av

Underwood, G T (w Ethel) pres City Bd of Education,
    h1227 Edgewater Dr
Welch, Vivian (wid Donald) sec Mayor George
    Markle, h1503 Pine Lake Rd
Wiese, Richard (w Inez) pres Wiese Realty, h800
    Ferndell Rd
Wilke, Eric (w Zola) investigator City Credit Bur,
    h4328 Melody La
Willey, Donald J (w Dolores) jtr city schls, h164
    Lauressa Av
Williams, James, pstr St Mark's Lutheran Ch, h539
    N Jackson Av
Wincek, Gerald (w Nettie) pres Golden Coach
    Limousine Serv, h315 Parr Av
" Roger (w Mary) slsm Belk's Sporting Goods,
    h112 Lake Av
Wiscoff, Sally, sec U.S. govt, h915 Vantage Dr
Wycoff, Andrew (w Mary) pres Wycoff Corp,
    h923 Riverview Dr